AAT

Qualifications and Credit Framework (QCF)

LEVEL 4 DIPLOMA IN ACCOUNTING

TEXT

Financial Performance

2010 Edition

First edition July 2010

ISBN 9780 7517 8566 1

British Library Cataloguing-in-Publication Data
A catalogue record for this book is available from the British
Library

Published by

BPP Learning Media Ltd
BPP House
Aldine Place
London
W12 8AA

www.bpp.com/learningmedia

Printed in the United Kingdom

CONTENTS

A NOTE ABOUT COPYRIGHT

INTRODUCTION

This is a time of great change for the AAT. From 1 July 2010 the AAT's assessments will fall within the **Qualifications and Credit Framework** and most papers will be assessed by way of an on demand **computer based assessment**. BPP Learning Media has reacted to this change by investing heavily to produce new ground breaking market leading resources. In particular, our **new suite of online resources** ensures that you are prepared for online testing by means of an online environment where tasks mimic the style of the AAT's assessment tasks.

The BPP range of resources comprises:

- **Texts**, covering all the knowledge and understanding needed, with numerous illustrations of 'how it works', practical examples and tasks for you to use to consolidate your learning. The majority of tasks within the texts have been written in an interactive style that reflects the style of the online tasks the AAT will set. Texts are available in our traditional paper format and, in addition, as E books which can be downloaded to your PC or laptop.

- **Question Banks**, including additional learning questions plus the AAT's practice assessment and a number of other full practice assessments. Full answers to all questions and assessments, prepared by BPP Learning Media Ltd, are included. For the first time our question banks are available in an online environment which mimics the AAT's testing environment. This enables you to familiarise yourself with the environment in which you will be tested

- **Passcards,** which are handy pocket sized revision tools designed to fit in a handbag or briefcase to enable students to revise anywhere at anytime. All major points are covered in the passcards which have been designed to assist you in consolidating knowledge

- **Workbooks,** which have been designed to cover the units that are assessed by way of project/case study. The workbooks contain many practical tasks to assist in the learning process and also a sample assessment or project to work through.

- **Lecturers' resources**, providing a further bank of tasks, answers and full practice assessments for classroom use, available separately only to lecturers whose colleges adopt BPP Learning Media material. The lecturers resources are available in both paper format and online in E format.

This Text for Financial Performance has been written specifically to ensure comprehensive yet concise coverage of the AAT's new learning outcomes and assessment criteria. It is fully up to date as at June 2010 and reflects both the AAT's unit guide and the practice assessment provided by the AAT.

Each chapter contains:

- Clear, step by step explanation of the topic

- Logical progression and linking from one chapter to the next

- Numerous illustrations of 'how it works'

- Interactive tasks within the text of the chapter itself, with answers at the back of the book. In general, these tasks have been written in the interactive form that students will see in their real assessments

- Test your learning questions of varying complexity, again with answers supplied at the back of the book. In general these test questions have been written in the interactive form that students will see in their real assessments

The emphasis in all tasks and test questions is on the practical application of the skills acquired.

If you have any comments about this book, please e-mail suedexter@bpp.com or write to Sue Dexter, Publishing Director, BPP Learning Media Ltd, BPP House, Aldine Place, London W12 8AA.

ASSESSMENT STRATEGY

The assessment will consist of two sections. Section 1 will consist of 8 questions covering the core topics of standard costing, forecasting, performance indicators, what if analysis and cost management techniques. Section 2 will consist of two written tasks one on variance analysis and one on performance analysis.

Learners will normally be assessed by computer-based assessment (CBA), which will include extended writing tasks, and will be required to demonstrate competence in both sections of the assessment. As this CBA will require both computer and human marking, results will normally be available approximately 6 weeks after the assessment *(this timing is provisional and may be subject to change)*.

Competency

Assessment strategy

Assessment name	Financial Performance
Level	4
Duration	2.5 hours
Competency	For the purpose of assessment the competency level for AAT assessment is set at 70 per cent. The level descriptor below describes the ability and skills students at this level must successfully demonstrate to achieve competence.
QCF Level descriptor	**Summary** Achievement at level 4 reflects the ability to identify and use relevant understanding, methods and skills to address problems that are well defined but complex and non-routine. It includes taking responsibility for overall courses of action as well as exercising autonomy and judgement within fairly broad parameters. It also reflects understanding of different perspectives or approaches within an area of study or work. **Knowledge and understanding** ■ Practical, theoretical or technical understanding to address problems that are well defined but complex and non routine ■ Analyse, interpret and evaluate relevant information and ideas ■ Be aware of the nature and approximate scope of the area of study or work ■ Have an informed awareness of different perspectives or approaches within the area of study or work

Application and action
■ Address problems that are complex and non-routine while normally fairly well defined
■ Identify, adapt and use appropriate methods and skills
■ Initiate and use appropriate investigation to inform actions
■ Review the effectiveness and appropriateness of methods, actions and results
Autonomy and accountability
■ Take responsibility for courses of action, including where relevant, responsibility for the work of others
■ Exercise autonomy and judgement within broad but generally well-defined parameters

AAT UNIT GUIDE

Financial Performance (FNPF)

Introduction

For the purpose of assessment both the Principles of Managing financial performance and the Measuring financial performance units will be combined and assessed together.

Purpose

The "Principles of Managing Financial Performance (Knowledge)" unit is about understanding the principles of managing financial performance. Learners will have the knowledge to be able to use a range of techniques to analyse information on expenditure. They will be able to make judgements to support decision making, planning and control by managers.

The "Measuring Financial Performance (Skills)" is about measuring financial performance. Learners will have the skills to collect and analyse information, monitor performance, and present reports to management.

In order for learners to be successful in the two financial performance units they will need to be able to explain, define, describe, calculate and analyse a range of fundamental concepts and techniques. Many of the concepts and techniques are interrelated and learners will need to understand how the concepts and techniques interrelate. They may also be required to explain and describe these relationships.

Learners will need to have a detailed understanding of the fundamental management accounting concepts and techniques in order to demonstrate competence in the learning outcomes. Learners will also need to be able to define and explain the following fundamental concepts (for the knowledge standards) and apply their knowledge to questions which may require the calculation or application of one or more of these fundamental concepts or techniques (for the skills standards).

Delivery guidance

1   **Cost classification, Cost recording, Cost reporting and Cost behaviour**

Knowledge – Learning outcomes 1, 2 and 3 and Assessment criteria 1.3, 1.4, 2.1, 2.5

Skills outcomes 1 and 3 and Assessment criteria 1.1, 1.2, 1.3, 1.4, 1.5, 3.1, 3.2, 3.3

(a)   Production costing and the elements of direct and indirect costs, cost classification into materials, labour, and overhead,

(b)   Cost classification by behaviour (fixed, variable, stepped fixed and semi variable) relevant range for fixed costs.

(c)   Calculation of variable and fixed costs using the high low method of cost estimation

    (d)   Prime cost, full production cost, marginal product cost,

    (e)   High low method of fixed and variable cost estimation

    (f)   Explain the types of cost centres, profit centres and investment centres

2   Marginal costing and Absorption costing

Knowledge – Learning outcomes 1, 2 and 3 and Assessment criteria 1.1, 1.3, 1.4, 2.3, 2.5

Skills – Learning outcomes 1 and 3 and Assessment criteria 1.1, 1.2, 1.3, 1.4, 1.5, 1.6,

    (a)   Absorption costing – definition, explanation and calculation of an overhead absorption rate, calculation of under and over absorption, explanation of the advantages and disadvantages of absorption costing – link with financial accounting requirements and price setting model.

    (b)   Marginal costing – definition, explanation and calculation of the marginal cost, explanation of the advantages and disadvantages of marginal costing, marginal costing and decision making, see link with contribution theory below.

    (c)   Marginal costing v Absorption costing – explain the differences between the treatment of costs, calculation of profit and effects of changing stock levels. Preparation of an absorption costing profit and loss account, a marginal costing profit and loss account, calculation of the changes in profit when stock levels change and a reconciliation between the marginal costing profit and the absorption costing profit.

    (d)   Absorption Costing v Marginal Costing in decision making. Learners need to understand how absorption costing and marginal costing can be used in tasks which measure performance and which consider ways of enhancing value. Absorption Costing may be relevant for measuring the performance of a business and it may also be appropriate to use absorption costing principles in enhancing value. A product may be re-engineered in order to reduce production costs and it would be perfectly appropriate to consider the full absorption cost of the redesigned product. Lifecycle Costing needs to consider both fixed and variable costs. However, it may be inappropriate to use absorption costing in certain circumstances. For example, if the business is considering contracting out the manufacture of a product, selling surplus capacity or other limiting factor decisions, then marginal costing is the appropriate method as fixed costs will not change as a result of the decision. However, Learners need to understand that certain fixed costs may well change and the marginal (incremental) cost may in these circumstances include both variable and fixed components.

    (e)   Practical limitations of cost classification, non linear behaviour

(f) Absorption Costing v Marginal Costing could feature in Standard Costing questions relating to performance measurement or as a stand alone

(g) Contribution analysis.

(h) Break even analysis and margin of safety.

3 Standard Costing and Variance Analysis

Knowledge – Learning outcomes 1, 2 and 3 and Assessment criteria 1.1, 1.2, 1.3, 1.4, 2.2, 2.3, 2.4, 2.5

Skills – Learning outcomes 1, 2 and 3 and Assessment criteria 1.1, 1.2, 1.3, 1.4, 1.5, 1.6, 1.7, 2.1, 2.2, 2.3,

(1) Explain how standard costs can be established, the different types of standard (ideal, target, normal, basic) and how the type of standard can affect the behaviour of the budget holder and workforce.

(2) Explain the role of standard costing in the planning, decision making and control process. Standard costing variances aid budgetary control systems by breaking down the simple variance identified in a budgetary control system into components based upon an expected outcome. Standard costing is a method of analysing a variance from a budget when standard costs are used in creating the budget.

(3) Extract relevant data from the question in order to calculate various requirements. Learners may be required to calculate any of the following:

(a) Standard quantity of inputs (materials, labour, overheads)

(b) Standard cost for given production volumes

(c) Actual quantity of inputs (materials, labour, overheads)

(d) Actual costs for given production volumes

(4) Explain and calculate the following variances

(a) Raw materials total, price, usage

(b) Labour total, rate, efficiency

(c) Labour idle time variance

(d) Fixed overhead expenditure variance

(e) Fixed overhead volume, capacity and efficiency.

(5) Prepare an operating statement under both absorption costing principles and marginal costing principles.

(6) Prepare a reconciliation of the budgeted material cost with the actual material cost using the material cost variances

(7) Prepare a reconciliation of the budgeted labour cost with the actual labour cost using the labour cost variances

(8) Prepare a reconciliation of budgeted fixed overheads with actual fixed overheads using fixed overhead variances.

(9) Prepare journal entries for the posting of variances.

(10) Break down variances using index numbers to isolate controllable and non- controllable parts.

(11) Break down variances, using additional information, into controllable and non-controllable variances.

(12) Prepare reports giving possible reasons for the variances, showing an understanding of the interrelationship between the variances.

(13) Comment on additional information provided by the budget holder as to reasons for the variance. For example, the production manager may say that the quality of raw materials or the old, poorly maintained machines or unskilled staff have caused the adverse raw material usage variance, when the raw materials price variance was adverse, implying that the material was of better than expected quality. This may not be the case - it could be that the buyer bought an inferior material but still paid more than the standard. It may be that an independent assessment of the quality of the material needs to be made.

(14) Explain how standards are developed and appreciate the concepts of Ideal standard, attainable (expected) standard and basic standard. Explain how the chosen standard may affect the behaviour on managers and staff.

(15) Explain the difference between controllable and non controllable variances, apply index numbers to variances in order to explain how general rising prices can cause variances, and adjust variances for changes in prices.

4   Performance indicators and "what if" analysis

Knowledge – learning outcomes 1, 2 and 3 and Assessment criteria 1.1, 1.2, 1.3, 1.4, 3.1, 3.2, 3.3, 3.4, 3.5

Skills – learning outcomes 1, 2 and 3 and assessment criteria 1.1, 1.2, 1.3, 1.4, 1.5, 1.6, 2.5, 2.6, 2.7, 2.8, 2.9, 3.1, 3.2, 3.3

(a)   Calculate performance indicators

Learners will be asked to calculate a range of performance indicators. Some, such as the return on capital employed or the current ratio, are applicable to many organisations, whilst others might be unique to a particular type of organisation. For example, if the task relates to a hotel, learners might be given data and asked to calculate the cost per room night, the percentage occupancy and the average discount given to customers.

The following is a list of the type of performance indicators learners might be asked to calculate.

(1) Financial (Profitability, Liquidity, Efficiency and Gearing)

    (a) Gross Profit Margin, Operating Profit Margin, Administration costs as a percentage of turnover, any cost as a percentage of turnover.

    (b) Current ratio, quick ratio.

    (c) Trade cycles (debtor days, stock days, creditor days)

    (d) Gearing ratio, debt to equity ratio.

    (e) Value added (Turnover less the cost of materials used and bought in services

(2) Efficiency, Capacity and Activity ratios

    (a) Labour efficiency ratio = standard hours for actual production/actual hours worked.

    (b) Capacity ratio = actual hours worked/ budgeted hours

    (c) Labour activity ratio = standard hours for actual production/ budgeted hours, or actual output/budgeted output.

(3) Indicators to measure efficiency, effectiveness and productivity

    (a) Measures of efficiency include ROCE, Operating Profit Margin and efficiency ratio for labour

    (b) Effectiveness measures include percentage of production free from defects, delivery times to customer, number of coaches, buses or trains on time, percentage of learners passing exams first time, number of times a class is cancelled, percentage of parcels delivered within the agreed time. Average waiting times.

    (c) Productivity measures are likely to be measured in units of output, or related to output in some way. Examples include number of, say, vehicles manufactured per week, operations undertaken per day, passengers transported per month, units produced per worker per day, rooms cleaned per hour or meals served per sitting.

(4) Indicators to measure quality of service and cost of quality

    (a) The number of defects/units returned/warranty claims/customer complaints, the cost of inspection/ repairs/re-working

(b) Prevention costs, appraisal costs, internal failure costs, external failure costs

(5) Learners may be asked to compare given indicators with performance indicators that they have calculated. They may have to undertake a benchmarking exercise and need to understand the purpose of benchmarking

(6) Learners need to recognise that a business has to select key performance indicators and monitor these in order to manage the business. The balanced scorecard is an approach often used and learners need to understand the concept of a balanced scorecard and may be asked to prepare one from given performance indicators.

(7) Tasks may require the calculation of specific performance indicators. If this is the case the calculation of the indicator will either be obvious or the formula for the indicator will be provided. For example, if the task is based on a hotel the occupancy rate calculation should be obvious given the number of rooms sold in the month divided by the total number of room nights available in the month. If the indicator is more complicated the formula will be given.

(b) Comment on the information generated from the calculation of the performance indicator

Learners need to be able to explain what the ratios are designed to show and analyse the ratio.

(c) Understand the interrelationships and limitations of the performance indicator

Learners need to be able to explain, describe the limitations of the ratios and the interrelationships. Learners may also be required to apply their understanding of the interrelationship in order to make recommendations to management.

(d) Prepare estimates of capital investment projects using discounted cash flow techniques

Learners need to be able to explain, describe and calculate discounted cash flow calculations of net present value, net present cost and net terminal cost and make recommendations to management.

(e) "What if" analysis

After having prepared performance indicators, Learners may be faced with taking or recommending action. They may be asked to do one or more of the following:

- Show what the results would have been if benchmark data had been achieved.

- Forecast the performance indicators for the next period based upon a set of assumptions.

- Re- calculate the performance indicators, taking account of given changes to the business, or perhaps select changes which will maximise given indicators.

- Work backwards through a ratio. For example, they may be asked, "What would the turnover need to have been for the asset turnover to be 3 times?", or "What would the operating profit need to have been for the ROCE to be 25%?". This is simple equation manipulation.

- Given several options, learners may be asked to evaluate and recommend a course of action. This could be to improve a key performance indicator like ROCE. They might also be asked to comment on options which cause an improvement in one indicator with a deterioration of another.

- Calculate indicators for 2 years and explain changes in performance

- Compare 2 businesses and comment on their relative performance.

- Identify potential improvements and estimate the value of them

- Suggest ways of improving the performance of a poorly performing business.

- Make recommendations.

- Make calculations and recommendations to management for any of the following scenarios

  - Make or buy decision – learners may be required to prepare workings and key ratios to aid the assessment of outsourcing manufacture

  - Limiting factor decision making – learners may have to adjust figures and recalculate ratios if a resource constraint limits production.

  - Break-even analysis and margin of safety – learners need to be able to calculate and comment on measures of risk, particularly where a business changes or proposes to change the fixed cost and variable costs of production.

- Closure of a business segment, transferring production overseas – learners may have to prepare calculations and make recommendations to management regarding the closure of a business segment

- Mechanisation – learners may be required to provide calculations and make recommendations to management regarding changing the production process from a labour intensive one to a machine intensive one. They may also be required to bring in break-even analysis in order to demonstrate the changing risk in the business.

With scenario planning or "what if" analysis, learners have to understand how elements of the profit and loss account and balance sheet are linked. For example, a 10% increase in sales volume will lead to a 10% increase in variable costs as more units are produced but no increase in fixed costs, assuming that capacity exists (fixed costs are fixed over the relevant range). A 10% increase in sales price, however, will not lead to any changes in costs. The increase in sales will change the profit and, if no dividends are paid, this will increase the net assets of the business. The change in sales will therefore affect several ratios.

(f) Key performance indicators and the behaviour of managers

Learners need to understand that the way in which business unit managers are assessed can have a great influence on the decisions they make. The use of key performance indicators such as ROCE can lead to a lack of goal congruence where managers make decisions which improve performance in certain indicators but which may not be best for the organisation as a whole.

For example, a manager may not be prepared to invest in new machinery if the increase in the net asset position will reduce the ROCE, even though the investment may reduce other costs, lead to zero defects or increase customer satisfaction.

5   Cost management

Knowledge – Learning outcomes 3 and Assessment criteria 3.6

Skills – Learning outcomes 1, 2 and 3 and Assessment criteria 1.1, 1.2, 1.3, 1.4, 1.5, 2.2, 2.4, 2.8, 2.9, 3.1, 3.2, 3.3

(a) Lifecycle costing and how it can be used to aid cost management. Learners may be required to calculate lifecycle costs for different options. Lifecycle cost calculations may require the use of discounted cash flow techniques.

(b) The concepts behind target costing (including value analysis/engineering). Learners may be required to explain target costing and prepare a target cost from information in the task. Learners may also have to analyse information provided from functional specialists like designers, engineers and marketing professionals.

(c)   Activity based costing and how it can be applied to an organisation. Learners may be given information and asked to calculate the absorption rates under activity based costing and comment on its applicability.

(d)   The principles of Total Quality Management. Learners may be provided with information about the various costs incurred to prevent faulty production and costs incurred to rectify faulty production and settle warranty claims. Learners may then be asked to calculate the cost of quality. Whilst the general theory is that organisations should plan to have zero defects, learners should be aware that there may be commercial justifications for allowing some defects, perhaps because of expensive quality assurance systems.

(e)   Product lifecycle and how costs change throughout the life of a product. Concepts of economies of scale, mechanisation, a switch from variable to fixed costs may be assessed.

(f)   Understanding of the planning, decision making and control stages in management accounting and how cost management techniques can aid the stages.

6   **Basic Statistical Methods:**

Knowledge – Learning outcomes 3 and Assessment criteria 3.4

Skills – Learning outcomes 1, 2 and 3 and Assessment criteria 2.1, 2.2, 2.3, 2.4

The learners must be able to explain the use and purpose of indexing, sampling and time series (e.g. moving averages, linear regression and seasonal trends).

Index numbers – learners must be able to calculate index numbers and use them to forecast costs and prices and also to subdivide variances. Learners must also be able to interpret indices and compare them with methods of securing contracts to reduce the risk of rising prices.

Moving averages – learners must be able to calculate moving averages and seasonal variations and use calculations to extrapolate a forecast of sales or costs.

Seasonal variations – learners need to understand types of variation from the trend and may be required to identify the seasonal variation or use the seasonal variation and a given trend to forecast sales volume, prices or cost information.

Regression Analysis

Learners will **not** be required to derive the regression equation $y = a + bx$ but they may be given the equation and asked to use it to calculate a and b, given y and x, for several points, or to calculate y and x, given a and b. The equation could then be used to predict prices, demand and costs.

chapter 1:
COSTS

─────── **chapter coverage** 📖 ───────

In this initial chapter we will introduce the concept of cost accounting by looking at the various ways that costs can be classified, recorded and reported.

The topics that are to be covered are:

✍ Overview of a costing system

✍ Classification of costs by behaviour

✍ Semi-variable costs

OVERVIEW OF A COSTING SYSTEM

One of the key concerns that the management of an organisation will have, will be how much the products that it produces, or the services that it provides, cost. This information will be vital for many purposes including the following:

- setting the selling price
- determining the quantities of production and sales
- continuing or discontinuing a product
- controlling costs
- controlling production processes
- appraising managers

Types of cost

Costs in both manufacturing and service industries are traditionally split between:

- material costs
- labour costs
- overheads (or expenses)

These costs in turn can be described as direct costs or indirect costs. This analysis depends upon whether the cost in question can be directly attributed to a unit of production or unit of service. The first stage in the cost allocation process then is to determine the cost units of the business.

In a manufacturing business the COST UNIT may be each unit of production or each batch of production. In a service business the identification of the cost unit may not be quite so straightforward but, for example, in a transport business the cost unit might be each lorry mile travelled or, in a restaurant, it might be each meal served.

Any material cost or labour cost or expense that can be directly related to the cost unit is a DIRECT COST of that cost unit. However many costs of the business cannot be directly attributed to a cost unit and these costs are initially taken to a cost centre.

A COST CENTRE is an area of the business, maybe a department such as the factory or canteen, for which costs are incurred that cannot be directly attributed to the cost units. These costs are known as INDIRECT COSTS or overheads and include, for example, the rent of the factory and the wages of the supervisor.

There are two types of cost centre – those that are directly involved in the production or provision of the cost unit, such as the factory, and these are known as PRODUCTION COST CENTRES. There are also cost centres that, while not actually producing the cost unit, do provide a service to the production cost centres, such as the canteen. These are known as SERVICE COST CENTRES.

Allocation and apportionment of overheads

The overheads of both the production and the service cost centres are part of the necessary cost of producing the cost units and therefore in some costing systems they are included in the overall cost of the cost unit. This is done by the following process:

- ALLOCATION of overheads that relate to just one cost centre, such as the depreciation of the factory machinery being allocated to the factory cost centre, or the food costs being allocated to the canteen.

- APPORTIONMENT of overheads that relate to a number of cost centres to each relevant cost centre on some fair basis, such as the apportionment of the rent of the building to each cost centre in the building on the basis of floor space occupied.

- re-apportionment of service cost centre costs to the production cost centres to ensure that all overheads are now included within the production cost centre costs.

- absorption of all of the overheads of each production cost centre into the cost of cost units on some fair basis, such as the number of labour hours or machine hours that each cost unit uses.

We can summarise this process in a diagram (this will be covered in more detail in chapter 2):

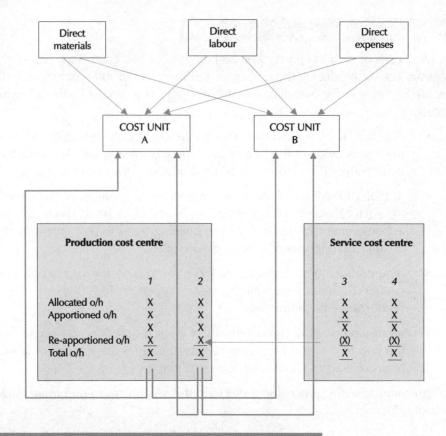

We have seen that a cost centre is an area or department of a business which incurs costs involved in the business operations. A PROFIT CENTRE is an area of the business which not only incurs costs but also earns revenue, for example a sales department in an organisation which earns revenue from sales but incurs costs such as a salesman's salary and commission. An INVESTMENT CENTRE is an area of the business which not only incurs costs and earns revenues but also accounts for its own capital investment. An example might be a separate division of the organisation which has a factory from which it produces goods, sells and despatches them.

CLASSIFICATION OF COSTS BY BEHAVIOUR

In order to be able to correctly deal with all of these different types of cost you must be able to recognise that different types of cost behave in different ways when the levels of activity in the organisation change. This is known as classification of costs by behaviour and the main classifications are:

- variable costs
- fixed costs
- stepped costs
- semi-variable costs

Each of these will be illustrated in this chapter and the concepts will then be used in later chapters in order to produce relevant management information.

Variable costs

VARIABLE COSTS are costs that vary directly in line with changes in the level of activity. Direct materials and direct labour are often viewed as variable costs. For example if 1 kg of a material is needed for each cost unit then 100,000 kg will be required for 100,000 units of production and 500,000 kg for 500,000 units of production.

The total variable cost can be expressed as:

Total variable cost = Variable cost per unit × number of units

A graph can be used to illustrate the total variable cost as activity levels change

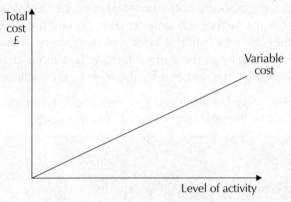

Direct costs such as materials costs may not always be true variable costs. For example, if a supplier offers a bulk purchasing discount for purchases above a certain quantity, then the cost per unit will fall if orders are placed for more than this quantity.

Fixed costs

A FIXED COST is one which does not change as activity levels alter. An example often used is that of the rent and rates of the factory. This will remain the same cost whether 100,000 units are produced or 500,000 units.

The behaviour of fixed costs can be shown graphically:

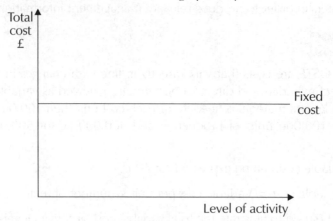

In practical terms fixed costs are only truly fixed over the RELEVANT RANGE. For example the rent of the factory will only remain constant provided that the level of activity is within the production capacity of the factory. If production levels increase above the capacity of the current factory then more factory space must be rented, thus increasing the rent cost for this level of production.

As the activity level increases the fixed cost remains fixed in total but the fixed cost per unit will fall as the total cost is spread over more units.

Task 1

A business incurs fixed costs of £100,000. Complete the table below showing the fixed cost per unit at each production levels?

Production level	Cost £
20,000 units	
40,000 units	
80,000 units	

Stepped costs

STEPPED COSTS are costs which are fixed over a relatively small range of activity but then increase in steps when certain levels of activity are reached. For example, if one production supervisor is required for each 30,000 units of a product that is made, then three supervisors are required for production of 90,000 units, four for production of up to 120,000 units, five for production up to 150,000 units and so on.

Stepped costs can be illustrated on a graph:

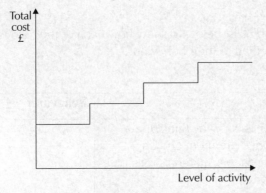

Stepped costs are really a fixed cost with a relatively short relevant range.

Task 2

Insert the missing term:

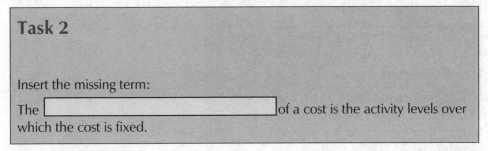

The ⬚ of a cost is the activity levels over which the cost is fixed.

Semi-variable costs

SEMI-VARIABLE COSTS are costs which have a fixed element and also a variable element. For example, the telephone bill includes a fixed element being the fixed line rental for the period and a variable element which will increase as the number of calls increase.

The total of a semi-variable cost can be expressed as:

Total cost = Fixed element + (variable cost per unit × number of units)

A semi-variable cost can be illustrated on a graph as follows:

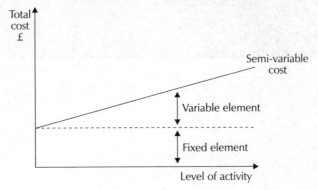

The calculation of the fixed and variable elements of a semi-variable cost will be considered in the next section of this chapter.

Task 3

Choose from the picklist below to show how each of the following costs would be classified according to their behaviour.

Cost	Behaviour
Stores department costs which include £5,000 of insurance premium and an average of £100 cost per materials receipt or issue	
Machinery depreciation based upon machine hours used	
Salary costs of lecturers in a training college, where one lecturer is required for every 200 students enrolled	
Buildings insurance for a building housing the stores, the factory and the canteen	
Wages of production workers who are paid per unit produced, with a guaranteed weekly minimum wage of £250	

Picklist

Variable

Fixed

Semi-variable

Fixed, then semi-variable

Stepped

HOW IT WORKS

The use of cost behaviour principles in product costing is illustrated in the following example.

Cameron Ltd produces one product which requires the following inputs:

Direct materials	1 kg @ £3.50 per kg
Direct labour	1 hour @ £6.00 per hour
Rent	£4,000 per quarter
Leased machines	£1,500 for every 4,000 units of production
Maintenance costs	£1,000 per quarter plus £1.00 per unit produced

Calculate the total cost of production and the cost per unit for each of the following production levels for the coming quarter:

(a)   4,000 units
(b)   10,000 units
(c)   16,000 units

Direct materials – these are a variable cost with a constant amount per unit (1kg x £3.50 = £3.50) therefore the total cost is found by multiplying the number of units by the unit cost:

£3.50 × 4,000 units	=	£14,000
£3.50 × 10,000 units	=	£35,000
£3.50 × 16,000 units	=	£56,000

Direct labour – another variable cost, with a unit cost of 1hr x £6 = £6:

£6.00 × 4,000 units	=	£24,000
£6.00 × 10,000 units	=	£60,000
£6.00 × 16,000 units	=	£96,000

Rent – this is a fixed cost and therefore provided we are still operating within the relevant range will remain at £4,000 whatever the production level.

Leased machines – this is a stepped cost and the number of machines leased will depend upon the quantity of production.

4,000 units	=	1 machine	=	£1,500
10,000 units	=	3 machines	=	£4,500
16,000 units	=	4 machines	=	£6,000

Maintenance costs – this is a semi-variable cost with a fixed element of £1,000 and a variable cost of £1 per unit. The total cost for each activity level is:

4,000 units	=	£1,000 + (4,000 × £1.00)	=	£5,000
10,000 units	=	£1,000 + (10,000 × £1.00)	=	£11,000
16,000 units	=	£1,000 + (16,000 × £1.00)	=	£17,000

Thus the total costs of production are:

	Production level – units		
	4,000	10,000	16,000
	£	£	£
Direct materials (variable)	14,000	35,000	56,000
Direct labour (variable)	24,000	60,000	96,000
Rent (fixed)	4,000	4,000	4,000
Leased machines (stepped)	1,500	4,500	6,000
Maintenance costs	5,000	11,000	17,000
Total cost	48,500	114,500	179,000
Number of units	4,000	10,000	16,000
Cost per unit	£12.13	£11.45	£11.19

The cost per unit is decreasing as the production quantity increases. This is because the fixed cost and the fixed element of the semi-variable cost are being spread over a larger number of units.

Variable costs with a discount

Suppose now that the supplier of the materials offers a bulk purchasing discount of 6% for all purchases if an order is placed for more than 8,000 kgs.

What is the direct materials cost in total and per unit at each level of production?

4,000 units

Total cost	4,000 × £3.50	=	£14,000
Cost per unit	£14,000/4,000	=	£3.50

10,000 units

Total cost	$10,000 \times (£3.50 \times 94\%)$	
Cost per unit	£32,900/10,000	=

16,000 units

Total cost	$16,000 \times (£3.50 \times 94\%)$	=	£52,640
Cost per unit	£52,640/16,000	=	£3.29

The direct materials are now not a true variable cost as the cost per unit falls once production is in excess of 8,000 units.

Task 4

A salesman receives a fixed salary of £800 per month plus commission of £20 for each sale confirmed in the month.

Complete the table to show the salesman's monthly salary for the month, if his confirmed sales are at each of the following levels.

Sales	Monthly salary £
4 sales	
8 sales	
15 sales	

Practical limitations of cost classifications

As we have seen in this chapter so far, it can be useful to classify costs according to their behaviour. However in order to have made these classifications we have assumed that the costs have a linear behaviour ie, are a straight line when drawn on a graph. This may not always be the case in practice. For example we have seen that if a discount is given for purchases above a certain level, then the materials purchases cost will not be a true variable cost. Thus unit variable costs may fall as economies of scale are achieved. Similarly although the direct labour cost is often viewed as a variable cost, if activity levels reach a certain amount then overtime might be incurred and this will mean that the cost is no longer a straight-forward variable cost.

assumption is normally that variable costs or the variable element of a semi-fixed cost will increase or decrease as activity levels in the form of units of output increase and fall. However the relevant level of activity may not always be units of output. For example an organisation's telephone bill is normally assumed to have a fixed element, the line rental, and a variable element, call costs, which increase as activity levels increase. In this case the relevant activity level causing the call cost to vary is the number of calls made. If we look at the call costs in relation to the level of output, in some organisations it may be the case that the call costs increase as the activity levels in terms of units of output fall, as the sales team will be trying to boost sales and therefore production.

Prime cost and full production cost

In the example above the costs were simply totalled, however for management accounting purposes it will sometimes be useful to categorise the costs in sub-totals.

The PRIME COST of a product is all the direct costs of producing that product.

The MARGINAL COST of a product is all the variable costs of producing that product (both direct eg materials and labour and indirect eg variable overheads)

The FULL PRODUCTION COST includes all the overheads or indirect costs of the production of the product, both fixed and variable.

HOW IT WORKS

Using the figures for the 4,000 units level of production from the previous example, we can now classify the costs as prime cost, marginal cost and full production cost.

	£
Direct materials	14,000
Direct labour	24,000
Prime cost	**38,000**
Variable maintenance costs	4,000
Marginal cost	**42,000**
Rent	4,000
Leased machines	1,500
Fixed maintenance costs	1,000
Full production cost	**48,500**

SEMI-VARIABLE COSTS

Semi-variable costs are more complex than variable and fixed costs as these costs have a fixed element which is not related to the level of activity, and a variable element which is related to the level of activity. For a semi-variable costs we need to be able to estimate, at any given level of activity, both the fixed element amount and the variable element rate.

Hi lo method of cost estimation

One method of estimating the fixed and variable elements of a semi-variable cost is to use the HI LO METHOD. Under this method historical data regarding the amount of the semi-variable cost at various activity levels is collected. A comparison is then made between the costs at the highest level of activity and at the lowest level of activity, in order to isolate the variable rate of increase in the cost and then to find the fixed element of the cost. This method assumes that there is a linear relationship between the cost and output at the highest and lowest activity levels.

HOW IT WORKS

The costs of the factory maintenance department for Kilman Ltd appear to be partially dependent upon the number of machine hours operated each month. The machine hours and the maintenance department costs for the last six months are given below:

	Machine hours	Maintenance cost £
June	4,000	104,000
July	4,800	127,000
August	4,200	111,000
September	4,500	119,000
October	3,800	107,000
November	4,100	107,000

Step 1

Find the highest and lowest levels of activity (note that this is the activity level and is not necessarily the highest and lowest cost).

In this case the highest level is 4,800 hours and the lowest level is 3,800 hours.

Compare the activity level and costs for each of these:

	Machine hours	Cost £
Highest	4,800	127,000
Lowest	3,800	107,000
Increase	1,000	20,000

This shows that for an increase in 1,000 machine hours there has been an increase of £20,000 of costs. Therefore the variable cost per machine hour can be estimated as:

Variable rate of increase   =   £20,000/1,000 hours

=   £20 per machine hour

Step 3

We can now find the fixed element of the cost, by substituting the variable rate into either the highest or lowest activity level, with the fixed element appearing as the balancing figure. This will provide you with the same answer whether you use the highest or lowest level of activity.

Highest level

	£
Variable element 4,800 hours × £20	96,000
Fixed element (balancing figure)	31,000
Total cost	127,000

Lowest level

Variable element 3,800 hours × £20	76,000
Fixed element (balancing figure)	31,000
Total cost	107,000

Therefore the fixed element of the maintenance department costs is £31,000 and the variable rate is £20 per machine hour.

Step 4

We can now use this analysis of the semi-variable cost to forecast figures for the maintenance department. The anticipated machine hours for the next three month period are as follows:

	Dec	Jan	Feb
Machine hours	4,000	4,500	5,000

The forecast maintenance department costs for these three months can be calculated:

	Forecast maintenance department costs
	£
Dec (4,000 × £20) + £31,000	111,000
Jan (4,500 × £20) + £31,000	121,000
Feb (5,000 × £20) + £31,000	131,000

Interpolation and extrapolation

In the previous example we used our calculated figures about the cost movement in order to estimate the future costs of the maintenance department. In order to find the variable and fixed elements of the cost we looked at an activity range of 3,800 hours to 4,800 hours and estimated how the costs moved within that range.

For January and February the anticipated machine hour levels fall within this range, therefore it is likely that our estimates of cost will be fairly accurate (although they do not coincide with the historical costs associated with those levels – our model is not totally accurate as it is based on the assumption of a linear relationship which is unlikely to apply perfectly in practice). When the levels being forecast are within the range considered this is known as INTERPOLATION.

However for March the machine hours are estimated to be 5,000. This is outside the range that we considered and therefore our estimate of future cost is known as EXTRAPOLATION. Extrapolation may not be as accurate as interpolation, as the activity level is outside our historical data range and therefore we do not know how the costs will behave outside of the range.

Task 5

The production costs at various levels of production for a business are given below:

Production level	Production costs
units	£
24,000	169,000
20,000	143,000
28,000	191,000

The variable rate of production costs is

The fixed amount of production costs is

CHAPTER OVERVIEW

- Direct costs are costs that can be related directly to a cost unit whereas indirect costs are initially allocated or apportioned to a cost centre, before being charged to cost units

- Costs are often classified according to their behaviour as activity levels change – the main classifications are variable costs, fixed costs, stepped costs and semi-variable costs

- Semi-variable costs include both a fixed element and a variable rate element – one method of calculating these two elements is to use the hi lo method

Keywords

Cost unit – the individual product or service for which costs are to be gathered

Direct costs – costs that can be directly attributed to cost units

Cost centre – an area of the business for which costs are to be gathered

Production cost centre - directly involved in the production of the cost unit

Service cost centre - provides a service to the production cost centres

Indirect costs – costs that cannot be attributed directly to a cost unit but are initially attributed to a cost centre

Allocation – overheads that relate to just one cost centre are charged directly to that cost centre

Apportionment – overheads that relate to a number of cost centres are shared between each relevant cost centre on some fair basis

Profit centre – an area of the business which incurs costs and earns revenues

Investment centre – an area of the business which incurs costs, earns revenues and is also responsible for its own capital investment

Variable costs – costs that increase/decrease directly in line with any changes in activity level

Fixed costs – costs that remain constant as activity levels change

Relevant range – the range of activity levels over which a fixed cost will not change

Stepped costs – costs which are fixed over a relatively small range and then increase in steps

Semi-variable costs – costs which have both a fixed element and variable element

Prime cost – all the direct costs of producing a product.

Marginal cost – all the variable costs of producing a product (both direct eg materials and labour and indirect eg variable overheads)

Full production cost – all the costs of producing a product, including the overheads or indirect costs of production

Hi lo method – a method of estimating the fixed and variable elements of a semi-variable cost using historic data

Interpolation – estimation of a forecast figure within the range of activity levels considered

Extrapolation – estimation of a forecast figure outside the range of activity levels considered

TEST YOUR LEARNING

1 The direct materials cost for 10,000 units is estimated to be £43,600 and for 12,000 is estimated to be £52, 320. This a variable cost.

True or false? Tick the correct answer.

True ☑

False ☐

2 A business expects to incur fixed costs of £64,000 in the following month.

Complete the table below to show the total fixed cost and the fixed cost per unit at each of the following activity levels.

Activity level	Total fixed cost £	Fixed cost per unit £
3,000 units	64 000	21.33
10,000 units	64,000	6.40
16,000 units	64,000	4 00

3 Given below are the activity levels and production costs for the last six months for a factory:

	Activity level	Production cost
	units	£
July	103,000	469,000
August	110,000	502,000
September	126,000	547,000
October	113,000	517,000
November	101,000	472,000
December	118,000	533,000

(a) The variable element of the production cost is

| 3.00 |

The fixed element of the production cost is

| 169.000 |

101.000 – 472.000
126.000   547 000
25.000   75.000

(b) Complete the following table to show the estimated production costs at each of the levels of production.

Level of production	Production cost £
120,000 units	529.000
150,000 units	619.000

(c) Comment upon which of the two estimates of production costs calculated in (b) is likely to be most accurate and why.

b, because 150,000 is
extrapolation.

chapter 2:
METHODS OF COSTING

---

chapter coverage 📖

In this chapter we will consider a variety of different methods of costing – absorption costing, marginal costing and activity based costing.

The topics that are to be covered are:

✎ Methods of costing

✎ Under- and over-absorption of overheads

✎ Activity based costing

METHODS OF COSTING

We have seen in outline how the cost of a cost unit is calculated. We will now move onto the different methods of calculating a cost per unit that a business may use. The method chosen will depend upon the type of business and the policy of management. There are three main methods of calculating a cost per unit:

- **ABSORPTION COSTING** – under this costing method a 'full' production cost per unit is calculated by including in the cost of the cost unit a proportion of the production overheads from each of the production and service cost centres. This is done by allocating, apportioning and absorbing the overheads.

- **VARIABLE OR MARGINAL COSTING** – under this method only the variable costs (or marginal costs) of production are included in the cost per cost unit. The fixed overheads are treated as period costs and not as part of the cost unit. The fixed overheads are charged to the income statement (profit and loss account) as an expense for the period.

- **ACTIVITY BASED COSTING** – this is a method of absorption costing which uses more sophisticated methods of allocating overheads to cost units than the normal methods of overhead allocation and apportionment. It does this by considering the activities that cause the overhead to be incurred and the factors that give rise to the costs (cost drivers).

HOW IT WORKS

Fenton Partners produce one product, the Fenton. The factory has two production departments, assembly and packing, and there is one service department, maintenance. 75% of the maintenance department's time is spent in the assembly department and the remainder in the packing department.

The expected costs of producing 100,000 units in the next quarter are as follows:

Direct materials	£24.00 per unit
Direct labour	2 hours assembly @ £7.00 per hour
	1 hour packing @ £6.00 per hour
Assembly overheads	£320,000
Packing overheads	£240,000
Maintenance overheads	£200,000

In each of the production and service departments it is estimated that 40% of the overheads are variable and the remainder are fixed. Overheads are absorbed on the basis of labour hours.

Calculate the cost per unit using the following costing methods:

(a) absorption costing
(b) marginal costing

Absorption costing

Production overheads

		Assembly	Packing	Maintenance
		£	£	£
Allocated and apportioned		320,000	240,000	200,000
Reapportioned – maintenance				
(75%/25%)		150,000	50,000	(200,000)
Total overhead		470,000	290,000	–
Total hours	2 × 100,000	200,000		
	1 × 100,000		100,000	
Absorption rate	=	$\dfrac{470,000}{200,000}$	$\dfrac{290,000}{100,000}$	
	=	£2.35 per labour hour	£2.90 per labour hour	

Interpretation:

For every one hour that the product is worked on in the assembly department, it is charged with a £2.35 share of the overheads incurred.

For every one hour that the product is worked on in the packing department, it is charged with a £2.90 share of the overheads incurred.

Unit cost

	£
Direct Materials	24.00
Direct labour – assembly 2 hours × £7.00	14.00
Direct labour – packing 1 hour × £6.00	6.00
Prime cost	44.00
Overheads – assembly 2 hours × £2.35	4.70
– packing 1 hour × £2.90	2.90
Total absorption cost per unit	51.60

Marginal costing

In this method only variable overheads are included in the cost per unit, so these must be ascertained:

		Assembly	Packing
		£	£
Total overhead		470,000	290,000
Variable element (40%)		188,000	116,000
Labour hours (as before)		200,000	100,000
Absorption rate	=	$\dfrac{188,000}{200,000}$	$\dfrac{116,000}{100,000}$
	=	£0.94 per labour hour	£1.16 per labour hour

Unit cost

	£
Direct materials	24.00
Direct labour – assembly	14.00
Direct labour – packing	6.00
Prime cost	44.00
Variable overhead – assembly (2 hours × £0.94)	1.88
– packing (1 hour × £1.16)	1.16
Marginal cost per unit	47.04

Task 1

A business expects to produce 5,000 units of its single product in the next month, with the following costs being incurred:

	£
Direct materials	12,000
Direct labour	15,000
Variable overheads	23,000
Fixed overheads	25,000

Complete the following table to show the cost per unit under both absorption costing and marginal costing methods.

Costing method	Cost per unit £
Absorption costing	
Marginal costing	

Marginal and absorption costing, inventory (stock) levels and profit

As we have just seen, the unit cost is very different under marginal costing from that calculated under absorption costing.

Under absorption costing the fixed overhead is absorbed into the units produced in the period, and therefore the full production cost of the units actually sold in the period is charged to the income statement (profit and loss account) as part of cost of sales.

However under marginal costing a lower value is assigned to cost of sales, as the cost per unit only includes variable costs. The fixed costs are then charged to the income statement (profit and loss account) as a period cost.

This difference is also reflected in the valuation of inventory (stock). Under absorption costing, inventory is valued at the full production cost, which includes the absorbed fixed overhead. However under marginal costing a lower value is assigned to the value of inventory (stock), as the cost per unit only includes variable costs.

If the opening inventory (stock) and closing inventory (stock) levels are the same (so that sales = production) then when we include revenue per unit and in total into our calculations, profit shown under both absorption costing and marginal costing will be the same. However if opening and closing inventory (stock) levels are different, ie there has been an increase or decrease in inventory (stock) levels, then absorption costing and marginal costing will not produce the same profit

25

figure, because of the differences in the treatment of fixed overheads and the valuation of inventory.

An important difference in this context between absorption and marginal costing, is that in the latter we calculate and focus on contribution per unit, which is revenue less variable costs per unit. We will look at the use of contribution for decision making in chapter 3.

HOW IT WORKS

Spa Ltd makes a single product and produces management accounts including a costing income statement (profit and loss account) each month. In both May and June 100,000 units of the product were produced.

The production costs in both May and June were:

	£
Direct materials	200,000
Direct labour	300,000
Fixed overheads	300,000
Total costs	800,000

There were no opening inventories (stock) at the start of May and all of the production for May was sold. However in June only 75,000 units of production were sold, leaving 25,000 units in inventory (stock).

Each unit is sold for £10.

(a) What is the cost per unit using:

    (i) absorption costing
    (ii) marginal costing?

(b) What is the profit for each month using:

    (i) absorption costing
    (ii) marginal costing?

(a) **Unit cost**

    (i) Absorption costing:

      £800,000/100,000 = £8 per unit

    (ii) Marginal costing:

      £500,000/100,000 = £5 per unit

(b) **Income statements (profit and loss accounts)**

(i) Absorption costing:

	May £	May £	June £	June £
Sales		1,000,000		750,000
Less: cost of sales				
Opening inventory (stock)	–		–	
Cost of production				
100,000 units × £8	800,000		800,000	
	800,000		800,000	
Less: closing inventory (stock)				
25,000 units × £8	–		(200,000)	
Cost of sales		800,000		600,000
Profit (Absorption costing)		200,000		150,000

(ii) Marginal costing:

	May £	May £	June £	June £
Sales		1,000,000		750,000
Less: cost of sales				
Opening inventory (stock)	–			
Cost of production				
100,000 units × £5	500,000		500,000	
	500,000		500,000	
Less: closing inventory (stock)				
25,000 units × £5	–		(125,000)	
Marginal cost of sales		500,000		375,000
Contribution to fixed costs		500,000		375,000
Less: fixed costs		300,000		300,000
Profit (Marginal costing)		200,000		75,000

In May the profit is the same under both costing methods, £200,000. This is because there is no movement in inventory (stock) during the period, since all of the production is sold.

In June however profit under absorption costing is £150,000, whereas it is only £75,000 under the marginal costing method. The reason for the £75,000 difference in profit, is that the closing inventory (stock) under absorption costing includes £75,000 (£300,000/100,000 × 25,000 units) of fixed costs that are being carried forward to the next accounting period, whereas under marginal costing they were all written off in June.

The rules are that:

(1) **if inventory (stock) levels are rising, then absorption costing will give higher profits** (as the fixed overheads are being carried forward into the next accounting period)

(2) **if inventory (stock) levels are falling, then absorption costing will give a lower profit figure** (as more fixed overheads from the previous period are charged to the income statement (profit and loss account) in this period)

(3) **where inventory (stock) levels are constant** (provided that unit costs are constant), **then absorption costing and marginal costing will give the same level of profit**

A reconciliation of the profit figures can be prepared:

	May	June
	£	£
Absorption cost profit	200,000	150,000
Change in inventory (stock) (sales = production)	0	
Increase in inventory (stock) (25,000 units – 0) × fixed cost per unit £3		(75,000)
Marginal cost profit	200,000	75,000

Task 2

A business operates a total absorption costing system. At the start of last month the business had 2,500 units in inventory (stock). During the month it produced another 23,000 units and sold 24,000. The cost per unit of the product is as follows:

	£
Direct Materials	10.00
Direct labour	14.00
Prime cost	24.00
Variable overheads	3.00
Fixed overheads	2.00
Total absorption cost per unit	29.00

The business reported a profit of £504,000.

The profit if the business used marginal costing would have been

£ [   ]

UNDER- AND OVER-ABSORPTION OF OVERHEADS

As we have seen using absorption costing, the overhead cost of output is found using the budgeted overhead costs for the period and the budgeted activity level. However using budgeted figures means that the actual overhead cost is unlikely to be the same as the overheads absorbed into production, as we are relying on two estimates:

- overhead costs
- activity levels

These will inevitably differ from the actual values that are experienced during the period. Consequently, at the end of the period when the income statement (profit and loss account) is drawn up, the profit figure will be wrong as the overhead charge will be the absorbed amount rather than the actual amount. The error in the profit figure results from one of two possibilities:

(1) If more overheads are absorbed than have actually been incurred, this is known as OVER-ABSORPTION.

(2) If fewer overheads are absorbed than have actually been incurred, this is known as UNDER-ABSORPTION.

The amount over- or under-absorbed is adjusted for in the income statement (profit and loss account) after the production cost has been charged. Under-absorption means that too little overhead has been charged in the production cost, so a deduction is made from profit. Over-absorption means that too much overhead has been charged, so there is a compensating addition to profit.

Note that over or under absorption is not a problem in marginal costing, as the fixed overhead is treated as a period cost and not absorbed into units.

HOW IT WORKS

Cowslip Limited budgeted to make and sell 10,000 units of their product for each of the next three months (February – April). The units are sold for £20 each and direct costs per unit are £6. Budgeted overheads were £15,000 per month, and overheads are recovered using a rate per machine hour basis. Each unit requires 3 hours of machine time, the budgeted machine hours being 30,000.

The actual overheads incurred over the next three months were:

	£
February	15,000
March	14,000
April	16,000

All other actual costs, revenues and quantities were as budgeted (i.e. only the overheads incurred differ from budget).

The overhead absorption rate (based on the budget) will be

$$= \frac{\text{Overheads}}{\text{Machine hours}}$$

$$= \frac{£15,000}{10,000 \text{ units} \times 3\text{h per unit}}$$

$$= £0.50 \text{ per machine hour}$$

or £1.50 per unit (3h @ £0.50)

In **February** a comparison of actual overheads and absorbed overheads will show that the two are the same:

	£
Actual overheads	15,000
Absorbed overheads	
(10,000 units × £1.50) or (30,000 hrs x £0.50)	15,000
Under/over absorption	Nil

In March, the production cost charged in the income statement (profit and loss account) will be the same as February, since 10,000 units were produced and the same number of machine hours have been used. But we can't leave profit at the same level as before: the actual overheads are only £14,000, so we should have a profit of £1,000 more. By including 30,000 machine hours at a cost of £0.50 per hour in the income statement (profit and loss account), we have absorbed more overheads than were actually incurred, which is an over absorption.

	£
Actual overheads	14,000
Absorbed overheads (30,000h × £0.50)	15,000
Over absorption	1,000

This over-absorption is credited to the income statement (profit and loss account) i.e. added back to profit.

In April actual overheads are £16,000

	£
Actual overheads	16,000
Absorbed overheads (30,000h × £0.50)	15,000
Under absorption	1,000

Thus the overheads absorbed in April are less than the actual overhead incurred. The under-absorbed overheads will be debited to the income statement (profit and loss account). Under-absorption means that not enough overheads have been charged against profits, so we deduct the under-absorption from profit to make up for this.

Note be very careful to calculate the under or over absorption based on actual v absorbed costs; budgeted costs are not brought into this calculation. This is particularly relevant when the actual amounts of both overheads and activity are different from budget.

Let's say that **in May**, the number of units produced and sold by Cowslip Limited is 12,000 – actual machine hours amounted to 38,000 and overheads actually incurred amount to £16,500. So this time both overheads and activity level are different from budget.

Calculate the overhead under- or over-absorbed as before, being careful to pick up the correct figures (highlighted).

	£
Actual overheads	**16,500**
Absorbed overheads (**38,000**h × £0.50)	19,000
Over absorption	2,500

The profit calculation will take account of the over absorption by adding £2,500 back to the profit for the period.

In summary, the under/over absorption is found by comparing:

	£
Actual overheads incurred for the period	X
Absorbed overheads:	
(actual units produced at absorption rate per unit) or	
(actual hours at absorption rate per hour)	X
Under/Over absorption	X

Task 3

Tulip Limited planned to make 30,000 units, each of which was expected to require two hours of direct labour. Budgeted overheads were £54,000. Actual production was 28,000 units, requiring a total of 55,000 direct labour hours. Actual overheads were £47,000.

(a) The overhead absorption rate based on direct labour hours is

         .90 p

(b) Use the picklists to complete the sentences:

     The over absorption of £ 2500 should be

     added profit

     Under

     Over

     £2,500

     £4,500

     Added to

     Deducted from

MARGINAL COSTING AND ABSORPTION COSTING COMPARED

Advantages of absorption costing:

- Fixed overheads have to be incurred to produce output so it is fair to charge each unit of product with a share of the fixed costs.

- Using full absorption cost to value stock is consistent with the closing inventory value that is required by accounting standards (IAS2/SSAP9) for the external financial statements.

- In the long term an organisation needs to covers its fixed costs to be profitable so when setting selling prices, an organisation needs to be aware of the full cost of the product.

Advantages of marginal costing:

- Fixed costs are the same regardless of output and therefore it makes sense to charge them in full as a period cost.

- It does not require apportionment of fixed costs which can be arbitrary.

- By charging fixed costs as a period cost it avoids the under or over absorption of fixed overheads.

- It focuses on variable costs and contribution which can be more useful for decision making (see chapter 3).

ACTIVITY BASED COSTING (ABC)

The final costing method to consider is that of activity based costing or ABC. This is a method of absorption costing which was developed in the 1970s and 1980s as an alternative to traditional absorption costing.

Under basic absorption costing, the production overheads of a cost centre are all absorbed on the same basis, usually labour hours or machine hours, no matter what the cause of the overhead. This could be viewed as quite an arbitrary approach to absorbing overheads, particularly as overheads now tend to form a very large part of product costs.

The principle of Activity Based Costing (ABC) is to breakdown the overheads into their constituent elements, for example costs incurred due to receiving materials, costs incurred due to issuing materials to production, costs incurred due to setting up machines for a production run (production setups), costs incurred due to quality control procedures etc.

Cost pools

Each of these elements that cause costs to be incurred are called ACTIVITIES and the costs associated with each activity are gathered together into COST POOLS.

For each cost pool what must then be identified is the factor that causes or drives these costs to change. This known as the COST DRIVER.

The total of the cost pool is then divided by the number of times the cost driver takes place and this gives an overhead rate per cost driver. The overheads from the cost pool are then allocated to different products depending upon their particular usage of the cost driver.

For example, a product that required frequent purchases of materials and frequent production set ups would have larger overheads allocated to it than a product that required few purchases and few production runs.

The diagram below illustrates in outline how ABC works:

Identify activities causing overheads	Activity 1	Activity 2
Gather all costs for each activity	Cost pool 1	Cost pool 2
Identify what causes the cost	Cost driver 1	Cost driver 2
Calculate cost driver rate	Cost pool 1 total / No. of cost drivers	Cost pool 2 total / No. of cost drivers
Apply to individual cost units	Use of cost driver × cost driver rate	Use of cost driver × cost driver rate

HOW IT WORKS

Caplan Ltd produces two products, the C and the P. The direct costs of the two products are given below:

	C	P
Direct materials	£3.50	£4.80
Direct labour	£2.00	£1.20

The budgeted production is for 120,000 units of C and 50,000 units of P.

The two main activities identified for the fairly simple production process are materials handling and production set-ups.

Product C requires only large production runs and large transfers of materials from stores. However product P is a more complex product with a number of different types of materials required and shorter and more frequent production runs.

The budgeted overheads for Caplan are £800,000 and they are made up as follows:

	£
Materials handling cost pool	300,000
Production set-up cost pool	500,000
	800,000

The use of these activities for each product is:

	C	P	Total
Number of materials requisitions	200	800	1,000
Number of production set-ups	100	400	500

Calculate the total costs incurred and the unit cost of each product, using the costing method of Activity Based Costing. Also calculate the direct (prime) cost and the overhead cost per unit.

Cost driver rate

Materials handling $\dfrac{£300,000}{1,000}$ = £300 per material requisition

Production set-ups $\dfrac{£500,000}{5,000}$ = £1,000 per production set-up

Total production costs and Cost per unit

	C £	P £
Direct materials		
120,000 × £3.50	420,000	
50,000 × £4.80		240,000
Direct labour		
120,000 × £2.00	240,000	
50,000 × £1.20		60,000

Materials handling overhead

200 × £300	60,000	
800 × £300		240,000

Production set-up overhead

100 × £1,000	100,000	
400 × £1,000		400,000
	820,000	940,000

Cost per unit

$$\frac{£820,000}{120,000 \text{ units}} \qquad \frac{£940,000}{50,000 \text{ units}}$$

£6.83 per unit   £18.80 per unit

Analysis of cost per unit

		C	-P
		£	£
Direct (or prime) costs	(3.50 + 2.00)	5.50	
	(4.80 + 1.20)		6.00
Materials handling overhead			
60,000/120,000		0.50	
240,000/50,000			4.80
Production set-up overhead			
100,000/120,000		0.83	
400,000/50,000			8.00
Unit cost		6.83	18.80

In this instance product C is charged with £1.33 of overhead, whereas the more activity intensive product P is charged with £12.80 of production overhead. Given that the direct labour cost of product P is only £1.20 compared to the £2.00 labour cost of product C, if the overheads had been apportioned according to labour hours, as with traditional absorption costing, then the picture would have been very different indeed.

Task 4

The costs of the quality control department of a manufacturing business are estimated to be £74,000 for the following quarter. During that period it is estimated that there will be 370 quality inspections of all the company's different products. Of these, Product A will require 25 inspections during the quarter and Product B 130 inspections.

Complete the table below to using activity based costing to show how much quality control overhead will be absorbed into Product A and Product B.

(a)

| Overhead included in Product A | £ | 5000 |
| Overhead included in Product B | £ | 26000 |

(b) It has been budgeted that 10,000 units of product A will be produced in the period and 13,000 units of product B.

Complete the table below to show the overhead cost per unit for Products A and B.

| Product A overhead cost per unit | £ | .50 |
| Product B overhead cost per unit | £ | 2.00 |

CHAPTER OVERVIEW

- Under absorption costing, all production overheads are allocated and apportioned to production cost centres and then absorbed into the cost of the products on some suitable basis

- Under marginal costing, the cost of the products is the variable cost of production with all fixed production costs being charged to the income statement (profit and loss account) as a period charge

- If inventory (stock) levels are constant then both absorption costing and marginal costing will report the same profit figure

- If inventory (stock) levels are increasing, absorption costing profit will be higher as **more** fixed overheads are carried forward to the following period in closing inventory (stock) than those brought forward in opening inventory (stock)

- If inventory (stock) levels are falling, marginal costing profit will be higher as **less** fixed overheads are carried forward under absorption costing in the closing inventory (stock) figure than those brought forward in opening inventory (stock)

- The difference in profit between absorption costing and marginal costing will be the fixed production overhead included in the increase/decrease in inventory (stock) levels under absorption costing

- Overhead absorption rates are based on budgeted values for activity levels and overheads incurred. In absorption costing, this results in under- or over-absorption of overheads which is adjusted for in the income statement (profit and loss account)

  - under-absorption is a deduction in the income statement (profit and loss account)

  - over-absorption is an addition in the income statement (profit and loss account)

- The under/over absorption is found by comparing the actual overhead incurred with the overhead absorbed in the period, where the overhead absorbed is calculated as:
  actual units produced at absorption rate per unit or actual hours at absorption rate per hour

- Activity based costing (ABC) considers the activities that cause overheads to be incurred and the factors that give rise to costs (cost drivers). It is a method of absorbing overheads into products on the basis of the amount of each activity that the particular product is expected to use in the period

Keywords

Absorption (full) costing – both variable and fixed production overheads are included in unit cost

Marginal (variable) costing – unit cost includes only variable production costs

Contribution – sales value less variable cost of the goods sold

Overhead absorption rate – the rate at which overheads are charged to cost units calculated by dividing overheads by the level of activity

Over-absorption – more overheads are absorbed into production than have actually been incurred

Under-absorption – less overheads are absorbed into production than were actually incurred

Activity based costing (ABC) – a more complex approach to absorption of overheads, based upon an analysis of the detailed causes of the overheads

Activities – the elements of the overhead cost which cause costs to be incurred

Cost pools – costs that can be attributed to each activity

Cost driver – the factor that causes the costs for each cost pool

TEST YOUR LEARNING

1   Overheads apportioned to two production departments have been worked out, along with estimates for labour hours and machine hours expected in the coming budget period. P1 is a labour intensive department, while P2 is highly mechanised with relatively few machine operatives. The budgeted figures are as follows.

	P1	P2
Overheads apportioned	£50,000	£60,000
Machine hours	800	4,000
Labour hours	2,500	600

(a)   The overhead absorption rate for department P1 is:

A   £62.50
B   £20.00 ✓
C   £15.00
D   £100.00

(b)   The overhead absorption rate for department P2 is:

A   £62.50
B   £20.00
C   £15.00 ✓
D   £100.00

2   Complete the following table to show the under- or over-absorption of
     overheads in each of the three cases below, and state whether this is an
     under or an over absorption and how this would be adjusted for in the
     income statement (profit and loss account).

	Amount of under/over absorption £	Under or over absorption	Add or subtract in income statement (P&L a/c)
An overhead absorption rate of £3 per unit, based on expected production levels of 500 units. Actual overheads turn out to be £1,600, and actual production is 650 units.	350	Over	+
The budget is set at 1,000 units, with £9,000 overheads recovered on the basis of 600 direct labour hours. At the end of the period, overheads amounted to £8,600, production achieved was only 950 units and 590 direct labour hours had been worked.	250	Over	+

3   Explain how fixed production overheads are treated in an absorption
     costing system and in a marginal costing system.

4   Given below is the budgeted information about the production of
     60,000 units of a single product in a factory for the following quarter:

Direct materials	£12.50 per unit
Direct labour – assembly	4 hours @ £8.40 per hour
– finishing	1 hour @ £6.60 per hour
Assembly production overheads	£336,000
Finishing production overheads	£84,000

It is estimated that 60% of the assembly overhead is variable and that
75% of the finishing overhead is variable.

Complete the table below to show the budgeted cost of the product
using each method of costing.

Method of costing	Budgeted cost £
Absorption costing	
Marginal costing	

5 Given below are the budgeted figures for production and sales of a factory's single product for the months of November and December:

	November	December
Production	15,000 units	15,000 units
Sales	12,500 units	18,000 units
Direct materials	£12.00 per unit	£12.00 per unit
Direct labour	£8.00 per unit	£8.00 per unit
Variable production cost	£237,000	£237,000
Fixed production cost	£390,000	£390,000

Overheads are absorbed on the basis of the budgeted production and the selling price of the product is £75.

There were 2,000 units of the product in inventory (stock) at the start of November.

(a) Prepare the budgeted income statements (profit and loss accounts) for each of the two months using:

(i) absorption costing

Absorption costing – income statement (profit and loss account)

	November		December	
	£	£	£	£
Sales	937500			1350000
Less: cost of sales				
Opening inventory (stock)	123600			278100
Production costs	927000			927000
	———		———	
Less: closing inventory (stock)	(278100)			(92700)
		772500		
				1112400
		———		———
Profit		165000		237600

(ii)   Marginal costing

Marginal costing – income statement (profit and loss account)

	November		December	
	£	£	£	£
Sales		937500		1350000
Less: cost of sales				
Opening inventory (stock)	71600			161100
Production costs	537000			537000
Less: closing inventory (stock)	(161100)			(53700)
				644400
Contribution		490000		705600
Less: fixed overheads		390000		(390.000)
Profit		100000		315600

(b)   Complete the table below to reconcile the absorption costing profit and the marginal costing profit for each of the two months

	November	December
	£	£
Absorption costing profit	165000	237600
Inventory (stock) changes		
Marginal costing profit		

6   A business produces two products, the LM and the NP. The direct costs of the two products are:

	LM	NP
Direct materials	£2.60	£3.90
Direct labour	£3.50	£2.70

The total overhead cost is made up as follows:

	£
Stores costs	140,000
Production set-up costs	280,000
Quality control inspection costs	180,000
	600,000

The budgeted production is for 50,000 units of LM and 20,000 units of NP.

Each product is expected to make the following use of the service activities:

	LM	NP	Total
Materials requisitions	100	220	320
Production set-ups	80	200	280
Quality control inspections	30	60	90

Complete the following table to show the budgeted cost per unit for each product using activity based costing and how much total budgeted overhead is included in the unit cost for each product.

Product	Budgeted cost per unit £	Budgeted overhead per unit £
LM		
NP		

chapter 3:
DECISION MAKING

USE OF MARGINAL COSTING AND CONTRIBUTION FOR DECISION MAKING

In the chapter on marginal costing we defined CONTRIBUTION as sales revenue less variable costs. We can look at contribution in total, as we did in marginal costing, or at contribution per unit.

Provided that the selling price and variable costs remain constant at different levels of activity, then contribution per unit will also be a constant figure at each level of activity. When we consider fixed costs however, we can see that as activity levels increase, although the fixed costs themselves remain constant, the fixed cost per unit falls as the fixed costs are spread over more units. This means that even though contribution per unit will remain constant with increasing levels of activity, the full production cost (absorption cost) per unit will decrease and profit per unit will increase.

HOW IT WORKS

J R Grantham & Partners are considering expanding their business from its current production and sales of 100,000 units per annum. Market research suggests that it will almost certainly be possible to increase sales to 150,000 and possibly even to 180,000 units per annum.

The single product that the partnership produces sells for £20 and has variable costs of production of £15. The fixed costs are currently £400,000 per annum and are not expected to increase.

We will look at the contribution per unit, full production cost per unit and profit per unit at each activity level.

	100,000	150,000	180,000
	£	£	£
Sales	2,000,000	3,000,000	3,600,000
Variable costs	1,500,000	2,250,000	2,700,000
Contribution	500,000	750,000	900,000
Fixed costs	400,000	400,000	400,000
Profit	100,000	350,000	500,000
Contribution per unit	£5	£5	£5

Full production cost per unit

(variable + fixed)

£15 + £400,000/100,000	£19		
£15 + £400,000/150,000		£17.67	
£15 + £400,000/180,000			£17.22
Profit per unit	£1	£2.33	£2.78

As we can see, there is a significant decrease in the full production cost per unit as the activity level rises, due to the fixed costs being spread over a larger number of units. This also therefore means that there is a significant increase in profit per unit as the activity level increases. However contribution per unit has remained constant.

This is one of the reasons why for decision making purposes contribution per unit is a much more meaningful figure than profit per unit, as the profit per unit figure is simply being affected by the spreading of the fixed costs.

HOW IT WORKS

A company produces a single product at a variable cost per unit of £20. During the year the company expects to make 100,000 units, all of which can be sold to existing customers for £30 per unit. The total fixed costs for the period are expected to be £4 per unit.

(i)   How much profit will the company make?

(ii) A customer has offered to buy an extra 5,000 units as a one-off order at a price of £23. Should the company accept (assuming it has spare capacity)?

(iii) What would the profit be if the company only made and sold 80,000 units (ignore the one- off order for this purpose)?

(i) The full cost per unit is £20 +£4 = £24

The profit per unit is £30 -£24 = £6 per unit, so the total profit from 100,000 units is £600,000.

(ii) The full absorption cost of the product is £24 so on the face of it at a selling price of £23 the product would make a loss.

However if we consider the additional revenue and costs involved for the order:

	£
Sales (5,000 x £23)	115,000
Variable costs (5,000 x £20)	100,000
Contribution	15,000

Since the fixed costs for the period are being incurred anyway the company should accept the one-off order as it increases contribution and therefore profit by £15,000.

However the company would not want to accept £23 as the regular selling price as in the long term it needs to cover the fixed overheads for the period.

Note: It is possible that the company might incur additional fixed costs relating specifically to the additional order, in which case these would need to be taken into account in determining whether to accept.

(iii) The profit from 80,000 units would not be 80,000 × £6 = £480,000 because if only 80,000 units are made the fixed overhead per unit would increase:

Total fixed costs were expected to be £4 × 100,000 units = £400,000.

Spread over 80,000 units this gives a fixed cost of £5 per unit and a new profit per unit of £30 – £25 = £5.

Hence total profit would be 80,000 × £5 = £400,000.

An alternative (and easier) calculation under marginal costing would be:

Contribution per unit = £30 – £20 = £10

Total contribution = 80,000 × £10 = £800,000, less fixed costs £400,000 = profit £400,000

Thus, for decision making purposes, you should always treat total profit as having two distinct elements:

1	Total contribution (= contribution/unit × units)	X
	Less:	
2	Fixed costs	(X)
		X

Element **1** (contribution) varies proportionately with volume, while element **2** (fixed costs) is a lump-sum period deduction.

As fixed costs in total are assumed to be constant for the period, whatever volume of products is made, maximisation of profit will be achieved by maximising contribution.

COST-VOLUME-PROFIT ANALYSIS

COST-VOLUME-PROFIT ANALYSIS is the general term for the analysis of the relationship between activity levels, costs and profit. One of the most common applications of this analysis is BREAK-EVEN ANALYSIS whereby the break-even point for a business is determined.

The BREAK-EVEN POINT is the level of activity where the sales revenue is equal to the total costs of the business, meaning that all costs are covered by sales revenue but no profit is made. This is obviously an important point for managers of a business to be aware of; if the activity level falls below the break-even point then losses will be made.

So the break-even point activity level can be expressed as the point where:

Sales revenue = Variable costs + Fixed costs

Alternatively

Sales revenue – Variable costs = Fixed costs

Remember that sales revenue minus variable costs is equal to contribution. So the relationship is that the break-even point is where:

Contribution = Fixed costs

Contribution per unit × break-even point (units) = Fixed costs

We saw in an earlier example in this chapter that, provided that selling price and variable costs remain constant at different levels of activity, then contribution per unit will also remain constant. We can therefore use this to calculate the break-even point.

$$\text{Break-even point} = \frac{\text{Fixed cost}}{\text{Contribution per unit}}$$

HOW IT WORKS

Reardon Enterprises sells a single product with a selling price of £10 per unit. The variable costs of producing the product are £6 per unit and the fixed costs of the business are £200,000.

What is the break-even point in units?

$$\text{Break-even point} = \frac{£200,000}{£10 - £6}$$

$$= 50,000 \text{ units}$$

We can prove that this is the point where no profit or loss is made:

	£
Sales (50,000 × £10)	500,000
Variable costs (50,000 × £6)	300,000)
Contribution (50,000 × £4)	200,000
Fixed costs	(200,000)
Profit	–

Therefore the management of Reardon Enterprises will know that they must ensure that sales volumes exceed 50,000 units per annum in order for the business to cover its total costs and make any profit.

Task 1

A business has a single product that it sells for £28. The variable costs of producing the product are £19 per unit and the fixed costs of the business are £360,000.

What is the break-even point in units?

☐ units

Target profit

It is also possible to extend the analysis using contribution per unit in order to determine the level of sales that are necessary in order to not only cover all of the costs but also to make a particular amount of profit, the target profit.

Thus we want:

Total contribution	X
Less: fixed costs	(X)
Target profit	X

Total contribution = contribution per unit x target number of units (activity level)

This needs to exactly cover fixed costs and generate the target profit.

Working back this gives us:

$$\text{Activity level} = \frac{\text{Fixed costs} + \text{target profit}}{\text{Contribution per unit}}$$

HOW IT WORKS

Returning to Reardon Enterprises the managing director, Anna Reardon, would like to ensure a profit of £100,000 for the coming year. What level of sales is required for this profit to be made?

$$\text{Activity level} = \frac{£200,000 + £100,000}{£10 - £6}$$
$$= 75,000 \text{ units}$$

Therefore if the business sells 75,000 units of the product a profit of £100,000 will be made. Again we can check this:

	£
Sales (75,000 × £10)	750,000
Variable costs (75,000 × £6)	(450,000)
Contribution	300,000
Fixed costs	(200,000)
Profit	100,000

Task 2

A business has fixed costs of £250,000. It sells just one product for a price of £80 and the variable costs of production are £60.

How many units of the product must be business sell in order to make a profit of £150,000?

[   ] units

Margin of safety

Another figure that management might be interested in is the MARGIN OF SAFETY. This is the difference between the budgeted or forecast sales or actual current sales and the break-even sales level. This is usually expressed as a percentage of the budgeted, forecast or actual sales. (In the assessment, make sure you express the margin of safety as a percentage of the budgeted, forecast or actual sales, not as a percentage of break-even sales.)

HOW IT WORKS

Remember that Reardon Enterprise's break-even sales volume was 50,000 units. If the budgeted sales for the forthcoming year are 70,000 units what is the margin of safety?

$$\text{Margin of safety} \quad = \quad 70,000 \text{ units} - 50,000 \text{ units}$$

$$= \quad 20,000 \text{ units}$$

This can be expressed as a percentage of budgeted sales, which should be used as the denominator in calculations.

$$\text{Margin of safety} = \frac{20,000}{70,000} \times 100$$

$$= 28.6\%$$

This tells management that sales can drop below the budgeted figure by 28.6% before losses start to be made.

Task 3

A business has budgeted to sell 75,000 units of its single product in the following year. The product sells for £32 and the variable costs of production are £24. The fixed overheads of the business are £480,000.

What is the margin of safety as a percentage?

☐ %

Profit volume ratio

When we were calculating the break-even point above, the figure that was derived using contribution per unit and fixed costs was the number of units that were required to be sold in order to break-even. However the break-even point can also be expressed in terms of the sales revenue required in order to break-even, by using the profit volume ratio (P/V) which can also be called the CONTRIBUTION TO SALES RATIO (C/S).

$$\text{Profit volume ratio} = \frac{\text{Contribution}}{\text{Sales}} \times 100$$

Thus the P/V ratio measures contribution per £ sales revenue rather than per physical sales unit.

Thus, at break-even sales revenue

Total contribution (P/V ratio × break-even sales revenue)	X
Less: fixed costs	(X)
Profit	0

The break-even point in terms of sales revenue can then be found as:

$$\text{Break-even point } (\pounds) = \frac{\text{Fixed cost}}{\text{Profit volume ratio}}$$

HOW IT WORKS

Reardon Enterprises sell their product for £10 and the variable costs are £6 per unit. Total fixed costs are £200,000.

$$\text{Profit volume ratio} = \frac{\pounds10 - \pounds6}{\pounds10} \times 100$$

$$= 40\%$$

$$\text{Break-even point } (\pounds) = \frac{200,000}{0.40}$$

$$= \pounds500,000$$

(which corresponds to a unit activity level of $\dfrac{\pounds500,000}{\pounds10} = 50,000$ as before)

Task 4

A business has a single product that it sells for £36. The variable costs of producing the product are £27 per unit and the fixed costs of the business are £360,000.

What is the break-even point in terms of sales revenue?

£ [   ]

LIMITING FACTOR ANALYSIS

Obviously the managers of a business will wish to produce and sell more than the break-even number of units in order to cover fixed costs and make a profit. However, in practice, the quantity that they can produce and sell may be limited by one or more factors, the LIMITING FACTOR(S).

In many cases the limiting factor will be market demand, or the amount of units that customers are prepared to buy. However, in other instances the limiting factor might be the amount of materials that are available or the number of machine or labour hours that are available.

HOW IT WORKS

A business sells a single product for £35. The variable costs of the product are:

Direct materials   3 kg per unit @ £3 per kg

Direct labour   2 hours per unit @ £7.50 per hour

The fixed costs of the business are £800,000.

Materials as limiting factor

If the supply of materials is limited to 360,000 kg, how many units can the business produce and how much profit will be made?

Number of units that can be produced	= 360,000 kg/3 kg per unit
	= 120,000 units

	£
Sales (120,000 × £35)	4,200,000
Variable costs (120,000 × (£9 + £15))	2,880,000
Contribution	1,320,000
Fixed costs	800,000
Profit	520,000

Labour hours as limiting factor

If materials are now not restricted, but the business only has 280,000 labour hours available for production, how many units can be made and what is the profit at this production level?

Number of units that can be produced	= 280,000 hours/2 hours per unit
	= 140,000 units

	£
Sales (140,000 × £35)	4,900,000
Variable costs (140,000 × £24)	3,360,000
Contribution	1,540,000
Fixed costs	800,000
Profit	740,000

MORE THAN ONE PRODUCT

We will now make the position a little more complicated by introducing a business that makes more than one product. If the availability of either materials or labour hours is the limiting factor, then it will be necessary to determine the optimum production mix.

In order to make a decision we must determine our criterion for the decision making process. In business the overriding criterion will normally be to make as much profit as possible. As fixed costs in total are assumed to be constant whatever combination of products is made, maximisation of profit will be achieved by maximising contribution.

If a business has more than one product, and one limiting factor, the technique to use in order to maximise contribution is to determine the contribution per unit of the scarce resource or limiting factor and concentrate upon the production of the product with the highest contribution per limiting factor unit.

HOW IT WORKS

Farnham Engineering makes three products A, B and C. The costs and selling prices of the three products are:

	A	B	C
	£	£	£
Direct materials @ £4 per kg	8	16	12
Direct labour @ £7 per hour	7	21	14
Variable overheads	3	9	6
Marginal cost	18	46	32
Selling price	22	54	39
Contribution	4	8	7

Sales demand for the coming period is expected to be as follows:

Product A	3,000 units
Product B	7,000 units
Product C	5,000 units

The supply of materials is limited to 50,000 kg during the period and the labour hours available are 28,000.

We have to decide firstly if there is a limiting factor other than sales demand. Consider the materials usage for each product if the maximum sales demand is produced. (You are not given the actual usage of materials of each product but you can work it out – for example the materials cost for A is £8 and as the materials are £4 per kg, product A must use 2 kg etc.)

	A	B	C	Total required
Materials (2/4/3kg)	6,000 kg	28,000 kg	15,000 kg	49,000 kg
Labour (1/3/2hrs)	3,000 hours	21,000 hours	10,000 hours	34,000 hours

As 50,000 kg of materials are available for the period and only 49,000 kg are required for the maximum production level, materials are not a limiting factor.

However, only 28,000 labour hours are available whereas in order to produce the maximum demand 34,000 hours are required. Therefore labour hours are the limiting factor.

The next stage is to calculate the contribution per limiting factor unit – so in this case the contribution per labour hour – for each product. Then rank the products according to how high the contribution per labour hour is for each one.

	A	B	C
Contribution	£4	£8	£7
Labour hours per unit	1 hour	3 hours	2 hours
Contribution per labour hour:			
£4/1	£4.00		
£8/3		£2.67	
£7/2			£3.50
Ranking	1	3	2

A makes the most contribution per unit of scarce resource (labour hours) and therefore in order to maximise contribution, we must concentrate first on production of A up to the maximum sales demand, then on C, and finally, if there are any remaining hours available, on B.

The optimal production plan in order to maximise contribution is:

	Units produced	Labour hours required
A	3,000	3,000
C	5,000	10,000
B (balance)	5,000*	15,000 (balancing figure)
		28,000

* Working: After making A and C there are 15,000 hours left. Each unit of B needs 3 hours so there is sufficient to make 15,000/3 = 5,000 units.

The contribution earned from this production plan is:

		£
A	(3,000 × £4)	12,000
B	(5,000 × £8)	40,000
C	(5,000 × £7)	35,000
Total contribution		87,000

Task 5

A business produces four products and the details are:

	P	Q	R	S
Contribution per unit	£12	£15	£9	£14
Materials per unit	3 kg	4 kg	1 kg	2 kg
Maximum demand (units)	2,000	6,000	1,000	4,000

Fixed costs amount to £30,000 each period, and the materials supply is limited to 30,000 kg.

(a) Complete the following table in order to determine the production plan that will maximise profit.

Product	Units produced

(b) The profit earned from this production plan will be £ [   ]

MAKE OR BUY DECISIONS

A make or buy problem involves a decision by an organisation about whether it should make a product or whether it should pay another organisation to do so. Here are some examples of applications of make or buy decisions.

(a) Whether a company should manufacture its own components, or else buy the components from an outside supplier

(b) Whether a construction company should do some work with its own employees, or whether it should sub-contract the work to another company

(c) Whether a service should be carried out by an internal department or whether an external organisation should be employed

Essentially the choice is between whether to do something in-house 'make' or contract it out 'buy'. The 'make' option should give management more direct control over the work, but the 'buy' option often has the benefit that the external organisation has a specialist skill and expertise in the work. Make or buy decisions should certainly not be based exclusively on cost considerations.

If an organisation has the freedom of choice about whether to make internally or buy externally and has no scarce resources that put a restriction on what it can do itself, the relevant costs for the decision will be the differential costs between the two options.

HOW IT WORKS

Shellfish Co makes four components, W, X, Y and Z, for which costs in the forthcoming year are expected to be as follows.

	W	X	Y	Z
Production (units)	1,000	2,000	4,000	3,000
Unit marginal costs	£	£	£	£
Direct materials	4	5	2	4
Direct labour	8	9	4	6
Variable production overheads	2	3	1	2
	14	17	7	12

Directly attributable fixed costs per annum and committed fixed costs:

	£
Incurred as a direct consequence of making W	1,000
Incurred as a direct consequence of making X	5,000
Incurred as a direct consequence of making Y	6,000
Incurred as a direct consequence of making Z	8,000
Other fixed costs (committed)	30,000
	50,000

A sub-contractor has offered to supply units of W, X, Y and Z for £12, £21, £10 and £14 respectively. Should Shellfish make or buy the components?

(a) The relevant costs are the differential costs between making and buying, and they consist of differences in unit variable costs plus differences in directly attributable fixed costs. Sub-contracting will usually result in some directly attributable fixed costs being saved.

	W	X	Y	Z
	£	£	£	£
Unit variable cost of making	14	17	7	12
Unit variable cost of buying	12	21	10	14
Differential variable cost	(2)	4	3	2
Annual requirements (units)	1,000	2,000	4,000	3,000

	£	£	£	£
Extra variable cost/(saving) of buying (per annum)	(2,000)	8,000	12,000	6,000
Fixed costs saved by buying	(1,000)	(5,000)	(6,000)	(8,000)
Extra total cost/(saving) of buying	(3,000)	3,000	6,000	(2,000)

(b) The company would save £3,000 pa by sub-contracting component W (where the purchase cost would be less than the marginal cost per unit to make internally) and would save £2,000 pa by sub-contracting component Z (because of the saving in fixed costs of £8,000). Financially it would not appear to be viable to sub-contract component X and Y, since this would increase costs.

(c) In this example, relevant costs are the variable costs of in-house manufacture, the variable costs of sub-contracted units, and the saving in fixed costs. Normally relevant costs are only variable costs but in instances like this, the savings in fixed costs must be taken into consideration as incremental costs as well.

(d) **Further considerations**

(i) If components W and Z are sub-contracted, the company will have spare capacity. How should that spare capacity be profitably used? Are there hidden benefits/costs to be obtained from sub-contracting? Would the company's workforce resent the loss of work to an outside sub-contractor, and might such a decision cause an industrial dispute? Alternatively can the spare capacity created be used for productive and profitable purposes.

(ii) Would the sub-contractor be reliable with delivery times, and would he supply components of the same quality as those manufactured internally?

(iii) Does the company wish to be flexible and maintain better control over operations by making everything itself?

(iv) Are the estimates of fixed cost savings reliable? In the case of product W, buying is clearly cheaper than making in-house. In the case of product Z, the decision to buy rather than make would only be financially beneficial if it is feasible that the fixed cost savings of £8,000 will really be 'delivered' by management. All too often in practice, promised savings fail to materialise!

Task 6

A business produces three products with the following costs per unit:

	A	B	C
	£	£	£
Direct materials	1.60	2.00	0.80
Direct labour	3.20	3.60	1.60
Direct overheads	0.80	1.20	0.40
Fixed overheads	1.60	2.00	0.80

An external firm has offered to make these components and sell them to the company at the following prices:

A   £5.50

B   £8.40

C   £4.00

On the basis of cost alone which if any products should be purchased from the external firm?

A   A only ✓

B   B only

C   C only

D   None of the products

CLOSURE OF A BUSINESS SEGMENT

Discontinuance or shutdown problems involve the following decisions:

(a) Whether or not to close down a product line, department or other activity, either because it is making losses or because it is too expensive to run.

(b) If the decision is to shut down, whether the closure should be permanent or temporary.

In practice, shutdown decisions may often involve longer-term considerations, and consideration of capital expenditures and revenues.

(a) A shutdown should result in savings in annual operating costs for a number of years into the future.

(b) Closure will probably release unwanted non-current (fixed) assets for sale. Some assets might have a small scrap value, but other assets, in particular property, might have a substantial sale value.

(c) Employees affected by the closure must be made redundant or relocated, perhaps after retraining, or else offered early retirement. There will be lump sum payments involved which must be taken into account in the financial arithmetic. For example, suppose that the closure of a regional office would result in annual savings of £100,000, non-current (fixed) assets could be sold off to earn income of £2 million, but redundancy payments would be £3 million. The shutdown decision would involve an assessment of the net capital cost of closure (£1 million) against the annual benefits (£100,000 pa).

It is possible, however, for shutdown problems to be simplified into short-run decisions, by making one of the following assumptions.

(a) Non-current (fixed) asset sales and redundancy costs would be negligible.

(b) Income from non-current (fixed) asset sales would match redundancy costs and so these capital items would be self-cancelling.

In such circumstances the financial aspect of shutdown decisions would be based on short-run relevant costs.

HOW IT WORKS

A company manufactures three products, Pawns, Rooks and Bishops. The present net annual income from these is as follows.

	Pawns £	Rooks £	Bishops £	Total £
Sales	50,000	40,000	60,000	150,000
Variable costs	30,000	25,000	35,000	90,000
Contribution	20,000	15,000	25,000	60,000
Fixed costs	17,000	18,000	20,000	55,000
Profit/loss	3,000	(3,000)	5,000	5,000

The company is concerned about its poor profit performance, and is considering whether or not to cease selling Rooks. It is felt that selling prices cannot be raised or lowered without adversely affecting net income. £5,000 of the fixed costs of Rooks are direct fixed costs which would be saved if production ceased (i.e. there are some attributable fixed costs). All other fixed costs, it is considered, would remain the same.

By stopping production of Rooks, the consequences would be a £10,000 fall in profits.

	£
Loss of contribution	(15,000)
Savings in fixed costs	5,000
Incremental loss	(10,000)

Suppose, however, it were possible to use the resources realised by stopping production of Rooks and switch to producing a new item, Crowners, which would sell for £50,000 and incur variable costs of £30,000 and extra direct fixed costs of £6,000. A new decision is now required.

	Rooks £	Crowners £
Sales	40,000	50,000
Less variable costs	25,000	30,000
	15,000	20,000
Less direct fixed costs	5,000	6,000
Contribution to shared fixed costs and profit	10,000	14,000

It would be more profitable to shut down production of Rooks and switch resources to making Crowners, in order to boost profits by £4,000 to £9,000 in total.

Timing of shutdown

An organisation may also need to consider the most appropriate timing for a shutdown. Some costs may be avoidable in the long run but not in the short run. For example, office space may have been rented and three months notice is required. This cost is therefore unavoidable for three months. In the same way supply contracts may require notice of cancellation. A month-by-month analysis of when notice should be given and when savings will be made will help the decision making process.

Qualitative factors

As usual the decision is not merely a matter of choosing the best financial option. Qualitative factors must once more be considered.

(a) What impact will a shutdown decision have on employee morale?

(b) What signal will the decision give to competitors? How will they react?

(c) How will customers react? Will they lose confidence in the company's products?

(d) How will suppliers be affected? If one supplier suffers disproportionately there may be a loss of goodwill and damage to future relations.

Transferring production overseas

In some cases management of an organisation may be considering shutting its UK operations and transferring its production operations overseas. This may be the case if key resources such as materials and labour are significantly cheaper in the foreign country. The quantitative and qualitative factors to be taken into account will tend to be very similar to those for a closure of a business segment. However there will also be other issues which are specific to setting up operations in a foreign country including:

- administrative / legal issues in setting up the operations

- the attitude of the host government to foreign investment

- the tax system in the country

- transportation issues involved in getting the products to their final destination.

Mechanisation decisions

In a similar way to decisions about closing a segment of the business, management may need information about changing the ways in which certain areas of the business operate. For example as technology plays a greater part in manufacturing, a business may be considering changing from a labour intensive production process to a machine intensive one.

There will be a number of aspects of costs that will need to be considered here:

- As with a closure of a business segment moving to a machine intensive production process will naturally mean a number of redundancy/early retirement costs

- However the reduction in the labour force will save on short term direct labour costs

- The investment in machinery will be very large and the methods of financing this investment should be considered

- In a machine based environment, it is likely that overheads in general will be much higher including machine maintenance, depreciation, power etc.

- Many of the additional overheads may be fixed overheads which may have an effect on the break-even point for the business. In order for the increased fixed overheads to be covered by contribution then more units may need to be sold. Break even analysis may be needed to determine whether the business can sell enough products to cover the additional fixed costs.

- If the level of fixed costs in the business increases as a proportion of total cost, the profits of the business will become more sensitive to changes in sales volumes. This is because if the sales of a business fall and its costs are mainly variable, the reduction in sales will lead to a corresponding reduction in costs. However if a business has mainly fixed costs, when sales volumes fall, the cost base remains largely the same and as a result there is a bigger impact on profits.

- There will also be qualitative factors to take into consideration, including the effect on the morale of the remaining workforce and any environmental issues involved in the mechanisation process.

HOW IT WORKS

A business is considering the purchase of a machine which will cost £475,000 and be depreciated on a straight-line basis over its 10 year life. The machine will allow the business to reduce the labour required to manufacture its product by 1.5 hours per unit. Currently the business makes and sells 4,000 units pa at £125 each and total annual fixed costs are £180,000.

The product's standard cost card shows the following variable costs:

Direct material	3kg @ £5	15
Direct labour	6hrs @ £10	60
		75

Assuming the business continues to make and sell 4,000 units we will consider the impact the machine purchase will have on the break-even point, the margin of safety, the profit for the year and the ratio of fixed costs to total costs.

Currently:

Contribution per unit = £125 – £75 = £50

Break-even = £180,000/50 = 3,600 units.

Margin of safety = 4,000 – 3,600/4,000 = 10%

Profit = (4,000 x £50) – £180,000 = £20,000

Fixed costs/Total costs = 180,000/(180000 + 4,000 @ £75) = 37.5%

With machine:

Contribution per unit becomes (£125 – £15 – £45) = £65

Note that the labour cost is now 4.5 hours @ £10 = £45

Fixed costs increase by £47,500 due to depreciation

Break-even = £227,500/65 = 3,500 units.

Margin of safety = 4,000 – 3,500/4,000 = 12.5%

Profit = (4,000 x £65) – £227,500 = £32,500

Fixed costs/Total costs = 227,500/(227,500 + 4,000 @ £60) = 48.7%

Here, the saving in direct labour (4,000 units at 1.5hrs x £10) £60,000 is greater than the increase in costs due to depreciation.

The break-even point and the margin of safety are increased but the business becomes more risky due to the increased proportion of fixed costs. This is known as having higher operating gearing.

DISCOUNTED CASH FLOWS

In this final section of the chapter, we move to looking at longer term decision making rather than the short-term decision making considered so far in this chapter. The purpose of using discounted cash flows (DCF) is to deal with the problem of the time value of money.

If we are offered £100 now or £100 in one year's time we are not comparing like with like. If interest rates are, say, 10% per annum then if the £100 received now were invested it would earn interest for a year at 10%. After one year the amount that we would have would be:

£100 × 1.10 = £110

Therefore we would definitely prefer the £100 now because it offers us an investment opportunity to earn £110 in one year's time.

Another way of looking at it would be that we would be indifferent between £100 now or £110 in one year's time. So we can say that the present value of £110 in one years' time is £100 now.

The present value of a future cash flow is calculated by applying a discount factor to the cash flow. The discount factor can be calculated as:

$$\frac{1}{(1+r)^n}$$

where: r =   the periodic interest rate or discount rate (expressed as a decimal)

   n =   the number of periods before the cash flow occurs

Fortunately you do not need to remember the formula as there are present value tables which have calculated the discount factors for each time period and each discount rate.

HOW IT WORKS

A company is to invest in a project with an immediate cash outflow of £20,000. The receipts from this project are £10,000 in one year's time, £14,000 in two years' time and finally £6,000 in three years' time.

The interest rate applicable to the company is 8% and the discount factors at this rate are given below.

	Discount factor
Period	8%
1	0.926
2	0.857
3	0.794

What is the present value of each of these cash flows?

Time	Cash flow	Discount factor	Present value
	£		£
0	(20,000)	1.000	(20,000)
1	10,000	0.926	9,260
2	14,000	0.857	11,998
3	6,000	0.794	4,764

Discounted cash flow and project appraisal

The computation of a present value is a discounted cash flow technique. We are finding the discounted present value of each individual cash flow.

The cash flows that are relevant are the future incremental cashflows that will arise as a result of the project that is being considered.

Note that for decision making we use cash flow and not profits, since these are less subjective. As a result, if you are given the expected profits from a project you will need to add back depreciation in order to estimate the cash flows.

If we are appraising a project, then the technique that we will use is to find the net present value of all of the cash flows of the project. We calculate the present value of each individual cash flow and then total them all, remembering that the initial cost of the project is a cash outflow. The total of the present values of the cash inflows minus the cash outflows is the NET PRESENT VALUE.

If the net present value (NPV) is positive, then the project should be accepted as this means that even after having taken account of the time value of money the cash inflows from the project exceed the cash outflows. If however the net present value is a negative figure, then the project should be rejected.

HOW IT WORKS

Returning to our previous example:

A company is to invest in a project with an immediate cash outflow of £20,000. The receipts from this project are £10,000 in one year's time, £14,000 in two years' time and finally £6,000 in three years' time.

The interest rate applicable to the company is 8% and the discount factors at this rate are given below.

Period	Discount factor 8%
1	0.926
2	0.857
3	0.794

What is the net present value of this project and should the company invest in it?

Time	Cash flow	Discount factor	Present value
	£		£
0	(20,000)	1.000	(20,000)
1	10,000	0.926	9,260
2	14,000	0.857	11,998
3	6,000	0.794	4,764
Net present value			6,022

The project has a positive net present value and therefore the company should invest in it.

Net present cost

In some instances you may be required just to calculate the present value of the costs of an operation or decision. This is done in exactly the same way as above but simply dealing with costs rather than revenues. This technique is often used to calculate the lifecycle cost of a machine that is regularly used by a business.

HOW IT WORKS

A company is to invest in a machine with an immediate cash outflow of £100,000. The machine will have annual running costs of £20,000 for the next three years paid in arrears. At the end of its three year life the machine will have an estimated residual value of £30,000.

The interest rate applicable to the company is 8% and the discount factors at this rate are given below.

Period	Discount factor 8%
1	0.926
2	0.857
3	0.794

What is the net present cost (lifecycle cost) of this machine?

Time	Cash flow £	Discount factor	Present value £
0	(100,000)	1.000	(100,000)
1	(20,000)	0.926	(18,520)
2	(20,000)	0.857	(17,140)
3 (30,000 – 20,000)	10,000	0.794	7 940
Net present cost			(127,720)

Net terminal value

Another method of looking at the cash flows of project, although not as common as using net present values, is to calculate the NET TERMINAL VALUE of a project. This is the value at the end of the project's life.

The terminal value method considers each cash inflow as if it was an investment and the compound interest on this inflow until the end of the project is added to the value of cash inflow.

For example suppose that £10,000 is received at time 1 and a project is a three period project with a discount rate of 10%.

The net terminal value of this receipt at time 3 would be £10,000 x 1.10 x 1.10 = 12,100. If this receipt of £10,000 had been invested for the remainder of the project life then it would have had a final or terminal value of £12,100.

HOW IT WORKS

Returning to our previous example:

A company is to invest in a project with an immediate cash outflow of £20,000. The receipts from this project are £10,000 in one year's time, £14,000 in two years' time and finally £6,000 in three years' time.

The interest rate applicable to the company is 8%.

Calculate the net terminal value of the project.

This will involve calculating the terminal value (the value at time 3) of each individual cash inflow and then deducting the terminal value of the cash outflow.

		Terminal value at time 3
Cash inflow at time 1 £10,000 x 1.08 x 1.08	=	£11,664
Cash inflow at time 2 £14,000 x 1.08	=	£15,120
Cash inflow at time 3	=	£6,000
		£32,784
Less: initial outflow (£20,000 x 1.08 x 1.08 x 1.08)		(£25,194)
Net terminal value		£7,590

Task 7

A business is considering replacing one of its current machines with a new machine.

Using the table below calculate the discounted lifecycle cost of purchasing the machine based upon the following:

- purchase price £400,000

- annual running costs of £45,000 for the next four years paid annually in arrears

- residual value of £150,000 at the end of the four years.

The discount factors at 5% are as follows:

Year 0   1.000

Year 1   0.952

Year 2   0.907

Year 3   0.864

Year 4   0,823

Year	0	1	2	3	4
Cash flow	(400,000)	(45000)	(45000)	(45000)	105·000
Discount factor	1.0	0,952	0,907	0·864	0·823·
Present value	(400,000)	(42840)	(40815)	(38880)	86415
Net present cost	(436120)				

CHAPTER OVERVIEW

- Due to the nature of fixed costs, total unit cost will tend to decrease as activity levels increase, as the fixed costs are spread over more units of production – however if selling price and variable costs remain constant then contribution per unit will remain constant as activity levels change

- As fixed costs in total are assumed to be constant for the period, whatever volume of products is made, maximisation of profit will be achieved by maximising contribution.

- Thus for decision making purposes we concentrate on marginal costing and contribution

- The break-even point in units is found by dividing the fixed costs by the contribution per unit

- If a target profit is required the unit sales to achieve this can be found by dividing the fixed costs plus target profit by the contribution per unit

- The difference between budgeted or actual sales and the break-even point is the margin of safety, which can be expressed as a percentage of budgeted or actual sales.

- The profit volume ratio can be used to find the break-even point in terms of sales revenue

    Break-even point (£) = Fixed cost/Profit volume ratio

- Normally production of products is limited by sales demand however in some instances factors such as the availability of material, labour hours or machine hours is the limiting factor

- Where there is more than one product and a limiting factor, overall profit is maximised by concentrating production on the products with the highest contribution per limiting factor unit

- In a make or buy decision with no limiting factors, the relevant costs are the differential costs between the two options. Typically this includes any variable costs incurred/saved as a result of the decision and any savings in attributable fixed costs.

- Shutdown/discontinuance problems can be simplified into short-run relevant cost decisions.

- Whether or not to move from a labour intensive production process to a machine intensive production process will also have many short and some long term effects.

- Discounted cash flows techniques are used in decision making to take account of the time value of money.

- Time value of money recognises that £1 today is worth more than £1 at a future time, because money can be reinvested to earn more money over time.

Keywords

Contribution – sales revenue or selling price per unit less variable costs

Cost-volume-profit analysis – analysis of the relationships between activity levels, costs and profits

Break-even analysis – calculations to determine the break-even point

Break-even point – level of sales whereby sales revenue is equal to total costs

Margin of safety – excess of budgeted or actual sales over the break-even point sales

Profit volume (P/V) ratio – ratio of contribution to sales

Contribution to sales (C/S) ratio – alternative name for the profit volume ratio

Limiting factor – a factor of production or sales that limits the amount of a product that can be produced or sold

Net present value – is the net total of the present value of a set of cash flows.

Net terminal value – the value of all cash flows as though invested until the end of the project less the original cash outflow

TEST YOUR LEARNING

1   If selling prices and variable costs remain constant at differing levels of activity explain why unit cost will tend to fall as activity levels increase.

2   A business has budgeted sales of its single product of 38,000 units. The selling price per unit is £57 and the variable costs of production are £45. The fixed costs of the business are £360,000.

The break-even point is [   ] units

The margin of safety is [   ] %

3   A business has fixed costs of £910,000. It sells a single product at a selling price of £24 and the variable costs of production and sales are £17 per unit.

How many units of the product must the business sell in order to make a profit of £500,000?

A   71,428 units

B   82,941 units

C   130,000 units

D   201,429 units

4   A business sells its single product for £40. The variable costs of this product total £32. The fixed costs of the business are £100,000.

The sales revenue required in order to make a profit of £200,000 is
£ [   ]

5   A business produces three products, the production and sales details of which are given below:

	Product		
	R	S	T
Direct materials @ £2 per kg	£16	£12	£10
Direct labour @ £9 per hour	£18	£36	£9
Selling price	£40	£60	£25
Machine hours per unit	6	4	3
Maximum sales demand	10,000 units	20,000 units	5,000 units

During the next period the supply of materials is limited to 250,000 kgs, the labour hours available are 120,000 and the machine hours available are also 120,000. Fixed costs are £50,000 per period.

(a) The limiting factor of production resources is materials/labour hours/machine hours? Select the appropriate answer

(b) Complete the following table to show the production plan which will maximise profit.

Product	Units produced

(c) The profit that will be earned under this production plan is £ [   ]

6   A business is considering investment in new machinery at a cost of £340,000 on 1 April 20X4. This machinery will be used to produce a new product which will give rise to the following net cash inflows:

31 March 20X5   £80,000

31 March 20X6   £70,000

31 March 20X7   £90,000

31 March 20X8   £120,000

31 March 20X9   £60,000

The new machinery is to be depreciated at 20% per annum on cost. The cost of capital is 7%.

Complete the table below to calculate the net present value of this project?

Year	Cash flows £	Discount factor at 7%	Present value £
0	(340 000)	1.000	(340,000)
1		0.9346	
2		0.8734	
3		0.8163	
4		0.7629	
5		0.7130	
Net present value			

7   A business is considering investment in new plant and machinery on 1 January 20X6 at a cost of £90,000. The company has a cost of capital of 11%. The cash cost savings are estimated to be:

31 December 20X6   £23,000

31 December 20X7   £31,000

31 December 20X8   £40,000

31 December 20X9   £18,000

(a)   Complete the table below to determine the net present value of this project?

Year	Cash flows £	Discount factor at 11%	Present value £
0		1.000	
1		0.9009	
2		0.8116	
3		0.7312	
4		0.6587	
Net present value			

(b)   Advise the business as to whether it should invest in the new plant and machinery and justify your advice.

chapter 4:
STATISTICAL METHODS

chapter coverage 📖

In this chapter we will look at some basic statistical methods that you may need to use for this Unit.

The topics that are to be covered are:

✍ Time series analysis

✍ Additive model

✍ Trend and seasonal variations

✍ Index numbers

✍ Linear regression

PREDICTING FUTURE COSTS AND REVENUES FROM HISTORIC DATA

A business may collect data about previous activities, costs and sales revenues and use it to help estimate future levels of activity, sales or costs. This chapter considers a number of statistical techniques that can be used in this way.

By studying the historic information it has captured, the business hopes to draw valid conclusions about the future. Sometimes this will require compromise, as the time and effort involved in examining all the data may outweigh the benefits and so a sample is selected. In order to provide a reasonable estimate, the sample of data on which such forecasts are made needs to be as representative as possible.

Techniques can be used to adjust the data for seasonal variations (time series) and also for changes in price levels (indexing).

TIME SERIES ANALYSIS

If we have collected cost or income data over a number of periods, such as sales revenue or production costs, this is known as a TIME SERIES. Such historic data may be used as a basis for forecasting future values. One of the key elements of information that management might require from a time series is an indication of the TREND. The trend is a feel for how the figure in question is changing over time – is it increasing rapidly, is it decreasing slightly?

The technique for determining the trend and other underlying components of a time series of figures is known as TIME SERIES ANALYSIS.

Elements of a time series

When considering results or costs over time there are four main elements that are likely to influence the figures:

- **Trend**

  The trend is the underlying movement of the figures over time. For example, sales may be erratic from month to month but in general terms are gradually rising.

- **Cyclical variations**

  Most economies will tend to have periods of growth and periods of recession. It is considered that such economic cycles typically take place over a seven to nine year period. Such long term economic cycles will cause alterations in the pattern of the actual results over time, known as CYCLICAL VARIATIONS. If the economy is growing then sales are likely to be increasing more rapidly but if the economy is in recession then sales growth may slow down or even reverse.

- **Seasonal variations**

  Most businesses will experience some sort of regular growth or reduction due to the seasonality of their business. This does not necessarily mean the actual seasons, summer, winter etc but some regular cycles for the particular business, repeated within a time frame of less than a year. These cycles are known as SEASONAL VARIATIONS. For example, a restaurant that is open 7 nights a week may generally experience peak numbers of customers on Friday and Saturday nights with lows on Monday and Tuesday.

- **Random variations**

  The actual results over time will also be influenced by random factors. For example in a manufacturing business if 30% of the workforce are affected by flu over a two week period then production will probably drop. These RANDOM VARIATIONS are totally unpredictable.

Task 1

What is the difference between a cyclical variation and a seasonal variation?

ADDITIVE MODEL

Under the additive model of time series analysis, it is assumed that the actual figure for each period of a time series is made up of the trend, the cyclical variation, the seasonal variation and any random variation added together. This can be expressed as follows:

Actual figure $= T + C + S + R$

where:

T	=	the trend
C	=	the cyclical variation
S	=	the seasonal variation
R	=	the random variation

You do not have to be concerned about calculations involving the cyclical variation or the random variation. Therefore we are left with the simpler expression:

Actual figure $= T + S$

We need only concern ourselves with the calculation of the trend and the seasonal variation.

There is also another model used in time series analysis, the multiplicative model, but this is not relevant for this syllabus.

TREND AND SEASONAL VARIATIONS

A simple way of detecting the trend from time series observations is to take averages over a certain period. If these averages change over time then there is evidence of a trend in the series.

Thus the technique that will be used is to take the actual figures from the time series and from these determine the trend using a technique of moving averages. Once the moving average (trend) has been identified it can be compared to the actual figure to ascertain the seasonal variation.

The expression above (Actual figure = T-S) can be altered slightly to read as follows:

Actual figure – T = S

Therefore by deducting the relevant trend figure from the actual figure the seasonal variation can be calculated.

We will consider first the calculation of the trend using moving averages.

Moving averages

The technique of calculating a MOVING AVERAGE is a key tool in time series analysis and is a method of finding averages for a number of consecutive periods. The number of periods' data to be included in the average is chosen such that a whole cycle of seasonal variations is included. Averaging these will thus smooth out seasonal variations. As each successive group of data is averaged, the underlying trend is highlighted.

HOW IT WORKS

Suppose that the sales figures for a business for the first six months of the year are as follows:

		£
January		33,000
February		39,000
March		36,000
April		44,000
May		35,000
June		49,000

It is felt that the sales cycle is on a quarterly basis – ie the seasonal variances repeat themselves every three months. What is required, therefore, is a three month moving average. This is done by firstly totalling the figures for January, February and March and then finding the average:

$$\frac{33,000 + 39,000 + 36,000}{3} = £36,000$$

Then we move on one month, and the average for February, March and April sales are calculated:

$$\frac{39,000 + 36,000 + 44,000}{3} = £39,667$$

Then the average for March, April and May:

$$\frac{36,000 + 44,000 + 35,000}{3} = £38,333$$

Then finally the average for April, May and June:

$$\frac{44,000 + 35,000 + 49,000}{3} = £42,667$$

Now we can show these moving averages together with the original figures – the convention is to show the moving average next to the middle month of those used in the average.

	Actual data	Moving average
	£	£
January	33,000	
February	39,000	36,000
March	36,000	39,667
April	44,000	38,333
May	35,000	42,667
June	49,000	

Task 2

Given below are the production costs for a factory for a six month period.

Complete the table to show the three month moving average for these figures.

Month	Actual	Three month moving average
	£	£
March	226,500	
April	251,600	238767
May	238,200	245800
June	247,600	242100
July	240,500	250300
August	262,800	

Centred moving averages

The trend for a time series is essentially the moving average for the time series. However, if the number of periods used in the moving average is an even number, such as the four quarters of the year, then there is a further calculation to make – the CENTRED MOVING AVERAGE. The reason for this is that if the moving average is based upon an even number of periods, then there is no central period to place the moving average against – a further average, the centred average, is required in order to find the trend.

HOW IT WORKS

The quarterly sales figures for Wrigley Partners for the last three years are given below:

		£
20X6	Quarter 1	88,900
	Quarter 2	100,300
	Quarter 3	63,800
	Quarter 4	75,200
20X7	Quarter 1	91,600
	Quarter 2	103,700
	Quarter 3	66,100
	Quarter 4	76,400
20X8	Quarter 1	95,400
	Quarter 2	106,000
	Quarter 3	68,800
	Quarter 4	77,100

By inspection, it would appear the sales figures exhibit seasonal variations over the four quarters of the year, for example quarter 2 is always the highest and quarter 3 the lowest. In order to find the trend of the time series a four quarterly centred moving average must first be calculated. Start with the four quarterly moving average:

First average:
$$\frac{88,900 + 100,300 + 63,800 + 75,200}{4} = 82,050$$

Second average:
$$\frac{100,300 + 63,800 + 75,200 + 91,600}{4} = 82,725$$

and so on.

		ACTUAL £	Moving average £
20X6	Quarter 1	88,900	
	Quarter 2	100,300	
			82,050
	Quarter 3	63,800	
			82,725
	Quarter 4	75,200	
			83,575
20X7	Quarter 1	91,600	
			84,150
	Quarter 2	103,700	
			84,450
	Quarter 3	66,100	
			85,400
	Quarter 4	76,400	
			85,975
20X8	Quarter 1	95,400	
			86,650
	Quarter 2	106,000	
			86,825
	Quarter 3	68,800	
	Quarter 4	77,100	

As the moving average being calculated is an even number, a four quarter moving average, then it is shown in between quarter 2 and 3 each time – the middle of the four quarters.

Now in order to find the trend line the centred moving average must be calculated. This entails taking each consecutive pair of moving average figures and in turn averaging them and showing them against quarter 3, quarter 4 etc.

First average: $\dfrac{82,050+82,725}{2} = 82,388$

Second average: $\dfrac{82,725+83,575}{2} = 83,150$

and so on.

		ACTUAL £	Moving average £	Centred moving average TREND £
20X6	Quarter 1	88,900		
	Quarter 2	100,300		
			82,050	
	Quarter 3	63,800		82,388
			82,725	
	Quarter 4	75,200		83,150
			83,575	
20X7	Quarter 1	91,600		83,863
			84,150	
	Quarter 2	103,700		84,300
			84,450	
	Quarter 3	66,100		84,925
			85,400	
	Quarter 4	76,400		85,688
			85,975	
20X8	Quarter 1	95,400		86,313
			86,650	
	Quarter 2	106,000		86,738
			86,825	
	Quarter 3	68,800		
	Quarter 4	77,100		

Calculating seasonal variations

We will now deal with identifying the seasonal variations. Remember the relationship between the actual figures, the trend and the seasonal variation in our simplified model:

Actual figure – trend = seasonal variation

We now include a final column on our table to show the seasonal variation for each quarter that can be directly compared to the trend.

For example, if the centred moving average (the trend) for 20X6 quarter 3 is 82,388 and the actual observation for the same period is 63,800, the difference, which is due to seasonal variation is – 18,588 (63,800 – 82,388), and is due to the seasonal variation.

		ACTUAL	Moving average	Centred moving average	Seasonal variation
				TREND	ACTUAL-TREND
		£	£	£	£
20X6	Quarter 1	88,900			
	Quarter 2	100,300			
			82,050		
	Quarter 3	63,800		82,388	−18,588
			82,725		
	Quarter 4	75,200		83,150	−7,950
			83,575		
20X7	Quarter 1	91,600		83,863	+7,737
			84,150		
	Quarter 2	103,700		84,300	+19,400
			84,450		
	Quarter 3	66,100		84,925	−18,825
			85,400		
	Quarter 4	76,400		85,688	−9,288
			85,975		
20X8	Quarter 1	95,400		86,313	+9,087
			86,650		
	Quarter 2	106,000		86,738	+19,262
			86,825		
	Quarter 3	68,800			
	Quarter 4	77,100			

The next stage is to find an average seasonal variation for each quarter, to get a representative seasonal variation for forecasting purposes. This is done by grouping the seasonal variations together, by quarter, in a table:

	Quarter 1	Quarter 2	Quarter 3	Quarter 4
20X6	−	−	−18,588	−7,950
20X7	+7,737	+19,400	−18,825	−9,288
20X8	+9,087	+19,262	−	−
Total	+16,824	+38,662	−37,413	−17,238
Average = total/2	+8,412	+19,331	−18,707	−8,619

The next stage is to ensure that the total seasonal variations total to zero:

+ 8,412 + 19,331 − 18,707 − 8,619 = +417

In this case they do not, therefore we must make minor adjustments to each of the seasonal variations by dividing the difference by 4:

417/4 = +104 (rounded)

and then deducting this figure from each of the seasonal variations.

	Quarter 1 £	Quarter 2 £	Quarter 3 £	Quarter 4 £
Unadjusted seasonal variation	+8,412	+19,331	−18,707	−8,619
Add adjustment	−104	−104	−104	−105
Adjusted seasonal variation	+8,308	+19,227	−18,811	− 8,724

We now have seasonal variations that total to zero (because of rounding differences, the quarter 4 adjustment used was 105 rather than 104 to ensure this).

Task 3

Given below are the annual sales figures for a business for the last eight years. Complete the table to calculate a four year moving average and trend using the centred moving average.

	Actual	Four year moving average	Centred moving average – trend
	£	£	£
20X1	226,700		
20X2	236,500		
		236500	
20X3	240,300		238175
		239850	
20X4	242,500		240988
		242125	2.....8
20X5	240,100		243038
		243950	
20X6	245,600		244663
		245375	
20X7	247,600		
20X8	248,200		

Graphing the time series and trend

Using our previous example. Wrigley Partners, at this stage it might be useful to draw the actual figures and the trend line onto a graph of the time series. When drawing a graph of a time series the time scale is always shown on the horizontal axis and the figures on the vertical axis.

Wrigley Partners – quarterly sales

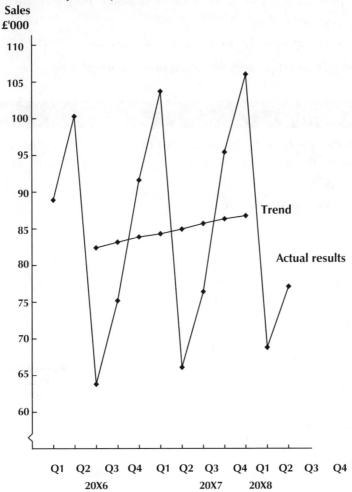

Using the trend

As you can see in the graph the sales of Wrigley Partners are irregular – quite high in quarters one and two, low in quarter three and higher again in quarter 4. This is known as a seasonal business.

The trend line (taken from the centred moving averages) however smoothes out the seasonal elements and shows how the sales are generally increasing over the three years.

The trend line can then be extended and the likely trend of sales in future periods can be read off from the graph as estimates. This process of estimating a future figure from a line on a graph is known as EXTRAPOLATION.

Using the seasonal variations

Once the trend line has been extrapolated and a trend figure read off the graph for a future period the trend figure must be adjusted by the relevant seasonal adjustment.

Remember: Actual figure = Trend +/– Seasonal variation

This will then give an estimate of the future period's actual sales.

HOW IT WORKS

Returning to the graph of the quarterly sales of Wrigley Partners we will extend the trend line for the four quarters in 20X9 by simply extending the trend line by hand on the graph.

Wrigley Partners – quarterly sales

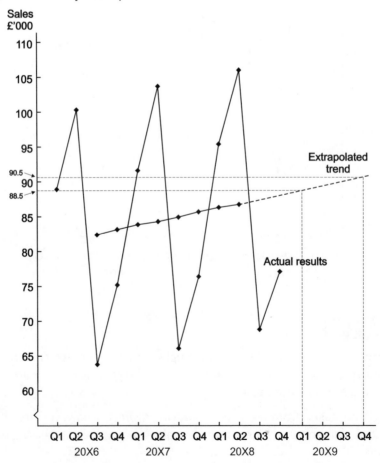

Once the trend line has been extended the estimated trend figures can then be read off from the graph (this will be easier if the graph is on graph paper):

20X9	Quarter 1	£88,500
	Quarter 2	£89,200
	Quarter 3	£89,900
	Quarter 4	£90,500

These figures however are not the expected sales for each quarter but the expected trend figure for each quarter. Quarter 1 and 2 are seasonally higher than the trend and Quarter 3 and 4 lower. Therefore we must apply the seasonal variation to the expected trend in order to find the anticipated sales figure.

		Trend	Seasonal variation	Forecast sales
		£	£	£
20X9	Quarter 1	88,500	+8,308	96,808
	Quarter 2	89,200	+19,227	108,427
	Quarter 3	89,900	–18,811	71,089
	Quarter 4	90,500	–8,724	81,776

Task 4

A manufacturing business has used its production costs for the last two years to identify a trend and monthly seasonal variations. Extrapolating the trend line has produced estimates of the trend in costs for the months of January to March 20X9 and the time series analysis has provided monthly seasonal variations.

	Estimated trend	Seasonal variations
	£	£
January	205,600	+23,200
February	208,600	+9,230
March	209,200	–3,500

Complete the table to calculate the anticipated production costs for January to March 20X9

Month	Cost £
January	228800
February	217830
March	205700

INDEX NUMBERS

We have seen how we can get a feel for how a time series is changing over time by plotting a trend line. Another simple and convenient method of doing this is to convert the actual figures to a series of INDEX NUMBERS.

Index numbers measure the change in value of a figure over time, by reference to its value at a fixed point.

This is done by determining firstly a BASE PERIOD which is the period for which the actual figure is equated to an index of 100. Each subsequent period's figure is converted to the equivalent index using the following formula:

$$\text{Index} = \frac{\text{Current period's figure}}{\text{Base period figure}} \times 100$$

HOW IT WORKS

The sales figures for a business for the first six months of the year are as follows:

	£
January	136,000
February	148,000
March	140,000
April	130,000
May	138,000
June	145,000

We will set the January figure as the base period, with an index of 100.

This means that the index for February is calculated as:

$$\frac{\text{Current period's figure}}{\text{Base period figure}} \times 100 = \frac{148,000}{136,000} \times 100 = 109$$

The index for March is:

$$\frac{140,000}{136,000} \times 100 = 103$$

The index for April is:

$$\frac{130,000}{136,000} \times 100 = 96$$

The index for May is:

$$\frac{138,000}{136,000} \times 100 = 101$$

The index for June is:

$$\frac{145,000}{136,000} \times 100 = 107$$

Interpreting an index

If the index for a period is greater than 100, this means that the current period figure is larger than the base period figure and if it is less than 100, the figure is lower than the base period figure. If the index is generally rising, then the figures are increasing over the base period but if the index is decreasing, the figures are decreasing compared to the base period.

Remember when interpreting an index that it represents the current period figure compared to the base period, not compared to the previous period.

HOW IT WORKS

We can show the actual sales together with the index for the previous example.

	£	Index
January	136,000	100
February	148,000	109
March	140,000	103
April	130,000	96
May	138,000	101
June	145,000	107

The index shows that although sales start to increase in February, they then fall again with April being lower than January. However by June the sales are again increasing, almost to the February level.

Task 5

The profit of a business for the last eight quarters is given below. Complete the table below to show the index for the profit figures using Quarter 1 20X7 as the base period.

		Profit £	Index
20X7	Quarter 1	86,700	100
	Quarter 2	88,200	101.7
	Quarter 3	93,400	107.7
	Quarter 4	90,500	104.4
20X8	Quarter 1	83,200	96.0
	Quarter 2	81,400	93.9
	Quarter 3	83,200	96.0
	Quarter 4	85,000	98.0

Retail price index

The Retail Price Index (RPI) is a measure of general price changes, which is published each month by the government.

A business can use the RPI to determine the extent to which its income and its costs have changed in line with general inflation.

HOW IT WORKS

A business has had the following sales for the last eight years:

	£
20X1	513,600
20X2	516,300
20X3	518,400
20X4	522,400
20X5	530,400
20X6	535,200
20X7	549,800
20X8	558,700

If we use 20X1 as the base year and then index the sales figures on that basis, the index will be as follows:

		Index
20X1	100.0	
20X2	516,300/513,600 × 100	100.5
20X3	518,400/513,600 × 100	100.9
20X4	522,400/513,600 × 100	101.7
20X5	530,400/513,600 × 100	103.3
20X6	535,200/513,600 × 100	104.2
20X7	549,800/513,600 × 100	107.0
20X8	558,700/513,600 × 100	108.8

This index shows a small but steady increase in sales revenue over the years. But is this due to an increase in sales volume, or simply the effects of inflation increasing the selling price?

We can consider the general increases in prices over the period by looking at the average Retail Price Index (RPI) for each of the years:

	RPI
20X1	140.7
20X2	144.1
20X3	149.1
20X4	152.7
20X5	157.5
20X6	162.9
20X7	165.4
20X8	170.2

We apply the RPI to the annual sales figures in order to show the RPI adjusted figures. This is done by using the following formula:

$$\text{Sales for current year} \times \frac{\text{RPI for year 1}}{\text{RPI for current year}}$$

20X1	Adjusted sales figure	=	513,600 × 140.7/140.7	= £513,600
20X2	Adjusted sales figure	=	516,300 × 140.7/144.1	= £504,118
20X3	Adjusted sales figure	=	518,400 × 140.7/149.1	= £489,194

and so on:

	Sales £	Adjusted sales £
20X1	513,600	513,600
20X2	516,300	504,118
20X3	518,400	489,194
20X4	522,400	481,347
20X5	530,400	473,824
20X6	535,200	462,263
20X7	549,800	467,696
20X8	558,700	461,863

In 'real' terms, i.e. without inflationary effects, sales have fallen. This could be due to:

- falling sales volumes
- selling prices failing to keep up with general inflation

or a combination of these.

What has been done here is to turn each period's sales into 20X1 price terms to illustrate that, in terms of the prices then prevailing, the sales over time have decreased.

We can now calculate an index based upon these adjusted sales figure which shows a very different picture from the earlier index:

	Sales £	Adjusted sales £	Index
20X1	513,600	513,600	100.0
20X2	516,300	504,118	98.2
20X3	518,400	489,194	95.2
20X4	522,400	481,347	93.7
20X5	530,400	473,824	92.3
20X6	535,200	462,263	90.0
20X7	549,800	467,696	91.1
20X8	558,700	461,863	89.9

This shows that the sales for the last eight years have in fact dramatically failed to keep up with the general rise in prices, as shown by the retail price index adjusted sales index.

Task 6

Given below are the monthly production costs for a business for the last year, together with the Retail Price Index for each month. Complete the table to show the adjusted production cost figures for the year based upon the Retail Price Index, in terms of June 20X7 prices.

		Costs	RPI	Restated costs
		£		£
20X7	June	133,100	171.1	133100
	July	133,800	170.5	134271
	Aug	133,600	170.8	133835
	Sept	134,600	171.7	
	Oct	135,800	171.6	
	Nov	135,100	172.1	
	Dec	135,600	172.1	
20X8	Jan	134,700	171.1	
	Feb	135,900	172.0	
	Mar	136,200	172.2	
	April	136,500	173.1	
	May	136,700	174.2	

Restating costs and income in current prices

In the previous example we took a series of sales figures and restated them in terms of prices prevailing in the earliest year of the time series. A further way of using the Retail Price Index is to restate earlier period's figures in terms of today's prices.

HOW IT WORKS

We will use the figures for sales which have been used earlier:

	£
20X1	513,600
20X2	516,300
20X3	518,400
20X4	522,400
20X5	530,400
20X6	535,200
20X7	549,800
20X8	558,700

The average Retail Price Index for each of these years was:

	RPI
20X1	140.7
20X2	144.1
20X3	149.1
20X4	152.7
20X5	157.5
20X6	162.9
20X7	165.4
20X8	170.2

In order to restate the sales in terms of year 20X8 prices the following formula is applied:

$$\text{Sales in current year} \times \frac{\text{RPI for 20X8}}{\text{RPI for the current year}}$$

The restated figures would appear as follows:

	Actual £	*In year 20X8 prices* £
20X1	513,600 × 170.2/140.7	621,284
20X2	516,300 × 170.2/144.1	609,814
20X3	518,400 × 170.2/149.1	591,762
20X4	522,400 × 170.2/152.7	582,269
20X5	530,400 × 170.2/157.5	573,169
20X6	535,200 × 170.2/162.9	559,184
20X7	549,800 × 170.2/165.4	565,756
20X8	558,700 × 170.2/170.2	558,700

We have now shown each year's sales in terms of year 20X8 prices. Again this shows that in real terms the sales have decreased over the period.

Task 7

Given below are the monthly production costs for a business for the last year, together with the Retail Price Index for each month. Complete the table to show the adjusted production cost figures for the year based upon the Retail Price Index, in terms of June 20X8 prices.

		Costs	RPI	Restated costs
		£		£
20X7	June	133,100	171.1	
	July	133,800	170.5	
	Aug	133,600	170.8	
	Sept	134,600	171.7	
	Oct	135,800	171.6	
	Nov	135,100	172.1	
	Dec	135,600	172.1	
20X8	Jan	134,700	171.1	
	Feb	135,900	172.0	
	Mar	136,200	172.2	
	April	136,500	173.1	
	May	136,700	174.2	

LINEAR REGRESSION

There is a further technique that can be used in forecasting costs and income and also, in assessments, is sometimes used for forecasting sales volumes. This technique is known as LINEAR REGRESSION. Regression analysis involves the prediction of one variable eg cost, based on another variable eg volume of output, on the assumption that there is a linear relationship (straight line on a graph) between the two variables.

The equation of a straight line

Given below is a straight line drawn onto a graph

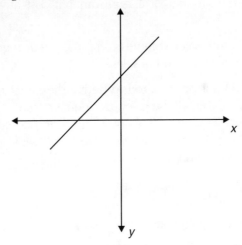

Any such straight line will have a defining equation in the following form:

$$y = a + bx$$

Both a and b are constants and represent specific figures:

- a is the point on the graph where the line intersects the y axis
- b represents the gradient of the line

We can now show a and b on the previous graph.

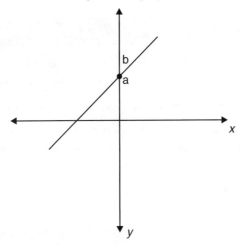

Using the equation of a straight line

The straight line drawn on the graphs above should remind you of two other straight line graphs that you have met earlier:

- the graph of a semi-variable cost
- the graph of a linear trend in a time series analysis

We can therefore use the equation for a straight line, or LINEAR REGRESSION EQUATION, in two possible ways in forecasting:

- to forecast the amount of a semi-variable cost at a given production level

- to forecast future sales volumes using the linear regression equation as the equation for the trend of sales.

In assessments you will not be required to derive the linear regression equation for a straight line. Either you will be given this equation and asked to find values of x and y, or you will be given values of x and y and asked to determine the values of a and b. However some care must be taken with what the variables x and y, and the constants a and b represent.

Dependent and independent variables

Given the equation of a straight line: $y = a + bx$:

- y is always the DEPENDENT VARIABLE

  (plotted on the VERTICAL axis)

- x is always the INDEPENDENT VARIABLE

  (plotted on the HORIZONTAL axis).

The dependent variable y can be calculated using the linear regression equation, provided that a value is known for the independent variable x.

HOW IT WORKS

(a) A linear regression equation expresses the relationship between the costs of producing a product and the quantity of production.

Which is the dependent variable and which the independent variable?

The cost of production is the dependent variable as this will depend upon the quantity. Therefore x represents the quantity of production and y represents the costs of production.

(b) A linear regression equation expresses the trend line for a time series of sales volumes.

Which is the dependent variable and which the independent variable?

The volume of sales depends upon the time period in which the sales were made, so volume is represented by y and time is represented on the x axis (note, time is ALWAYS an independent variable!).

Task 8

A linear regression equation expresses the relationship between advertising costs and sales volume. Which is the dependent variable and which is the independent variable?

Determining a and b in a linear regression equation

We have seen that the linear regression equation is $y = a + bx$, where a is the point where the line intersects the y axis and b is the gradient of the line.

If we are considering the equation of a straight line depicting the relationship between cost(y) and output(x), say

$y = 10,500 + 5x$

then

a = £10,500, which represents the fixed costs (incurred even if output is zero)

and b = £5 , which represents the variable costs per unit.

If you are given a number of figures for x and y, then it is possible to draw the linear regression line on a graph and determine the amounts represented by a and b.

HOW IT WORKS

A business has been monitoring its monthly production costs and has discovered the following:

- if production is 2,000 units then the cost of production is £7,000

- if production is 3,000 units then the cost of production is £9,000

If we assume that this relationship is linear, then the quantity of production will represent x and the cost of production will represent y. We can now plot these figures on a graph with the quantity of production on the x axis and the cost of production on the y axis.

- the first point to plot is where x = 2,000 units of production and production costs are £7,000

- the second point to plot is where x = 3,000 units of production and production costs are £9,000

Once these two points have been plotted, then a line can be joined between them.

Production cost £

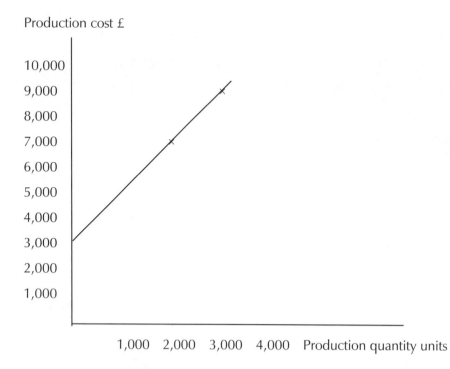

1,000   2,000   3,000   4,000   Production quantity units

We can now easily read off the graph the figure for a in the linear regression equation. This is the point where the regression line meets the y axis, so in this case £3,000. The figure for b requires a little more thought. This is the gradient of the line. We can see from our two points plotted that the cost of production increases by £2,000 (from £7,000 to £9,000) with a 1,000 unit increase in production (2,000 to 3,000). Therefore for every 1,000 increase in units there is £2,000 increase in costs giving a gradient of 2, therefore the figure for b is 2.

Forecasting semi-variable costs

If we are given the linear regression equation for a semi-variable cost, then provided that we know our forecast level of activity, x, we will be able to calculate the forecast level of cost, y.

HOW IT WORKS

The linear regression equation for the canteen costs (y) of a business for a month is as follows:

$$y = 20,000 + 45x$$

The variable x represents the number of employees using the canteen – the independent variable.

It is anticipated that the number of employees using the canteen in the next three months is as follows:

	Number of employees
January	840
February	900
March	875

What are the forecast canteen costs for each period?

		£
January	20,000 + (45 × 840)	57,800
February	20,000 + (45 × 900)	60,500
March	20,000 + (45 × 875)	59,375

Task 9

The linear regression equation for production costs (y) for a business is:

$$y = 63,000 + 3.20\,x$$

If production is expected to be 44,000 units in the next quarter, what are the anticipated production costs?

£ [   ]

Forecasting sales

If we are given a linear regression equation which represents the trend for sales, then we can use this to estimate sales for future periods. The x variable is the time period and therefore this is normally given a sequential number starting with 1 for the first period of the time series. Given the trend equation we can then calculate the trend for sales for any future period. Note that this will only give meaningful results if the trend is observed to be approximately linear, ie a straight line, from its graph.

HOW IT WORKS

The trend for sales volume for one of Trinket Ltd's products is given:

$$y = 16.5 + 0.78\,x$$

Where y is the volume of sales in thousands in any given time period and x is the time period.

The time series is based upon quarterly sales volumes starting in quarter 1 of 20X6.

The seasonal variations for each quarter are:

Quarter 1	−2,660
Quarter 2	+4,250
Quarter 3	+2,130
Quarter 4	−3,720

Estimate the sales volume for each quarter of 20X9.

Step 1

Find the values of x for the four quarters in 20X9.

Q1	20X6	x = 1
Q2	20X6	x = 2
Q3	20X6	x = 3
Q4	20X6	x = 4
Q1	20X7	x = 5

and so on until

Q1	20X9	x = 13

Step 2

Calculate the trend for each quarter before seasonal adjustments using the linear regression equation.

20X9	x value	y = 16.5 + 0.78 x
Q1	13	26.64
Q2	14	27.42
Q3	15	28.20
Q4	16	28.98

Step 3

Adjust the trend figures for the seasonal variations to find the seasonally adjusted sales volume.

Quarter	Trend ('000 units)	Seasonal adjustment volume	Seasonally adjusted sales (units)
Q1	26.64	−2,660	23,980
Q2	27.42	+4,250	31,670
Q3	28.20	+2,130	30,330
Q4	28.98	−3,720	25,260

Interpolation and extrapolation

Again we have to consider that interpolation, an estimation within the historical range, is more reliable than extrapolation, an estimation beyond the historical range.

When using linear regression analysis to estimate future sales from a trend line, this is always extrapolation and this means that there is an underlying assumption that the current trend will continue into the future.

Task 10

The linear regression equation for the trend of sales in thousands of units based upon time series analysis of the monthly figures for the last two years is:

$$y = 4.8 + 1.2 x$$

What is the estimated sales trend for each of the first three months of next year?

Month 1

Month 2

Month 3

CHAPTER OVERVIEW

- A series of cost or income data collected over a number of periods, such as sales revenue or production costs, is known as a time series. Such historic data may be used as a basis for forecasting future values.

- The four elements that make up the actual figures in a time series are the trend, cyclical variations, seasonal variations and random variations

- The additive model for time series is that the actual figure is made up of the trend plus the cyclical variation plus the seasonal variation plus the random variation – for this Unit only the trend and seasonal variation need be considered

- The trend is found by calculating a moving average for the actual figures – if the moving average is based upon an even number of periods, then the trend is actually found by calculating a centred moving average

- The seasonal variation for each period is calculated as the actual figure minus the trend – the average seasonal variation is then found for each period and adjustments are made to ensure that the total seasonal variation adds to zero

- The actual figures and the trend can be plotted on a time series graph with the time scale always shown on the horizontal axis

- Forecasts of future figures can be found by extending the trend line on the graph, reading off the estimated trend figure for the future period and then adjusting for the seasonal variation in that future period

- Another fairly simple method of showing whether income or expenditure has increased or decreased is to calculate an index – this is done by comparing each period's figures with those of the designated base period – the base period has an index of 100 and each period's index relates to that

- If the index for a period is above 100 then the income or expense is greater than the base period, but if it is below 100 then it is lower than in the base period – an increasing index shows a growth in the figures and vice versa

- The Retail Price Index can be used to determine whether income or costs have changed in line with general changes in inflation by adjusting each period's figures for changes in the RPI

- The RPI can be used either to turn the figures into prices based upon the earliest year or prices based upon the current year (or any year in between for that matter), however the resulting trend of figures will always be the same

- Regression analysis involves the prediction of one variable e.g. cost, based on another variable e.g. volume of output, on the assumption that there is a linear relationship between the two variables.

- Linear regression analysis can be used in order to estimate either semi-variable costs at a particular activity level or future sales volumes at a particular point in time, based on a linear trend

- The linear regression line, $y = a + bx$, will always be given to you in an assessment, you will not need to derive it, however care should be taken with the variables x and y – x is always the independent variable and y is the dependent variable

Keywords

Time series – a series of income or expense figures recorded for a number of consecutive periods

Trend – the underlying movements of the time series over the period

Time series analysis – a method of calculating the trend and other relevant figures from a time series

Cyclical variations – the effect on figures due to long term economic cycles

Seasonal variations – the regular short-term pattern of increases or decreases in figures that repeats due to the nature of the business

Random variations – the effects on the figures due to totally random events or circumstances

Moving average – the calculation of an average figure for the results of consecutive periods of time

Centred moving average – the average of two consecutive moving averages when the period for the moving average is an even number

Extrapolation – estimation of a future figure outside the range of data previously observed e.g. predicting future sales from a line on a graph

Index number – conversion of actual figures compared to a base period where the base year period is expressed as 100

Base period – the period for which the index is expressed as 100 and against which all other period figures are compared

Retail Price Index (RPI) – a measure of general price changes, which is published each month by the government.

Linear regression – a technique for forecasting semi-variable costs or future sales using the equation for a straight line

Linear regression equation – $y = a + bx$

where a is the point on the graph where the line intersects the y axis

b is the gradient of the line

Dependent variable – y is always the dependent variable

Independent variable – x is always in the independent variable

TEST YOUR LEARNING

1 Given below are the production cost figures for a business for the last year. Complete the table to calculate a three month moving average for these figures.

	Actual	Three month moving average
	£	£
July	397,500	
August	403,800	
September	399,600	
October	405,300	
November	406,100	
December	408,500	
January	407,900	
February	410,400	
March	416,000	
April	413,100	
May	417,500	
June	421,800	

2 Given below are the quarterly sales figures for a business for the last three and a half years. Complete the table to calculate a four quarter moving average, the trend using a centred moving average and the seasonal variations. Then adjust the seasonal variations as necessary.

		Actual	Four quarter moving average	Centred moving average – TREND	Seasonal variations
		£	£	£	£
20X5	Quarter 1	383,600			
	Quarter 2	387,600			
			365400		
	Quarter 3	361,800		365688	-3888
			365975		
	Quarter 4	328,600		366575	-37975
			367175		
20X6	Quarter 1	385,900			
	Quarter 2	392,400			
	Quarter 3	352,500			
	Quarter 4	338,800			
20X7	Quarter 1	392,500			
	Quarter 2	410,300			
	Quarter 3	368,900			
	Quarter 4	344,400			
20X8	Quarter 1	398,300			
	Quarter 2	425,600			

Seasonal variations:

	Quarter 1	Quarter 2	Quarter 3	Quarter 4
	£	£	£	£
20X5			− 3888	− 37935
20X6	+ 19887	+ 26275	− 15725	− 32488
20X7	+ 16925	+ 31975	− 10850	− 37988
Average	+ 18406	29125	− 10154	− 36150
Adjustment required				

1227 ÷ 4

=

	Quarter 1	Quarter 2	Quarter 3	Quarter 4
	£	£	£	£
Unadjusted				
Adjustment				
Seasonal variation				

3   Given below are the materials costs of a business for the last six months. Complete the table to calculate the index for each month's costs using January as the base month.

	Cost	Index
	£	
January	59,700	100
February	62,300	104.4
March	56,900	95.3
April	60,400	101.2
May	62,400	104.5
June	66,700	111.7

4 (a) Given below are the wages costs of a business for the last six months together with the retail price index for those months. Complete the table to calculate the RPI adjusted wages cost figures for each of the six months, with all costs expressed in terms of June prices.

	Wages cost	RPI	Adjusted cost
	£		£
January	126,700	171.1	126848
February	129,700	172.0	12
March	130,400	172.2	31085
April	131,600	173.0	
May	130,500	172.1	
June	131,600	171.3	

(b) Using the adjusted RPI wages costs complete the table to calculate an index for the wages costs for each month with January as the base year.

	Adjusted cost	Index
	£	
January	126848	
February	129172	101.8
March		
April		
May		
June		

5 The linear regression equation for costs of the stores department of a business is given as follows:

$$y = 13,000 + 0.8x$$

Where x is the number of units produced in a period.

The anticipated production levels for the next six months are given below. Complete the table to calculate the forecast stores department costs for the next six months.

	Production	Costs
	Units	£
January	5,400	17320
February	5,600	
March	5,700	
April	6,000	
May	5,500	
June	6,100	

6 A time series analysis of sales volumes each quarter for the last three years, 20X6 to 20X8, has revealed that the trend can be estimated by the equation:

$$y = 2,200 + 45 x$$

Where y is the sales volume and x is the time period.

The seasonal variations for each quarter have been calculated as:

Quarter 1	−200
Quarter 2	+500
Quarter 3	+350
Quarter 4	−650

Use the table below to estimate the sales volume for each quarter of 20X9.

	Value of x	Trend	Seasonal variation	Forecast sales
Quarter 1 20X9	13	2785	−200	2565
Quarter 2 20X9	14	2830	+500	3330
Quarter 3 20X9	15	2875	+350	3225
Quarter 4 20X9	16	2920	−650	2270

chapter 5:
STANDARD COSTING

chapter coverage 📖

In this chapter we will introduce the important concept of standard costing. We will look at how standards are developed and their uses in a management control system. We will then move on to the calculation of all of the basic variances, before considering further aspects of calculating variances in the next chapter.

The topics that are to be covered are:

✍ How standard costs are set

✍ Types of standard

✍ Introduction to standard costing systems

✍ Direct materials variances

✍ Direct labour variances

✍ Fixed overhead variances

✍ Fixed overhead efficiency and capacity variances

✍ Fixed overhead variances – absorption costing

✍ Reconciliation of total standard cost to total actual cost

✍ Marginal costing variances

INTRODUCTION TO STANDARD COSTING SYSTEMS

A STANDARD COSTING SYSTEM is one in which the expected cost of each unit of production is set out in a standard cost card and the actual cost of the units actually produced is compared in detail to this standard cost card. VARIANCES, the difference between the actual costs of the production and the standard costs, are then calculated and are used by management in running the business efficiently.

There are several areas involved in a standard costing system:

- setting the standards – see below

- calculating the variances – we will concentrate on this aspect in this chapter

- interpreting the variances – this will be considered in the next chapter

- reporting variances to management and management action – again this will be considered in the next chapter.

Uses of a standard costing system

Many manufacturing organisations and some service industries make use of standard costing systems, as they can be advantageous to management in a variety of different ways and can provide management with information to aid their three principal tasks of planning, decision making and control.

- the standard quantities of materials and labour required for production can be useful when planning future operations and setting budgets

- the standard costs of production can be useful for decision making – for example in comparing the costs of two similar products or setting selling prices

- Standard costing variances aid control by breaking down the overall variance into its individual components. The variances calculated by comparing actual costs to standard costs can provide management with information about areas of the business which require monitoring or some action to be taken.

Variances to be calculated

The variances to be calculated for this Unit are set out in the diagram below:

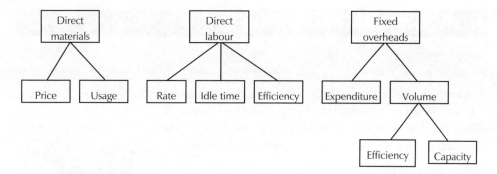

Absorption costing

You will remember from Chapter 2, that under a system of absorption costing the overheads of the business are absorbed into the cost units on the basis of a pre-determined overhead absorption rate. This means that the cost of the unit of production is a 'full' cost including its share of production overheads.

For this Unit, the only overheads that are to be considered are the fixed overheads. The diagram above illustrates the fixed overhead variances that will need to be calculated – the total variance is split into an expenditure variance and a volume variance and the volume variance in turn can be analysed into an efficiency variance and a capacity variance.

Marginal costing

Again you should remember from Chapter 2, that under a marginal costing accounting system the cost of cost units is made up of their variable costs only. The fixed overheads are treated as period costs and are written off to the income statement as an expense of the period, rather than being included in the cost of the cost units.

For the purposes of this Unit, the direct materials and direct labour will be treated as variable costs. The fixed overheads are not absorbed into the cost units or included on the standard cost card for the products. Therefore the fixed overhead variances to be calculated for marginal costing are reduced to just the fixed overhead expenditure variance, with no further analysis required.

Therefore the diagram summarising the variances required under a marginal standard costing system will be rather simpler than the earlier diagram:

Variances summary

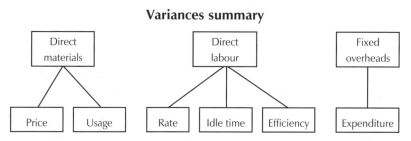

HOW STANDARD COSTS ARE SET

Standard costs

A standard cost is the planned unit cost of a product or service. This is usually documented in a standard cost card. Standard costing is a method of analysing a difference between actual performance and budget (known as a variance), when standard costs have been used to create the budget.

A standard cost card shows full details of the standard cost of each product.

The standard cost of product 1234 is set out below.

STANDARD COST CARD – PRODUCT 1234

	£	£
Direct materials		
Material X – 3 kg at £4 per kg	12	
Material Y – 9 litres at £2 per litre	18	
		30
Direct labour		
Grade A – 6 hours at £7 per hour	42	
Grade B – 8 hours at £8 per hour	64	
		106
Standard prime cost		136
Fixed production overhead – 14 hours at £4.50 per hour		63
Standard full production cost		199

Notice how the total standard cost is built up from standards for each cost element: standard quantities of materials at standard prices, standard quantities of labour time at standard rates and so on. It is therefore determined by management's estimates of the following.

- The expected prices of materials, labour and expenses
- Efficiency levels in the use of materials and labour
- Budgeted overhead costs and budgeted volumes of activity

We will now think about how each of the standard costs on the standard cost card are set.

Direct materials standard cost

The standard cost for the direct materials in a product is made up of two elements:

- the amount of material expected to be used in one unit
- the price of the material per kg, litre etc

The amount of material required for each unit of a product can be found from the original product specification – the amount originally considered necessary for each unit.

This figure may however be amended over time as the actual amount used in production is monitored.

The basic price of the material can be found from suppliers' quotations or invoices. However when setting the standard, the following should also be taken into account:

- general inflation rates
- any foreseen increases in the price of this particular material
- any seasonality in the price
- any discounts available for bulk purchases
- any anticipated scarcity of the material which may mean paying a higher price

Direct labour standard cost

The standard cost of the direct labour for a product will be made up of:
- the amount of time being spent on each unit of the product
- the hourly wage rate for the employees working on the product

The information for the amount of labour time for each unit may come from time sheets, clock cards, computerised recording systems on the machines being used or from formal observations of the operations, known as work study or more commonly a 'time and motion' study. Factors that should be taken into account when setting the standard for the amount of labour time include:
- the level of skill or training of the labour used on the product
- any anticipated changes in the grade of labour used on the product
- any anticipated changes in work methods or productivity levels
- the effect on productivity of any bonus scheme to be introduced

The hourly rate for the direct labour used on the product can be found from the payroll records. However consideration should be given to:

- anticipated pay rises
- any anticipated changes of the grade of labour to be used
- the effect of any bonus scheme on the labour rate
- whether any overtime is anticipated and whether the premium should be built into the hourly rate

Fixed overhead standard cost

The fixed overhead standard cost will be based on the total of the budgeted costs for each of the elements of the fixed overhead. Under marginal costing there is no further calculation to be done.

Under absorption costing the total budgeted fixed overhead must then be used to calculate the standard overhead absorption rate. This is found by dividing the total budgeted fixed overhead by the budgeted activity level, which may be measured in terms of:

- number of units produced
- direct labour hours
- machine hours

The information for determining the total budgeted fixed overhead will come from bills or invoices for past periods plus any anticipated price changes, either based upon specific indices or a general measure of inflation such as the Retail Price Index.

TYPES OF STANDARD

As you will have seen above when we looked at how standards are set, there are various bases that can be used, for example, are expected price rises included in the standard, are the effects of changes in work practices included in the standard etc?

There are therefore a number of different figures that can be calculated as the standard cost.

Ideal standards

IDEAL STANDARDS are standard costs that are set on the basis that ideal working conditions applying. Therefore there is no allowance for wastage, inefficiencies or idle time when setting the materials and labour cost standards.

There are two main problems with ideal standards:

Planning – if ideal standards are used for planning purposes, it is likely that the results will be inaccurate, as the standard does not reflect the reality of the working conditions. Therefore if a labour cost standard is set with no allowance for any inefficiency or idle time in the operations, the reality is that the operations will take longer or will require more employees than that which has been planned for.

Control – if ideal standards are compared to actual costs then this will always result in adverse variances as the reality is that there will be some inefficiencies and wastage. This can be demotivational to managers and employees who will feel that in reality these standards can never be met and therefore they may stop trying to meet them. A further problem with these adverse variances is that they will be viewed as the norm and be ignored, meaning that any corrective action that might be required is not taken.

Attainable standards

ATTAINABLE STANDARDS are ones which better reflect the reality of the workplace and which allows for small amounts of normal wastage and inefficiency. An attainable standard is one that is achievable; however, it will only be met if the operations are carried out efficiently and cost-effectively.

If attainable standards are well set, then the variances that result will tend to be a mixture of favourable and adverse variances as sometimes the standard will be exceeded and sometimes it will not quite be met. Attainable standards are often viewed as motivational to managers and employees, as they are not out of reach in the way that ideal standards are but they can be met if all goes to plan.

Current standards

CURRENT STANDARDS are based on **current working conditions** (current wastage, current inefficiencies). The disadvantage of current standards is that they do not attempt to improve on current levels of efficiency. Standards set are on a short term basis and frequent revisions may be necessary.

Basic standards

BASIC STANDARDS are the historical standard costs, probably the ones set when the product was first produced. As such, they are likely to be out of date, as they will not have taken account of inflation or any changes in working practices.

If basic standards are used to compare to actual costs, then this will tend to result in large variances, both adverse and favourable, depending upon how out of date the basic standard is. These variances will therefore be little more than meaningless. For this reason basic standards are rarely used for variance analysis but may still be kept as historical information alongside other more up-to-date standards.

Task 1

What are the potential problems of using ideal standards to calculate variances?

DIRECT MATERIALS VARIANCES

The TOTAL MATERIAL VARIANCE is the difference between the actual cost of the materials used in the production and the standard cost for the actual level of production.

Note that we are using the standard cost for the actual level of production as our comparison for the actual costs of production even if the actual level of production is different from that which was budgeted. This is an example of flexing a budget.

For example suppose that 1,000 units were budgeted to be produced with a total standard material cost of £1,000. If 1,500 units were produced with a total material cost of £1,400 it would be meaningless to compare £1,400 to £1,000 as they are for different numbers of units. Only by flexing the budget, to show the standard cost of the actual production of 1,500 units at £1,500, can a meaningful comparison be made.

The total direct material variance can be either favourable or adverse. If the actual cost of the materials is more than the standard cost for that level of production then there will be an ADVERSE VARIANCE (also known as unfavourable), as the production has cost more than anticipated. However if the actual cost of the materials is less than the standard cost for that level of production then the variance will be a FAVOURABLE VARIANCE. In our earlier illustration, as the standard material cost for 1,500 units of production is £1,500 and the actual cost was £1,400 this is a favourable variance of £100.

The total direct material variance can then be split into the MATERIAL PRICE VARIANCE and the MATERIAL USAGE VARIANCE.

Direct materials price variance

This variance is calculated to show the difference between the standard price due to be paid for the materials actually used and the actual price paid.

As we are comparing the standard price to the actual price, we must base this upon the same quantities. The quantity to be used for the price variance is the actual quantity used. The price variance can therefore be expressed as follows:

	£
Actual quantity at standard price	X
Actual quantity at actual price	X
Direct material price variance	X

If the actual price is more than the standard price, the variance will appear as a negative figure indicating an adverse variance. Whereas if the actual price is less than the standard price, the variance will be a positive figure, a favourable variance. However when determining whether a variance is adverse or favourable it is normally advisable to consider the logic of the situation – is the actual price more or less than the standard price?

Direct materials usage variance

This variance will indicate whether the amount of materials actually used in the production is more or less than the standard usage for that level of production. In this case we are comparing the actual quantity to the standard quantity for the actual level of production and therefore when valuing these quantities, the same price must be used – this is the standard price of the materials.

The price variance can be expressed as:

	£
Standard quantity of material for actual production at the standard price	X
Actual quantity of material for actual production at the standard price	X
Direct materials usage variance	X

Again if the actual quantity is more than the standard quantity, the variance will be adverse but if the actual quantity is less than the standard quantity, the variance will be favourable.

HOW IT WORKS

The standard cost card for one of Lawson Ltd's products, the George, is shown below:

	£
Direct materials 4 kg @ £2.00 per kg	8.00
Direct labour 2 hours @ £7.00 per hour	14.00
Fixed overheads 2 hours @ £3.00 per hour	6.00
Total standard absorption cost	28.00

The budgeted level of production for July was 20,000 units but in fact only 18,000 units were produced.

The actual quantity of materials used in July was 68,000 kg and the total cost of the materials was £142,800.

We will now determine the direct materials cost variances.

Total materials cost variance

	£
Standard materials cost for actual production 18,000 units × 4 kg × £2.00	144,000
Actual materials cost	142,800
Total materials cost variance	1,200 Fav

As the actual cost is less than the total standard cost (based on the flexed budget) the variance is favourable.

Materials price variance

	£
Actual quantity at standard price 68,000kg × £2.00	136,000
Actual quantity at actual price	142,800
Materials price variance	6,800 Adv

As the actual price is more than the standard, the variance is adverse.

The 68,000 kg were actually purchased for a price of £142,800 which is £2.10 per kg (£142,800/68,000) whereas the standard price is only £2.00 per kg.

Materials usage variance

	£
Standard quantity for actual production at standard price	144,000
18,000 × 4 kg × £2.00	
Actual quantity for actual production at standard price	136,000
68,000 kg × £2.00	
Materials usage variance	8,000 Fav

As the actual quantity total is less than the standard quantity total, then the variance is favourable.

For the production of 18,000 units the requirement should have been for 72,000 kg (18,000 × 4 kg), whereas the production level was achieved using only 68,000 kg.

We can finally just check our calculations by ensuring that the sum of the price and usage variances equals the total materials variance:

Materials price variance	6,800 Adv
Materials usage variance	8,000 Fav
Total materials cost variance	1,200 Fav

Task 2

A product has a standard usage of 12 litres of material, at a standard price of £20.50 per litre. The production of the product during the last month was 24,000 units, for which 312,000 litres were used at a total cost of £6,240,000.

(a)   What is the total materials cost variance?

Total materials cost variance £ _____

(b)   What is the materials price variance?

Materials price variance £ _____

(c)   What is the materials usage variance?

Materials usage variance £ _____

Material inventory (stock)

Sometimes a business will purchase more material than it uses in production for the period which results in material inventory (stock). In this situation the material price variance is based on the quantity of material purchased whereas the usage variance is based on the quantity actually used in production.

HOW IT WORKS

Studley Ltd makes a product that requires 3kg of material at £5/kg. During March 4,000 kgs of material were purchased at a price of £19,200. In the period 1,200 units of product were made using 3,800 kgs of the material.

We will now determine the direct materials cost variances.

Materials price variance

	£
Actual quantity purchased at standard price	20,000
4,000kg × £5.00	
Actual quantity purchased at actual price	19,200
Materials price variance	800 Fav

As the actual price is less than the standard, the variance is favourable.

Materials usage variance

	£
Standard quantity for actual production at standard price	18,000
1,200 × 3 kg × £5.00	
Actual quantity used for actual production at standard price 3,800 kg × £5.00	19,000
Materials usage variance	1,000 Adv

As the actual quantity total is more than the standard quantity total, then the variance is adverse.

Note: The difference between the actual quantity purchased and used is an increase in inventory (stock) of 200 kgs (4,000-3,800).

Task 3

A company manufactures a product that requires 5kg of material at £10/kg. During June 8,000 kgs of material were purchased at a price of £75,000. In the period 1,500 units of product were made using 7,700 kgs of the material.

(a)   What is the materials price variance?

Materials price variance £ [   ]

(b)   What is the materials usage variance?

Materials usage variance £ [   ]

DIRECT LABOUR VARIANCES

The TOTAL LABOUR VARIANCE is the difference between the actual cost of labour for the period and the standard cost of labour for the actual production in the period. Note again, that as with the materials cost, we are comparing the actual cost to the standard cost for the actual quantity of production (the flexed budget).

The total direct labour cost variance can then be split into the LABOUR RATE VARIANCE and the LABOUR EFFICIENCY VARIANCE. The rate variance is very similar to the materials price variance and the efficiency variance mirrors the materials usage variance, and therefore the calculations of these variances are the same as for the equivalent materials variance.

Labour rate variance

The labour rate variance shows the difference between the actual cost of the labour for the hours worked and the standard cost for those hours worked. As the actual rate of pay and the standard rate of pay are being compared, then the hours used must remain constant – the actual hours paid.

The variance can be expressed as:

	£
Actual hours at standard rate	X
Actual hours at actual rate	X
Labour rate variance	X

If the actual rate is greater than the standard rate, the variance is adverse and if the actual cost is less than the standard the variance is favourable.

Labour efficiency variance

The labour efficiency variance, just like the materials usage variance, is used to calculate whether the hours actually worked in order to produce the actual quantity of output are more or less than the standard hours needed for the actual quantity of production – did the labour force work efficiently or not?

As the standard hours are being compared to the actual hours, they must be valued at the same hourly rate – the standard rate of pay.

This can be expressed as:

	£
Standard hours for actual production at the standard rate	X
Actual hours for actual production at the standard rate	X
Labour efficiency variance	X

If the actual hours are more than the standard hours for the actual level of production, then the workforce has been inefficient and the variance will be adverse. If the actual hours are less than the standard hours, then the employees have worked efficiently and the variance is favourable.

HOW IT WORKS

The standard cost card for the George is given again below:

	£
Direct materials 4 kg @ £2.00 per kg	8.00
Direct labour 2 hours @ £7.00 per hour	14.00
Fixed overheads 2 hours @ £3.00 per hour	6.00
Total standard absorption cost	28.00

Remember that the actual production was 18,000 units, rather than the 20,000 units originally budgeted for.

The total cost of the labour for the month was £254,600 for 38,000 hours.

Total direct labour cost variance

	£
Standard labour cost for actual production	
18,000 × 2 hours × £7.00	252,000
Actual labour cost	254,600
Total labour cost variance	2,600 Adv

As the actual cost is greater than the standard total cost, the variance is adverse.

Labour rate variance

	£
Actual hours at standard rate 38,000 hours × £7.00	266,000
Actual hours at actual rate	254,600
Labour rate variance	11,400 Fav

The actual rate is less than the standard rate, therefore the variance is favourable.

The actual labour rate per hour that was paid was £6.70 per hour (£254,600/38,000) compared to the standard rate of £7.00 per hour.

Labour efficiency variance

	£
Standard hours for actual production at standard rate	
18,000 × 2 hours × £7.00	252,000
Actual hours for actual production at standard rate	
38,000 hours × £7.00	266,000
Labour efficiency variance	14,000 Adv

As the actual hours are greater than the standard hours, the variance is adverse.

Production of 18,000 units should have taken 36,000 hours (18,000 × 2) whereas in fact the production was inefficient and took 38,000 hours.

Finally, a check to ensure that the sub-variances total back to the total labour cost variance.

	£
Labour rate variance	11,400 Fav
Labour efficiency variance	14,000 Adv
Total labour variance	2,600 Adv

Task 4

A product has a standard requirement of 4 hours of direct labour per unit at a standard hourly rate of £6.50. During the last month production was 12,000 units using 45,000 hours at a total cost of £306,000.

(a)   What is the total direct labour cost variance?

Total direct labour cost variance £ [   ]

(b)   What is the labour rate variance?

Labour rate variance £ [   ]

(c)   What is the labour efficiency variance?

Labour efficiency variance £ [   ]

Idle time variance

A company may operate a costing system in which any idle time is recorded. Idle time may be caused by machine breakdowns or not having work to give to employees, perhaps because of bottlenecks in production or a shortage of orders from customers. When idle time occurs, the labour force is still paid wages for time at work, but no actual work is done. Time paid for without any work being done is unproductive and therefore inefficient. In variance analysis, idle time is always an adverse efficiency variance.

When idle time is recorded separately, it is helpful to provide control information which identifies the cost of idle time separately, and in variance analysis, there will be an idle time variance as a separate part of the total labour efficiency variance. The remaining efficiency variance will then relate only to the productivity of the labour force during the hours spent actively working.

HOW IT WORKS

The standard direct labour cost of product X is as follows.

2 hours of grade Z labour at £5 per hour = £10 per unit of product X.

During the period, 1,500 units of product X were made and the cost of grade Z labour was £17,500 for 3,080 hours. However, there was a shortage of customer orders and 100 hours were recorded as idle time.

Calculate the following variances.

(a) The direct labour total variance
(b) The direct labour rate variance
(c) The idle time variance
(d) The direct labour efficiency variance

Variances

(a) **The direct labour total variance**

	£
1,500 units of product X should have cost £10 per unit (standard labour cost for actual production)	15,000
but did actually cost	17,500
Direct labour total variance	2,500 (A)

Actual cost is greater than standard cost. The variance is therefore adverse.

(b) **The direct labour rate variance**

The rate variance is a comparison of what the hours paid should have cost and what they did cost.

	£
3,080 hours of grade Z labour should have cost £5 per hour (actual hours at standard rate)	15,400
but did actually cost (actual hours at actual rate)	17,500
Direct labour rate variance	2,100 (A)

Actual cost is greater than standard cost. The variance is therefore adverse.

(c) **The idle time variance**

The idle time variance is the hours of idle time, valued at the standard rate per hour.

Idle time variance = 100 hours (A) × £5 = £500 (A)

Idle time is always an adverse variance.

(d) The direct labour efficiency variance

The efficiency variance considers the hours actively worked (the difference between hours paid for and idle time hours). In our example, there were (3,080 − 100) = 2,980 hours when the labour force was not idle. The variance is calculated by taking the amount of output produced (1,500 units of product X) and comparing the time it should have taken to make them, with the actual time spent actively making them (2,980 hours). Once again, the variance in hours is valued at the standard rate per labour hour.

1,500 units of product X should take 2hrs each	3,000 hrs
(standard hours for actual production)	
but did take (3,080 − 100)	2,980 hrs
Direct labour efficiency variance in hours	20 hrs (F)
× standard rate per hour	× £5
Direct labour efficiency variance in £	100 (F)

(e) **Summary**

Direct labour rate variance	2,100 (A)
Idle time variance	500 (A)
Direct labour efficiency variance	100 (F)
Direct labour total variance	2,500 (A)

FIXED OVERHEAD VARIANCES

Under an absorption costing system fixed overheads are absorbed into the actual units of production on the basis of a pre-determined overhead absorption rate. This standard absorption rate may be expressed as an amount per unit or as an amount per direct labour hour or direct machine hour.

However the absorption rate is expressed the following figures will always be compared:

| Fixed overheads incurred | v | Fixed overheads absorbed |

If the total fixed overheads incurred are exactly as budgeted and the units of production or hours worked are also exactly as budgeted then these two figures will be equal.

However in practice it is likely that one of three situations may occur:

(a) the fixed overheads are greater or smaller than the budgeted amount

(b) the actual production or the hours worked are more or less than budgeted; or

(c) there is a combination of both of the first two situations.

When any of these occur then the fixed overheads incurred and the fixed overheads absorbed will be different. There will either be an UNDER-ABSORPTION OF OVERHEADS or an OVER-ABSORPTION OF OVERHEADS. This under- or over-absorption is the TOTAL FIXED OVERHEAD VARIANCE.

As we have seen any under- or over-absorption of overheads will be due to either the amount incurred being different to the budgeted figure or the amount absorbed being different to budget. The total fixed overhead variance can therefore be analysed into these two possible causes by calculating the FIXED OVERHEAD EXPENDITURE VARIANCE and the FIXED OVERHEAD VOLUME VARIANCE.

Fixed overhead expenditure variance

Remember that fixed overheads are, by definition, not expected to alter if the level of production is different to that which is budgeted. Therefore any difference between the budgeted fixed overhead and the actual fixed overhead must be caused by unexpected changes in prices of one or more of the elements of cost in the total fixed overhead.

The fixed overhead expenditure variance is therefore simply:

	£
Budgeted fixed overhead	X
Actual fixed overhead	X
Fixed overhead expenditure variance	X

If the actual overhead is greater than the budgeted overhead, this is an adverse variance but if the actual overhead is less than the budgeted figure, this is a favourable variance.

Fixed overhead volume variance

In chapter 2 we saw that when using absorption costing, the standard absorption rate per unit of output is found using the budgeted overhead costs for the period and the budgeted activity level. However using budgeted figures means that the actual overhead cost is unlikely to be the same as the overheads absorbed into production, as we are relying on two estimates:

- overhead costs
- activity levels

The fixed overhead expenditure variance measures the difference between actual and budgeted fixed overhead.

The fixed overhead volume variance measures the fact that if the actual level of activity differs from the budget more or less fixed overhead will be absorbed than was budgeted for.

Together the two variances equal the over- or under-absorption of fixed overhead that we calculated in chapter 2.

The calculation of the fixed overhead volume variance will depend upon the absorption rate that is used for fixed overheads.

If fixed overheads are absorbed on the basis of units of production then the calculation is:

	£
Actual production at standard absorption rate per unit	
(= Fixed OH absorbed)	X
Budgeted production at standard absorption rate per unit	
(= Budgeted fixed OH)	X
Fixed overhead volume variance	X

If the actual production is greater than the budgeted production then this is a favourable outcome and therefore a favourable volume variance. If actual production is less than budgeted then this is not so good and the volume variance will be adverse.

Note that these variances do not represent an actual cost saving or overrun – this is dealt with by the expenditure variance. They show the necessary adjustments arising from over/under-absorption of fixed overheads due to differences in the level of activity compared to the budget. For example, if actual production is greater than budgeted, this will lead to a fixed overhead over-absorption, ie cost of production will be charged with too much fixed overhead, which will ultimately go through to profit. To compensate for this a favourable fixed overhead volume variance (one that increases profits again) is added back.

Again think through the logic of the outcome in order to determine whether the variances are favourable or adverse rather than relying on getting the formula the right way round.

If the fixed overheads are absorbed on the basis of labour hours or machine hours it is important that you use the standard hours for the actual production and not the actual hours. Under this basis of absorption the fixed overhead volume variance would be calculated as:

	£
Standard hours for actual production at the standard absorption rate per hour	X
Standard hours for the budgeted production at the standard absorption rate per hour	X
Fixed overhead volume variance	X

Again if the actual production expressed in standard hours is greater than budgeted the variance is favourable but if the actual production is less than budgeted the variance is adverse.

HOW IT WORKS

Using our example of Lawson Ltd's production of the George for the month of July it can be seen that the same results will be obtained whichever method of absorption is used.

The standard cost card for the George is given below:

	£
Direct materials 4 kg @ £2.00 per kg	8.00
Direct labour 2 hours @ £7.00 per hour	14.00
Fixed overheads 2 hours @ £3.00 per hour	6.00
Total standard absorption cost	28.00

The actual production was 18,000 units rather than the budgeted figure of 20,000 and this production took a total of 38,000 labour hours.

The actual fixed overhead incurred in the period was £115,000.

Fixed overhead variances – absorption basis – per unit

The fixed overhead absorption basis will initially be taken to be per unit. From the standard cost card we can see that the standard absorption rate is £6.00 per unit.

In order to find the total fixed overhead variance we need to find the under- or over-absorbed overhead.

Total fixed overhead variance

	£
Fixed overhead incurred	115,000
Fixed overhead absorbed (18,000 units × £6.00)	108,000
Overhead under-absorbed	7,000 Adv

As there is an under-absorption of overhead this is an adverse variance as more fixed overhead needs to be charged to the income statement (profit and loss account).

Fixed overhead expenditure variance

In order to find the fixed overhead expenditure variance, the budgeted fixed overhead is required. By returning to the standard cost card and the budgeted production information we can deduce this figure.

The standard cost card shows the standard fixed overhead absorption rate to be £6.00 per unit. This was based upon planned production of 20,000 units therefore the budgeted fixed overhead must have been:

20,000 units × £6.00 per unit = £120,000

The fixed overhead expenditure variance is therefore:

	£
Budgeted fixed overhead	120,000
Actual fixed overhead	115,000
Fixed overhead expenditure variance	5,000 Fav

As the actual fixed overhead is less than the budgeted figure this is a favourable variance.

Fixed overhead volume variance

As the fixed overheads are being absorbed on a unit basis the calculation is:

	£
Actual production at standard absorption rate 18,000 units × £6.00 per unit	108,000
Budgeted production at standard absorption rate 20,000 units × £6.00 per unit	120,000
Fixed overhead volume variance	12,000 Adv

The variance is adverse, as actual production is less than budgeted production, and has therefore absorbed less than it should have done. The shortfall is made up by this adverse variance being charged to the income statement (profit and loss account).

We will now check that the fixed overhead expenditure and volume variances add back to the fixed overhead total variance:

	£
Fixed overhead expenditure variance	5,000 Fav
Fixed overhead volume variance	12,000 Adv
Fixed overhead total variance	7,000 Adv

Fixed overhead variances – absorption basis – labour hours

If the fixed overheads were to be absorbed on a labour hour basis, we can see from the standard cost card that the standard absorption rate is £3.00 per direct labour hour.

Total fixed overhead variance

To find the total fixed overhead variance, that is the under- or over-absorbed fixed overhead, the fixed overhead incurred is compared to the fixed overhead absorbed. The fixed overhead is absorbed not on the basis of the actual labour hours worked (38,000) but on the basis of the standard labour hours for the actual production which in this case would be 18,000 units × 2 hours = 36,000 hours.

	£
Fixed overhead incurred	115,000
Fixed overhead absorbed (36,000 hours × £3.00 per hour)	108,000
Overhead under-absorbed	7,000 Adv

As there is an under-absorption of overhead this is an adverse variance, as more fixed overhead needs to be charged to the income statement (profit and loss account).

Fixed overhead expenditure variance

As this variance has nothing to do with overhead absorption, then the figures are exactly the same as before.

The fixed overhead expenditure variance is therefore:

	£
Budgeted fixed overhead	120,000
Actual fixed overhead	115,000
Fixed overhead expenditure variance	5,000 Fav

As the actual fixed overhead is less than the budgeted figure, this is a favourable variance.

Fixed overhead volume variance

As the fixed overheads are being absorbed on a direct labour hour basis then again the actual absorption is based upon the standard labour hours for the actual production. The calculation is:

	£
Standard hours for actual production at standard absorption rate	
36,000 hours × £3.00 per hour	108,000
Budgeted production hours at standard absorption rate	
20,000 units × 2hrs x £3.00 per hour	120,000
Fixed overhead volume variance	12,000 Adv

The variance is adverse as standard hours for actual production are less than budgeted production hours.

As you can see the variances are exactly the same whichever basis of absorption is used, but if the absorption basis is labour hours or machine hours then the absorption must be based upon the standard hours for the actual production not the actual labour hours worked or the machine hours worked.

Task 5

During the month of September a business incurred fixed overheads of £26,000. The actual production of the business's single product was 2,500 units taking 5,500 direct labour hours. Budgeted production had been for 2,400 units each requiring 2 standard direct labour hours. Fixed overheads are absorbed on the basis of £5.00 per direct labour hour.

Calculate the following figures:

(a) the budgeted fixed overhead

Budgeted fixed overhead £ [ ]

(b) the total fixed overhead variance

Total fixed overhead variance £ [ ]

(c) the fixed overhead expenditure variance

Fixed overhead expenditure variance £ [ ]

(d) the fixed overhead volume variance

Fixed overhead volume variance £ [ ]

FIXED OVERHEAD EFFICIENCY AND CAPACITY VARIANCES

If the fixed overheads are absorbed on a unit basis then the only fixed overhead variances that can be calculated are the expenditure and volume variances. However, if the overheads are absorbed on an hourly basis then the fixed overhead volume variance can be analysed further into a FIXED OVERHEAD EFFICIENCY VARIANCE and a FIXED OVERHEAD CAPACITY VARIANCE.

This analysis of the fixed overhead volume variance helps to explain the causes of the volume variance:

- was the volume variance due to the workforce working more or less efficiently than budgeted? – the efficiency variance

- was the volume variance due to the workforce working for more or less total hours than budgeted? – the capacity variance.

Fixed overhead efficiency variance

This variance considers how efficiently the workforce produced the goods by comparing the time the actual production should have taken to the time it actually took, all valued at the hourly absorption rate. It is calculated in a similar way to the labour efficiency variance.

The calculation is:

	£
Standard hours for actual production at standard absorption rate	X
Actual hours for actual production at standard absorption rate	X
Fixed overhead efficiency variance	X

If the actual hours are greater than the standard hours then the workforce has been inefficient and the variance is adverse. However if the actual hours are less than the standard hours, the workforce have worked efficiently and the variance is favourable.

Fixed overhead capacity variance

The capacity variance measures whether all of the available hours were used or indeed if more hours were worked than were budgeted for. These hours are all valued at the standard hourly absorption rate.

The calculation is:

	£
Actual hours worked at standard absorption rate	X
Budgeted hours at standard absorption rate	X
Fixed overhead capacity variance	X

If the actual hours worked are greater than the budgeted hours then this is good for the business and is therefore a favourable variance. If the actual hours worked are less than those that were budgeted for, the variance is adverse.

HOW IT WORKS

Let's return to Lawson Ltd and the July production of the George.

The standard cost card is again shown:

	£
Direct materials 4 kg @ £2.00 per kg	8.00
Direct labour 2 hours @ £7.00 per hour	14.00
Fixed overheads 2 hours @ £3.00 per hour	6.00
Total standard absorption cost	28.00

Budgeted production was 20,000 units and actual production was 18,000 units taking 38,000 hours. The fixed overhead incurred in the month was £115,000.

The fixed overhead variances calculated so far are:

	£
Fixed overhead expenditure variance	5,000 Fav
Fixed overhead volume variance	12,000 Adv
Total fixed overhead variance	7,000 Adv

We will now analyse the fixed overhead volume variance into its constituent elements.

Fixed overhead efficiency variance

	£
Standard hours for actual production at standard absorption rate	
18,000 units × 2 hours × £3.00 per hour	108,000
Actual hours for actual production at standard absorption rate	
38,000 hours × £3.00 per hour	114,000
Fixed overhead efficiency variance	6,000 Adv

As the actual production took more hours than the standard hours for that level of production then this is an adverse efficiency variance.

Fixed overhead capacity variance

For this calculation, the total budgeted hours must be deduced from the standard cost card. The budgeted production was for 20,000 units and each unit has standard hours of 2 direct labour hours, therefore the budgeted labour hours were 40,000.

	£
Actual hours worked at standard absorption rate	
38,000 hours × £3.00 per hour	114,000
Budgeted hours at standard absorption rate	
40,000 × £3.00 per hour	120,000
Fixed overhead capacity variance	6,000 Adv

Only 38,000 hours were worked although 40,000 hours had been budgeted for, therefore this is an adverse capacity variance, since not all the productive capacity has been used.

Now we can check that the efficiency and capacity variances total back to the volume variance:

	£
Fixed overhead efficiency variance	6,000 Adv
Fixed overhead capacity variance	6,000 Adv
Fixed overhead volume variance	12,000 Adv

The total fixed overhead variances can be presented as follows:

	£	£
Fixed overhead expenditure		5,000 Fav
Fixed overhead efficiency	6,000 Adv	
Fixed overhead capacity	6,000 Adv	
Fixed overhead volume		12,000 Adv
Total fixed overhead variance		7,000 Adv

Task 6

During the month of September a business incurred fixed overheads of £25,000. The actual production of the business's single product was 2,500 units taking 5,500 direct labour hours. Budgeted production had been for 2,400 units each requiring 2 standard direct labour hours. Fixed overheads are absorbed on the basis of £5.00 per direct labour hour.

Calculate the following figures:

(a) the budgeted direct labour hours for the month

Budgeted direct labour hours [   ] hours

(b) the fixed overhead efficiency variance

Fixed overhead efficiency variance £ [   ]

(c) the fixed overhead capacity variance

Fixed overhead capacity variance £ [   ]

FIXED OVERHEADS VARIANCES – ABSORPTION COSTING

We can now summarise the fixed overhead variances that can be calculated under an absorption costing system using the figures from Lawson Ltd.

Remember that it is only when fixed overheads are absorbed on an hourly basis that we can analyse the volume variance further, into efficiency and capacity variances.

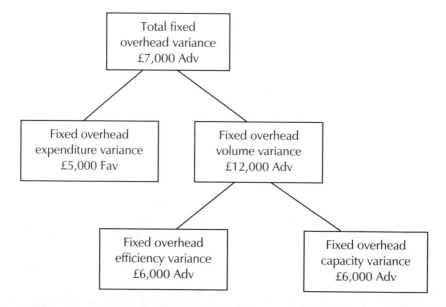

RECONCILIATION OF TOTAL STANDARD COST TO TOTAL ACTUAL COST

Once all of the cost variances have been calculated, it is then useful to summarise the total standard cost, variances and total actual cost using a RECONCILIATION STATEMENT (sometimes called an OPERATING STATEMENT).

It is common practice to start with the total standard cost for the actual production, then adjust this for the variances calculated in order to finish with the total actual cost of production. This can be illustrated as follows:

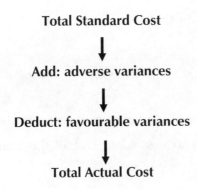

Total Standard Cost

↓

Add: adverse variances

↓

Deduct: favourable variances

↓

Total Actual Cost

When preparing the operating statement or reconciliation, think about the addition and subtraction of variances. Adverse variances are added to the total standard cost, as this means that the actual cost is higher than the standard cost (or amount absorbed in the case of fixed overheads). Favourable variances are deducted from the standard cost, as this means that the actual cost is less than the standard/absorbed cost.

HOW IT WORKS

We will now summarise all of the variances calculated for Lawson Ltd.

	£
Materials price variance	6,800 Adv
Materials usage variance	8,000 Fav
Total materials cost variance	1,200 Fav

	£
Labour rate variance	11,400 Fav
Labour efficiency variance	14,000 Adv
Total labour cost variance	2,600 Adv

	£	£
Fixed overhead expenditure variance		5,000 Fav
Fixed overhead efficiency variance	6,000 Adv	
Fixed overhead capacity variance	6,000 Adv	
Fixed overhead volume variance		12,000 Adv
Fixed overhead total variance		7,000 Adv

We will also need the standard cost card for the George:

	£
Direct materials 4 kg @ £2.00 per kg	8.00
Direct labour 2 hours @ £7.00 per hour	14.00
Fixed overheads 2 hours @ £3.00 per hour	6.00
Total standard absorption cost	28.00

Remember that the actual production costs for July were:

	£
Direct materials	142,800
Direct labour	254,600
Fixed overhead	115,000

We will now produce the reconciliation or operating statement.

Firstly we must calculate the total standard cost of the actual production of 18,000 units:

	£
Direct materials 18,000 × £8.00	144,000
Direct labour 18,000 × £14.00	252,000
Fixed overhead 18,000 × £6.00	108,000
Total standard production cost	504,000

Alternatively this figure for total standard cost of production can be calculated as 18,000 x £28 which is the total standard cost of each product from the standard cost card.

We need to reconcile this figure to the total actual production cost:

	£
Direct materials	142,800
Direct labour	254,600
Fixed overhead	115,000
Total actual production cost	512,400

Reconciliation statement – July

	Variances		
	Adverse	Favourable	
	£	£	£
Total standard cost			504,000
Variances:			
Materials price	6,800		
Materials usage		8,000	
Labour rate		11,400	
Labour efficiency	14,000		
Fixed overhead expenditure		5,000	
Fixed overhead efficiency	6,000		
Fixed overhead capacity	6,000		
	32,800	24,400	
Add: adverse variances			32,800
Less: favourable variances			(24,400)
Total actual cost			512,400

Task 7

If you are producing a reconciliation statement which reconciles the standard cost of production to the actual cost, explain whether favourable cost variances are added or subtracted and why.

MARGINAL COSTING

In a standard marginal costing system the standard cost card will only include the variable costs of production as the fixed overheads are not included in the cost of the cost units, but are written off as a period cost.

The calculations of the materials and labour variances are exactly the same as in an absorption costing system. The only difference is that there is only one fixed overhead variance – the expenditure variance – as all of the other fixed overhead variances are due to absorption which does not take place under marginal costing.

HOW IT WORKS

If Lawson Ltd operated a marginal costing system then the standard cost card for the George would appear as follows:

	£
Direct materials 4 kg @ £2.00 per kg	8.00
Direct labour 2 hours @ £7.00 per hour	14.00
	22.00

The actual production was 18,000 compared to budgeted production of 20,000 units. The budgeted fixed overhead was £120,000 and the fixed overhead incurred was £115,000.

The materials and labour variances would be calculated in exactly the same manner as before, giving the same figures:

	£
Materials price variance	6,800 Adv
Materials usage variance	8,000 Fav
Total materials cost variance	1,200 Fav

	£
Labour rate variance	11,400 Fav
Labour efficiency variance	14,000 Adv
Total labour cost variance	2,600 Adv

The fixed overhead expenditure variance is, as before, the difference between the budgeted and actual fixed overhead £5,000 favourable (£120,000 − £115,000).

A reconciliation or operating statement can now be prepared between the standard marginal cost of production and the actual cost of production.

First we must calculate the standard production cost under marginal costing:

	£
Direct materials 18,000 × £8.00	144,000
Direct labour 18,000 × £14.00	252,000
Marginal cost of production (18,000 x £22)	396,000
Fixed overheads	120,000
Total cost under marginal costing	516,000

As before, the actual cost of production was £512,400.

Reconciliation statement – July

	Adverse £	Favourable £	£
	Variances		
Total standard cost			516,000
Variances:			
Materials price	6,800		
Materials usage		8,000	
Labour rate		11,400	
Labour efficiency	14,000		
Fixed overhead expenditure		5,000	
	20,800	24,400	
Add: adverse variances			20,800
Less: favourable variances			(24,400)
Total actual production cost			512,400

STANDARD COST BOOKKEEPING

When an organisation runs a standard costing system, the variances need to be included in the ledger accounts. This is known as standard cost bookkeeping.

In a standard costing bookkeeping system variances are recorded as follows:

- the materials price variance is recorded in the stores control account
- the labour rate variance is recorded in the wages control account

- the following variances are recorded in the work in progress control account:
  - materials usage variance
  - labour efficiency variance
  - idle time variance
- the production overhead expenditure variance will be recorded in the production overhead control account
- the production overhead volume variance will be recorded either in the production overhead control account or in the work in progress control account
- the balance of variances in the variance accounts will be written off to the income statement (profit and loss account).

Adverse variances are debited to the variance account as an expense and favourable variances are credited to the variance account.

HOW IT WORKS

Zed Co operates an integrated accounting system and a standard absorption costing system and prepares its final accounts monthly.

The following variances have been calculated for the month of October.

Direct material price variance	£40 Fav
Direct material usage variance	£80 Adv
Direct labour rate variance	£45 Adv
Direct labour efficiency variance	£360 Fav
Fixed overhead expenditure variance	£100 Fav
Fixed overhead volume variance	£50 Adv

The Journal entries to record these variances are as follows:

Direct material price variance

Debit	Stores control account	£40	
Credit	Variance account		£40

Direct material usage variance

Debit	Variance account	£80	
Credit	Work in progress control account		£80

Direct labour rate variance

Debit	Variance account	£45
Credit	Wages control account	£45

Direct labour efficiency variance

Debit	Work in progress control account	£360	
Credit	Variance account		£360

Fixed overhead expenditure variance

Debit	Production overhead control account	£100	
Credit	Variance account		£100

Fixed overhead volume variance

Debit	Variance account	£50	
Credit	Production overhead control account		£50

In some accounting systems there is a separate account for each type of variance rather than a single variance account.

Task 8

A firm uses standard costing and an integrated accounting system. The double entry for an adverse material usage variance is

A   DR stores control account

   CR work-in-progress control account

B   DR material usage variance account

   CR stores control account

C   DR work-in-progress control account

   CR material usage variance account

D   DR material usage variance account

   CR work-in-progress control account

CHAPTER OVERVIEW

- The direct materials standard cost is set by determining the estimated quantity of material to be used per unit and the estimated price of that material

- The direct labour standard cost is set by determining the estimated labour time per unit and the estimated rate per hour

- The fixed overhead standard cost is determined by finding a realistic estimate of each of the elements of the fixed overhead

- The standards that can be set include ideal standards, attainable standards and basic standards

- A standard costing system allows the standard cost of production to be compared to the actual costs and variances calculated. This can help management perform their three main roles of decision making, planning and control

- For this Unit materials, labour and fixed overhead variances must be calculated and reconciliations of standard cost to actual cost prepared in both a standard absorption costing system and a standard marginal costing system

- The total direct materials cost variance can be split into a materials price variance and a materials usage variance.

- The total direct labour cost variance can be split in a similar manner into the labour rate variance and the labour efficiency variance

- The total fixed overhead cost variance in an absorption costing system is the amount of fixed overhead that has been under- or over-absorbed in the period

- The total fixed overhead variance can then be analysed into the fixed overhead expenditure variance and fixed overhead volume variance

- If fixed overheads are absorbed on an hourly basis then care must be taken when calculating the volume variance as the standard hours for the actual production should be used rather than the actual hours worked

- Only if fixed overheads are absorbed on an hourly basis can the fixed overhead volume variance be further analysed into an efficiency variance and a capacity variance

- A reconciliation of the standard cost for the actual production to the actual cost of production can be performed by adding the adverse variances to the standard cost and deducting the favourable variances. This is also sometimes called an operating statement.

- In a standard marginal costing system the materials and labour variances are calculated in exactly the same manner as in an absorption costing system – however there is only one fixed overhead variance, the fixed overhead expenditure variance

- In a standard cost bookkeeping system, the variances are recorded as follows:

  - The material price variance is recorded in the stores control account.

  - The labour rate variance is recorded in the wages control account.

  - The following variances are recorded in the work in progress account.

    - Material usage variance
    - Idle time variance
    - Labour efficiency variance

  - The production overhead expenditure variance will be recorded in the production overhead control account.

  - The production overhead volume variance may be recorded in the fixed production overhead account. (Note. Alternatively, you may find the volume variance recorded in the work in progress account.)

  - The balance of variances in the variance accounts at the end of a period may be written off to the income statement.

- Adverse variances are debited to the relevant variance account; favourable variances are credited in the relevant variance account.

Keywords

Standard cost card – document detailing the estimated cost of a unit of a product

Ideal standards – standards set on the basis of perfect working conditions

Attainable standards – realistically achievable standards into which are built elements of normal wastage and inefficiency

Current standards – standards based on current working conditions

Basic standards – historical standards that are normally set when the product is initially produced

Standard costing system – a system which assigns standard costs to each cost unit and allows a comparison of standard costs to actual costs and the calculation of variances

Variances – the difference between the standard costs and the actual costs for a period

Total material variance – the difference between the standard materials cost for the actual production and the actual cost

Adverse variance – where the actual cost is greater than the standard cost

Favourable variance – where the actual cost is less than the standard cost

Material price variance – the difference between the standard price of the materials purchased and their actual cost

Material usage variance – the difference between the standard quantity of material for the actual production and the actual quantity, valued at the standard price of material

Total labour variance – the difference between the standard labour cost for the actual production and the actual cost

Labour rate variance – the difference between the standard rate of pay for the actual hours and the actual cost

Labour efficiency variance – the difference between the standard hours for the actual production and the actual hours, valued at the standard labour rate per hour

Labour idle time variance – an adverse efficiency variance – the difference between the actual hours paid for and the actual hours of productive labour, valued at the standard labour rate per hour

Under-absorption of overheads – where the amount of fixed overhead absorbed into cost units for the period is less than the overhead incurred

Over-absorption of overheads – where the amount of fixed overhead absorbed into cost units for the period is more than the overhead incurred

Total fixed overhead variance – the under or over absorbed fixed overhead for the period

Fixed overhead expenditure variance – the difference between the budgeted fixed overhead and the actual fixed overhead

Fixed overhead volume variance – the difference between actual production level and budgeted production level, valued at the standard absorption rate per unit

Fixed overhead efficiency variance – the difference between the standard hours for the actual production and the actual hours, valued at the standard labour hour absorption rate

Fixed overhead capacity variance – the difference between the actual hours worked and the hours budgeted to be worked, valued at the standard labour hour absorption rate

Reconciliation or operating statement – a statement which uses the variances for the period to reconcile the standard cost for the actual production to the actual cost

TEST YOUR LEARNING

1   Explain where the information for setting the direct labour cost standard would be found and what factors should be taken into consideration when setting it.

2   Explain the difference between ideal standards, attainable standards and basic standards.

3   A business budgeted to produce 1,600 units of one of its products, the YG, during the month of October. The YG uses 7 kg of raw material with a standard cost of £6.00 per kg. During the month the actual production was 1,800 units of YG using 12,000 kg of raw materials costing £70,800.

Calculate the following figures:

(a)   the total materials cost variance

Total materials cost variance £ [4800 F]

(b)   the materials price variance

Materials price variance £ [1200 F]

(c)   the materials usage variance

Materials usage variance £ [1800 F]

4   Production of product FFD for the month of December in a manufacturing business was 15,400 units using 41,000 hours of direct labour costing £265,200. The standard cost card shows that the standard input for a unit of FFD is 2.5 hours at a rate of £6.80 per hour.

Calculate the following figures:

(a)   the total labour cost variance

Total labour cost variance £ [3400 A]

(b)   the labour rate variance

Labour rate variance £ [13600 A]

(c)   the labour efficiency variance

Labour efficiency variance £ [17000 F]

5   A business incurred fixed overheads of £56,000 in the month of May. The fixed overheads are absorbed into units of production at the rate of £2.50 per direct labour hour. The actual production during the month was 6,400 units although the budget had been for 7,000 units. The standard labour cost for the production is 3 hours per unit at an hourly rate of £7.20. During the month 20,000 labour hours were worked at a total cost of £148,600.

Calculate the following figures:

(a) the budgeted fixed overhead for the month

Budgeted fixed overhead £ 52500

(b) the fixed overhead expenditure variance

Fixed overhead expenditure variance £ 3500 A.

(c) the fixed overhead volume variance

Fixed overhead volume variance £

(d) the fixed overhead efficiency variance

Fixed overhead efficiency variance £

(e) the fixed overhead capacity variance

Fixed overhead capacity variance £

6 The standard cost card for a business's product, the MU, is shown below:

	£
Direct materials 4.2 kg at £3.60 per kg	15.12
Direct labour 1.5 hours at £7.80 per hour	11.70
Fixed overheads 1.5 hours at £2.80 per hour	4.20
	31.02

The budgeted production was for 1,800 units of MU. The actual costs during the month of June for the production of 1,750 units of the MU were as follows:

	£
Direct materials 7,500 kg	25,900
Direct labour 2,580 hours	20,600
Fixed overheads	8,100

You are to:

(a) calculate the materials price and usage variances

Materials price variance £

Materials usage variance £

(b) calculate the labour rate and efficiency variances

Labour rate variance £

Labour efficiency variance £

(c) calculate the fixed overhead expenditure, efficiency and capacity variances

Fixed overhead expenditure variance £ _____

Fixed overhead efficiency variance £ _____

Fixed overhead capacity variance £ _____

(d) complete the table to prepare a reconciliation statement reconciling the standard cost of the production to the total cost

Reconciliation statement

	Adverse variances	Favourable variances	
	£	£	£
Standard cost of production			54285
Variances			
Materials price		1100	
Materials usage	540		
Labour rate	476		
Labour efficiency		351	
Fixed overhead expenditure	540		
Fixed overhead efficiency	15	126	
Fixed overhead capacity	336		
Add: adverse variances	1892		
Less: favourable variances		1577	
Actual cost of production			56600

7 A business operates a marginal standard costing system and the cost card for its single product is given below:

	£
Direct materials 12 kg @ £4.80	57.60
Direct labour 3 hours @ £8.00	24.00
	81.60

The budgeted output for the period was 2,100 units and the budgeted fixed overhead was £95,000.

The actual production in the period was 2,400 units and the actual costs were as follows:

	£
Direct materials 29,600 kg	145,000
Direct labour 6,900 hours	56,200
Fixed overhead	92,000

You are to:

(a) calculate the total direct materials cost variance and the materials price and usage variances

Direct materials cost variance £ ☐

Materials price variance £ ☐

Materials usage variance £ ☐

(b) calculate the total direct labour cost variance and the labour rate and efficiency variances

Direct labour cost variance £ ☐

Labour rate variance £ ☐

Labour efficiency variance £ ☐

(c) calculate any relevant fixed overhead variances

Fixed overhead expenditure variance £ ☐

(d) complete the table to produce a reconciliation statement reconciling the standard cost of the production to the actual cost.

	Adverse variances	Favourable variances	
	£	£	£
Standard cost of actual production			
Variances			
Materials price			
Materials usage			
Labour rate			
Labour efficiency			
Fixed overhead expenditure			
Add adverse variances			
Less: favourable variances			
Total actual cost			

8   Which three of the following variances are recorded in the work-in-progress control account in a standard cost bookkeeping system?

- Material price variance
- Material usage variance
- Labour rate variance
- Variable overhead efficiency variance
- Sales variance
- Idle time variance

chapter 6:
STANDARD COSTING – FURTHER ASPECTS

chapter coverage 📖

We will now take standard costing a little further and look at the reasons for variances and how to break down some variances further to determine their causes and in particular those causes that are controllable and those that are not.

The topics that are to be covered are:

✍ Reasons for variances

✍ Interdependence of variances

REASONS FOR VARIANCES

When reporting variances to management a simple operating (reconciliation) report as illustrated in the last chapter is a useful starting point. However management will also wish to know the reasons for the variances. Before we look at a specific example we will consider some of the possible reasons for each type of variance:

Materials price variance – adverse

- an unexpected price increase from a supplier
- loss of a previous trade or bulk buying discount from a supplier
- purchase of a higher grade of materials

Materials price variance – favourable

- negotiation of a better price from a supplier
- negotiation of a trade or bulk purchase discount from a supplier
- purchase of a lower grade of materials

Materials usage variance – adverse

- greater wastage due to a lower grade of material
- greater wastage due to use of a lower grade of labour
- problems with machinery

Materials usage variance – favourable

- use of a higher grade of material which led to less wastage
- use of more skilled labour leading to less wastage than normal
- new machinery which provides greater efficiency

Labour rate variance – adverse

- unexpected increase in labour costs
- use of a higher grade of labour than anticipated
- unexpectedly high levels of overtime

Labour rate variance – favourable

- use of a lower grade of labour than budgeted for
- less overtime than budgeted for

Labour efficiency variance – adverse

- use of a less skilled grade of labour
- use of a lower grade of material which takes longer to work on
- more idle time than budgeted
- poor supervision of the workforce
- problems with machinery

Labour efficiency variance – favourable

- use of a more skilled grade of labour
- use of a higher grade of material which takes less time to work on
- less idle time than budgeted
- use of new more efficient machinery

Fixed overhead expenditure variance – adverse or favourable

- an unexpected increase or decrease in the cost of any element of fixed overheads

Fixed overhead volume variance – adverse or favourable

- an unexpected increase or decrease in production volume. If absorption is done on the basis of labour or machine hours, analysis of the volume variance into the efficiency and capacity variances can help to find reasons for the volume variance.

Fixed overhead efficiency variance – adverse or favourable

- if the absorption basis is that of labour hours then the fixed overhead efficiency variance will be due to the same causes as the labour efficiency variance

- if the absorption basis is that of machine hours then the fixed overhead efficiency variance will reflect how efficiently the machinery has been used to produce the cost units

Fixed overhead capacity variance – adverse or favourable

- if the absorption basis is that of labour hours,

- this variance measures whether more or less hours were worked than originally budgeted

- if the absorption basis is that of machine hours, the capacity variance measures whether more or less machine hours were operated than originally budgeted

Task 1

If a business has a favourable labour rate variance of £2,500, which of the following might have been the cause of this?

A   more overtime paid than budgeted

B   use of a lower grade of material which takes longer to work on

C   more idle time than budgeted

D   use of a lower grade of labour than anticipated

INTERDEPENDENCE OF VARIANCES

You may have noticed from some of the possible causes of variances given above, that many of these are likely to be inter-related. This is known as the INTERDEPENDENCE OF VARIANCES.

For example, a favourable material price variance that is caused by purchasing a lower grade of material may lead directly to an adverse materials usage variance, as the lower grade of material means that there is greater wastage.

A further example might be the use of a lower grade of labour on a job than budgeted, leading to a favourable labour rate variance but an adverse materials usage variance, as the less skilled labour cause more materials wastage.

Responsibility for variances

Investigating the causes of variances and determining any interdependence between the variances is an important aspect of management control, as in a system of responsibility accounting the managers responsible for various elements of the business will be held accountable for the relevant variances.

Take the example of a favourable material price variance caused by purchasing a lower grade of material which leads directly to an adverse materials usage variance. The initial reaction might be to praise the purchasing manager for the favourable variance and to lay blame for the adverse usage variance on the production manager. However, the true picture is that, in the absence of any further reasons for the variance, the responsibility for both variances lies with the purchasing manager.

When asked to explain a variance, the budget holder may provide information that is inaccurate or ignores any interdependence. In this case, the holder of the materials budget, the purchasing manager, may suggest that the favourable material price variance is due to better price negotiations with the supplier. However an independent assessment of quality by the production manager may lead to the true cause of the variance (the lower grade of material) and its impact elsewhere in the business in terms of adverse usage, being revealed

Other reasons for variances

As well as the reasons suggested so far for variances that might occur, one fundamental reason for a variance, particularly one that recurs each period, may be that the standard is out of date. If the standard does not reflect the reality of the cost or usage of materials, labour or overheads then this will be a significant cause of any variances.

Standards should be regularly reviewed, at least annually, and kept up-to-date in terms of the costs of materials, labour and fixed overheads and in terms of the usage of materials and labour hours required for each product.

Further causes of variances may be one-off events such as a power cut, breakdown of machinery or annual staff holidays.

Alteration of standard costs

The decision to alter a standard cost should be not be taken lightly and should only be done when there is a long term or permanent change in the cost of the resource or the usage.

For example, suppose a material price variance has been caused by a change of supplier due to the fact that the normal supplier was out of supplies. Purchases will continue to be made from the normal supplier in future. In this case the standard should not be changed. However if there is a general price increase for the material in question, no matter which supplier is used, then the standard direct materials cost should be revised.

HOW IT WORKS

Given below is the absorption cost reconciliation or operating statement for Lawson Ltd for the production of the George in July 20X8, showing all of the variances calculated in the previous chapter.

Reconciliation or operating statement – July

	Variances		
	Adverse	Favourable	
	£	£	£
Total standard cost			504,000
Variances:			
Materials price	6,800		
Materials usage		8,000	
Labour rate		11,400	
Labour efficiency	14,000		
Fixed overhead expenditure		5,000	
Fixed overhead efficiency	6,000		
Fixed overhead capacity	6,000		
	32,800	24,400	
Add: adverse variances			32,800
Less: favourable variances			(24,400)
Total actual cost			512,400

Upon investigation of the variances, the following is discovered:

- the supplier of the materials has permanently increased its prices but has also significantly improved the quality of the material

- some of the workforce used in the period were of a lower grade than normal and they were not as familiar with the production process as the normal labour force

- during the period there was a machine breakdown which caused a significant amount of idle time when the workforce was not actually able to make the product

- due to the machine breakdown, the power costs for the period were lower than anticipated

- Lawson Ltd has recently reduced the amount of factory space that it rents but the standard rental cost has not been adjusted.

You are to write a report to the Operations Manager identifying possible causes of the variances and making any suggestions for action that should be taken.

REPORT

To: Operations Manager, Lawson Ltd
From: An Accountant
Date: August 20X8
Subject: Variances

The direct materials, direct labour and fixed overhead variances for the period have been calculated.

There is an adverse materials price variance, caused by the supplier of the materials permanently increasing his prices. However, the quality of the material has also been improved, which will have played a part in the favourable materials usage variance. We should consider other suppliers for the supply of our materials, but if their prices are the same as our supplier's, or the material quality is not as good, then the standard cost of the materials should be altered. If it can be shown that the higher quality material has caused the favourable usage variance then consideration should also be given to alteration of the direct materials usage per unit on the standard cost card.

The favourable labour rate variance will be due to the use of lower grade labour than normal for some of the period and this may also have partly caused the adverse labour efficiency variance. The labour efficiency variance is also partly due to the machine breakdown during the period, which has meant that labour hours have been paid for when no productive work was achieved (idle time). The machine breakdown is a one-off event which should not be built into the standard costs. However, if it is anticipated that the lower grade of labour will now normally be used for the production, then the standard labour rate and hours should be changed.

The fixed overhead expenditure variance was favourable due to lower power costs, due to the machine breakdown and also a reduction in factory rental. The reduction in rent is a permanent reduction and therefore the budgeted fixed overhead should be altered to reflect this in future periods.

The fixed overhead efficiency variance is due to the adverse labour efficiency variance and the factors that caused it, as discussed above. The adverse capacity variance shows that not all the available labour hours in the original budget were worked and the reasons for this should be investigated. One possible explanation may be that there are not enough employees who are skilled enough to produce the George.

Task 2

A business has recently taken on a new contract which required it to hire new workers. In its first period the results for the contract showed a favourable labour rate variance of £2,500, but an adverse labour efficiency variance of £6,250 and an adverse material usage variance of £5,750.

The manager responsible for hiring labour has suggested that the favourable labour rate variance was due to them managing to agree a lower rate per hour with the workforce.

What other possible explanations could there be for the favourable labour rate variance which might also explain the adverse labour efficiency and materials usage variances? What action could be taken to ascertain the true picture?

FURTHER ANALYSIS OF VARIANCES

In assigning responsibility for variances, managers should only be held accountable for factors that are within their control. Variances are caused by two basic factors:

- planning factors – when setting standards and formulating budgets for how much will be produced, we are engaged in planning. A great deal of planning is actually (well-informed) guesswork, and it is useful to try to separate out a variance caused by a guess that turns out to be wrong (and therefore to an extent uncontrollable), from variances caused by other decisions

- control factors – as the production period goes on, managers must make a great many control decisions, such as buying material of a lower grade than planned, or taking advantage of a discount offered, which had not been anticipated at the planning stage. It is therefore useful to separate out variances caused by control decisions from those caused by planning assumptions

It is sometimes the case that a variance can be split into two parts:

- the part that is caused by some particular factor that is known, such as actual change in materials prices (sometimes called a planning or uncontrollable variance since it is attributable to a failure in planning, rather than an operational decision)

- the part that is caused by other factors that we do not specifically know about (sometimes called a control variance, since it is attributable to factors experienced in actual operations)

Examples of variances that might be split into planning and control variances include the following:

- materials price variance – analysed between the element due to a specific price change (planning) and that due to other factors (control)

- materials price variance – analysed between the element due to a seasonal change in price of the material (planning) and that due to other factors (control)

- materials usage variance – analysed between the element due to the learning process for the workforce (planning) and that due to other factors (control)

- labour rate variance – analysed between the element due to specific wage increases (planning) and that due to other factors (control)

- labour efficiency variance – analysed between the element due to the learning process or training period (planning) and that due to other elements (control)

Materials price changes

The standard materials cost will often be set based upon the anticipated materials price during the period. However the actual price of the materials may have been materially different during the period, meaning that the materials price variance may not show the true picture of what is happening.

The materials price variance is calculated as follows:

	£
Standard price for actual quantity used	X
Actual cost of materials	X
Materials price variance	X

This can then be analysed into:

Price variance due to known price change (planning variance)		Price variance due to other factors (control variance)	
	£		£
Standard price for actual quantity used	X	Price-adjusted cost for actual quantity used	X
Price-adjusted cost for actual quantity used	X	Actual cost	X
	X		X

HOW IT WORKS

The standard direct materials cost for a business's product is:

4 kg @ £5.00 per kg = £20.00

During the month of October production was 12,000 units of the product and the actual materials cost was £248,000 for 45,600 kg. The market price of the materials has been unexpectedly increased to £5.50 per kg for the whole month, due to shortages.

Calculate the total materials price variance and then show how it can be analysed between the planning element (caused by the price increase) and the control element (caused by other factors).

Total materials price variance

	£
Standard price for actual quantity 45,600 kg × £5.00	228,000
Actual quantity at actual price	248,000
	20,000 Adv

Planning variance due to price increase

	£
Standard price for actual quantity 45,600 kg × £5.00	228,000
Adjusted price for actual quantity 45,600 kg × £5.50	250,800
	22,800 Adv

Control variance due to other factors

	£
Adjusted price for actual quantity 45,600 × £5.50	250,800
Actual cost	248,000
	2,800 Fav

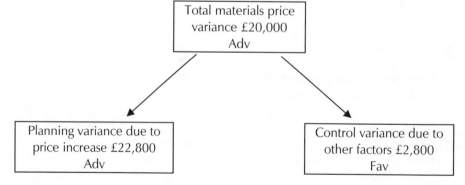

The total materials price variance shows an adverse price variance of £20,000. However when we analyse the price variance, we can see that all of that was caused by the new higher price (the planning variance) and that indeed the control variance caused by other factors was in fact favourable. Therefore the purchasing manager should be praised for the favourable control variance and not blamed for the uncontrollable adverse planning variance.

Task 3

A business's product has a standard direct material cost of £24.60 (3 kg @ £8.20 per kg). During the month of September the total production of the product was 1,500 units using 4,600 kg of materials at a total cost of £40,800. During the month the price was unexpectedly increased due to a shortage of the material to £9.00 per kg.

(a)   The total materials price variance was £ [   ]

(b)   The planning variance due to the price increase was £ [   ]

        The control variance due to other factors was £ [   ]

Seasonal variations in price

In some businesses, material prices will tend to be different at different times of the year, due to availability or other factors. When considering the materials price variance, it may be useful to analyse this into the planning price variance due to the season and the control price variance due to any other factors.

HOW IT WORKS

A business makes a product which uses a raw material which has a standard price of £20.00 per kg. Each unit of the product requires 3 kg of this material. The price of the materials for the last 6 years has been subjected to a time series analysis and the following seasonal variations have been seen to occur.

Jan – Mar	–£2.00
Apr – Jun	+£1.00
Jul – Aug	+£3.00
Sep – Dec	–£2.00

During February 10,000 units of the product were made and the price paid for the 32,000 kg of material was £560,000.

What is the total materials price variance and how can this be analysed to show the planning variance due to the season and the control variance due to other factors?

Total materials price variance

	£
Standard cost for actual quantity 32,000 kg × £20	640,000
Actual cost	560,000
	80,000 Fav

Planning variance due to seasonality

	£
Standard cost for actual quantity 32,000 kg × £20	640,000
Adjusted price for actual quantity 32,000 kg × (£20 –£2.00)	576,000
	64,000 Fav

Control variance due to other factors

	£
Adjusted price for actual quantity 32,000 kg × (£20 –£2.00)	576,000
Actual cost	560,000
	16,000 Fav

The total favourable price variance of £80,000 can now be seen only partly to be due to the seasonal factors. There is also £16,000 of favourable control variance due to other factors.

Task 4

The standard cost of direct materials for a product is made up of 5 kg of material at an average standard cost of £6.00 per kg. It has been noted over the years that the cost of the material fluctuates on a seasonal basis around the average standard cost as follows:

Jan – June   –£0.90

July – Dec   +£0.90

In the month of October the actual production was 2,000 units and 10,300 kg of material were used at a cost of £69,500.

(a)   The total materials price variance was £ ⬚

(b)   The planning variance due to the seasonal price change was £ ⬚

The control variance due to other factors was £ ⬚

Labour efficiency variances

It is often the case that a labour force will have to learn how to produce a product, so their level of production will be lower in the early days of production and should increase in later periods. If the productivity of the workforce is affected by still being in this learning or training period, then the total labour efficiency variance may be misleading.

In exactly the same way as we did for the materials price variance, we can analyse the labour efficiency variance into the element that has been caused by the learning process (and which should be anticipated at the planning stage) and the element caused by other controllable factors.

HOW IT WORKS

A business has just started production of a new product, with a long-run standard labour cost of 4 hours per unit at an hourly rate of £8.00.

However, in this first learning period of production, it is anticipated that each unit will take 20% longer to make than the long-run standard time.

The production in the first period was 2,000 units and the actual hours worked were 10,000 at a cost of £75,000.

What is the total labour efficiency variance, the planning variance caused by the learning process and the control variance caused by other factors?

Total labour efficiency variance

	£
Standard hours for actual production at standard rate	
2,000 × 4 hours × £8.00	64,000
Actual hours at standard rate 10,000 × £8.00	80,000
	16,000 Adv

Planning variance due to learning process

	£
Standard hours for actual production at standard rate 2,000 × 4 hours × £8.00	64,000
Adjusted hours for actual production at standard rate 2,000 × (4 hours × 1.20) × £8.00	76,800
	12,800 Adv

Control variance due to other factors

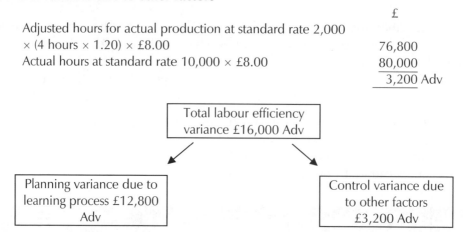

	£
Adjusted hours for actual production at standard rate 2,000 × (4 hours × 1.20) × £8.00	76,800
Actual hours at standard rate 10,000 × £8.00	80,000
	3,200 Adv

Total labour efficiency variance £16,000 Adv

Planning variance due to learning process £12,800 Adv

Control variance due to other factors £3,200 Adv

The total adverse efficiency variance is made up of only £12,800 that relates to the learning process – the remaining £3,200 of adverse variance is due to other control factors.

Task 5

A business has just had its first month of production of a new product. During the period 12,000 units were produced in 48,000 hours costing £288,000 in direct labour. The standard labour cost has been set at 3.5 hours for each unit of production at a rate of £6.20 per labour hour. However it is anticipated that the first month's production will take 25% longer than the standard hours.

(a)   The total labour efficiency variance was £ ▢

(b)   The planning variance due to the early production problems was
£ ▢

The control variance due to other factors was £ ▢

Using indices to update standard costs

In some instances you may be given information about indices, either specific indices relating to the materials the business uses or indices regarding the labour rates. These index numbers can then be used to update an old standard cost.

HOW IT WORKS

A business has the following standard direct materials cost for its product:

> 10 kg @ £3.40 per kg = £34.00

The standard cost of the material was set when the price index for the material stood at 170. During the month of July, 4,000 units of the product were made, using 38,000 kg, at a total cost of £135,000. For July, the price index for the material was 185.

Calculate the total materials price variance and analyse it into the planning variance that relates to the price increase and the control variance that is related to other factors.

Total materials price variance

	£
Standard price of actual materials 38,000 kg × £3.40	129,200
Actual cost	135,000
	5,800 Adv

Planning variance relating to price increase

	£
Standard price of actual materials 38,000 kg × £3.40	129,200
Adjusted price for actual materials	
38,000 kg × (£3.40 × 185/170)	140,600
	11,400 Adv

Control variance relating to other factors

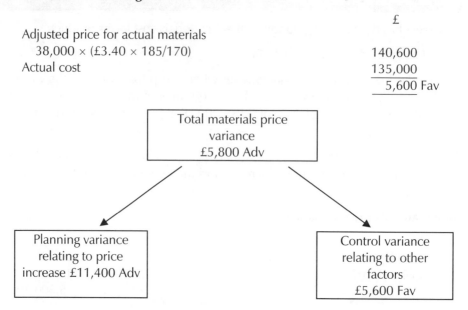

	£
Adjusted price for actual materials	
38,000 × (£3.40 × 185/170)	140,600
Actual cost	135,000
	5,600 Fav

Total materials price variance
£5,800 Adv

Planning variance relating to price increase £11,400 Adv

Control variance relating to other factors £5,600 Fav

Although the price variance is only £5,800 adverse, this is due to the fact that there is a favourable control variance due to other factors of £5,600, which has been netted off against the £11,400 adverse planning variance caused by the price increase.

Task 6

A business has a direct labour standard cost of 4 hours per product at a standard hourly rate of £7.50. This standard labour rate was set when the relevant labour index stood at 120. The labour rate index is now 130. During the period the actual production was 5,000 products using 21,000 hours costing £160,000.

(a)   The total labour rate variance was £ [   ]

(b)   The planning variance due to the specific index of labour rate increases was £ [   ]

    The control variance due to other factors was £ [   ]

CHAPTER OVERVIEW

- Each type of variance can have a variety of causes – often the variances are interdependent meaning that a factor that caused one variance is also the factor that causes other variances

- Once the reasons for the variances have been discovered, then responsibility for the variances, both favourable as well as adverse, can be assigned to the relevant managers

- A business may need to carry out an independent investigation of the reasons for a variance, in order to ascertain whether the explanation of the variance provided by the budget holder is reasonable. This may help them decide whether there is any interdependence and assess who should be held responsible.

- Some variances may be due to the setting of the standard and therefore be uncontrollable by the relevant manager – in some circumstances the standard will need to be altered if there has been a long term or permanent change in the cost or usage of the resources

- If the actual price of materials is significantly different to standard price, due to a problem with the standard, then this can have an effect on materials price variance that can appear misleading – the materials price variance can then be analysed into the planning variance caused by the price increase (uncontrollable) and the control variance caused by other factors

- The materials price variance can also be affected by any seasonality of materials prices – again the total price variance can be analysed into the planning variance which is due to the seasonal element of the price and the control variance caused by other factors

- There may be occasions when the labour efficiency variance does not give a true picture of the situation, particularly in the early stages of production when the workforce are still learning how to make the product – in such cases the labour efficiency variance can be analysed into the planning variance caused by the learning process and the control variance caused by other factors

- If a standard cost is based upon an index for a particular material or labour price then the standard cost can be updated using the current value of the index in order to analyse the materials price or labour rate variance into planning and control variances

KEY WORDS

Interdependence of variances – this is where the factor which causes one variance can also be the cause of another variance

System of responsibility accounting – where the managers responsible for various elements of the business will be held accountable for the variances within their control.

Planning variances – the part of the variance that is due to the standard cost used at the planning stage being wrong. This variance is often considered uncontrollable.

Control variances – the part of the variance that is due to other controllable operational factors or decisions

TEST YOUR LEARNING

1 Given below is the operating statement for one of the factories of a business for the month of November, reconciling the total standard cost to the total actual cost for the month.

Operating statement – November

	Variances Adverse £	Variances Favourable £	£
Total standard cost			634,200
Variances:			
Materials price	9,200		
Materials usage	14,600		
Labour rate		15,400	
Labour efficiency	13,200		
Fixed overhead expenditure	7,200		
Fixed overhead efficiency	11,500		
Fixed overhead capacity		6,000	
	55,700	21,400	
Add: adverse variances			55,700
Less: favourable variances			(21,400)
Total actual cost			668,500

You also discover the following information:

- due to staff shortages a more junior grade of labour than normal, from one of the other factories, had to be used in the production process, giving rise to inefficiencies and additional wastage

- the material price has been increased by all suppliers and it is doubtful that the materials can be purchased more cheaply than this in future

- due to its inventory (stock)-holding policy the factory has had to rent some additional space but this has not been recognised in the standard fixed overhead cost

- due to the inefficiencies of labour, more hours had to be worked than normal in the month

Write a report to the Managing Director explaining the possible reasons for the variances for the month and making any suggestions about future actions that should be taken.

2   The standard direct materials cost for a product is:

12 litres @ £2.40 per litre = £28.80

During week 23, the total production was 1,200 units of the product which used 14,000 litres of material. The price of the material has suddenly increased to £2.80 per litre and the business paid £38,500 during the month for materials.

(a)   The total materials price variance was £ [＿＿＿＿＿＿]

(b)   The planning variance due to the price increase was £ [＿＿＿＿＿]

The control variance caused by other factors was £ [＿＿＿＿＿]

3   A business makes a product that requires 6.5 kg of material input, which has been assigned a standard cost of £8.00 per kg. However the price of the material fluctuates throughout the year and the seasonal variations have been monitored over a number of years using time series analysis. The seasonal variations in price are:

Jan – Mar	−£1.84
Apr – June	−£0.40
July – Sept	+£0.64
Oct – Dec	+£1.60

During June the output was 1,800 units of finished product using 12,300 kg of material. The total material cost was £95,200.

(a)   The total materials price variance was £ [＿＿＿＿＿＿]

(b)   The planning variance due to the seasonal variation was £ [＿＿＿＿＿＿]

The control variance due to other factors was £ [＿＿＿＿＿＿]

4   A business has just started to produce a new product which it is anticipated will require 11 direct labour hours per unit for the first month of production. However as the employees become used to making the product it is thought that the labour time per unit will reduce to 9 hours, which is the figure which has been used for the standard cost of the direct labour together with a labour rate of £6.80 per hour.

During the first month of production 2,400 units were produced, taking 27,000 hours to produce and the labour cost was £182,600.

(a)   The total labour efficiency variance was £ [＿＿＿＿＿＿]

(b)   The planning variance due to the learning process in production was £ [＿＿＿＿＿＿]

The control variance due to other factors was £ [＿＿＿＿＿＿]

5   A business set the standard cost for its materials at 7 kg per unit at a price of £6.50 per kg when the index for those particular material prices stood at 130. During the month of November 14,000 units of the product were produced using 100,000 kg of materials and the total cost was £670,000. In November the index for the materials price stood at 138.

(a)   The total materials price variance was £ [   ]

(b)   The planning variance due to the price increase was £ [   ]

      The control variance due to other factors was £ [   ]

chapter 7:
PERFORMANCE INDICATORS

chapter coverage 📖

In this chapter we will look at the calculation and meaning of a variety of performance indicators, both financial and non-financial.

The topics we shall cover are:

🖎 What is meant by performance indicators

🖎 Productivity

🖎 Value added

🖎 Control ratios: efficiency, capacity and activity

🖎 Gross and net profit margins

🖎 Return on capital employed

🖎 Asset turnover and non-current (fixed) asset turnover

🖎 Working capital ratios

🖎 Ratio analysis

🖎 Limitations of ratio analysis

🖎 The balanced scorecard

🖎 Service organisations

🖎 What if analysis

PERFORMANCE INDICATORS

In the previous two chapters we considered standard costing as a method of providing information for management to allow them to control costs and hence performance. In this chapter we will consider other methods of summarising both financial and non-financial information about a business, for the purposes of management's control of costs and enhancement of value. This information for management will be provided by calculating a variety of performance indicators.

PERFORMANCE INDICATORS are methods of summarising the performance of all or parts of the organisation for a period. Performance indicators are ways of summarising performance using a formula. Some of the performance indicators will be expressed as absolute figures, such as inventory (stock) turnover period in days, whereas others will be expressed as relative figures or percentages, for example, a gross profit percentage where gross profit is expressed as a percentage of sales.

Financial and non-financial data

Some of the performance indicators will be based upon financial data. For example, a gross profit margin is calculated using figures for gross profit and sales, both taken from the income statement (profit and loss account). However other performance indicators will be based upon non-financial data, such as calculation of the number of units produced per hour.

Using the performance indicators

The performance indicators that we will consider in this chapter are vital tools of management as they serve as summaries of the performance of the business during the period. For example, if the production director is informed that productivity is 50 units per hour for the month then this has summarised information about the number of units produced and the number of hours worked, without the need for management to have these detailed figures.

However none of these performance indicators is of much significance on their own. They are only useful if they are being compared to other figures. The comparisons that are useful are:

- comparison to previous period's performance measures
- comparison to budgeted performance measures or target measures
- comparison to industry average performance measures
- comparison to other similar organisations' measures

The latter three comparisons are all forms of BENCHMARKING.

Comparability

If the performance indicators are to be used in comparison with another measure then it is important that we are comparing like with like. In general, performance indicators are a good method of providing consistent information; provided the same formula is used in each period, the performance indicators can be compared over time in order to discover the trend of performance.

However, care must be taken to ensure that the figures used are strictly comparable. For example, if the performance indicators of a business are being compared with those of another business and the businesses have different accounting policies regarding, say, depreciation, then the resulting comparison may be distorted.

A further problem may be when figures are being compared over a period of time during which there has been an increase in prices. In such instances, before the performance indicators are calculated the figures should be made comparable by using an appropriate index (this was considered in detail in Chapter 4).

PRODUCTIVITY

PRODUCTIVITY is a measure of how hard the employees are working or how productive they are being in their hours at work and is likely to be measured in terms of units of output.

As with many performance indicators, productivity can be measured in different ways but the basic calculation is to discover how many units of product or service are being produced either each hour or by each employee.

HOW IT WORKS

Harris Engineering has two factories which each make single and similar products. The production figures for the two factories for the month of June are given below:

	Factory A	Factory B
Units produced	285,000	146,000
Number of production workers	30	16
Hours worked	4,800	2,600

The productivity of the two factories could be expressed in two ways: productivity per hour or productivity per employee.

Method 1 – Productivity per labour hour

$$\text{Productivity per labour hour} = \frac{\text{Output in the period}}{\text{Hours worked in the period}}$$

	Factory A	*Factory B*
$=$	$\dfrac{285,000\,\text{units}}{4,800\,\text{hours}}$	$\dfrac{146,000\,\text{units}}{2,600\,\text{hours}}$
$=$	59.4 units per hour	56.2 units per hour

Obviously the productivity of the two factories can be compared (provided that the units produced are similar) and these figures indicate that productivity per labour hour is slightly higher in Factory A than in Factory B.

This productivity level could also then be compared with previous months' and with budgeted figures.

Suppose that the budgeted figures for the month for Factory A were 250,000 units of production in 4,400 labour hours.

$$\text{Budgeted productivity} = \frac{250,000\,\text{units}}{4,400\,\text{hours}}$$

$$= 56.8 \text{ units per labour hour}$$

In this case, the actual productivity during June is high compared to the standard or budgeted productivity.

Increase in productivity

An increase in productivity means that more units can be produced in one hour or by one employee. This will normally mean a reduction in costs, as the same number of units can be produced in less hours and therefore with reduced labour costs, machine costs and overheads.

HOW IT WORKS

Returning to Harris Engineering, in Factory B 146,000 units were produced in 2,600 hours in June resulting in productivity of 56.2 units produced per hour. Labour is paid at a rate of £10 per hour. If the productivity of Factory B could be increased to 59 units per hour (as in Factory A) what effect would this have on the labour cost of Factory B?

Suppose that 146,000 units are to be produced next month. If productivity increases to 59 units per hour then this production will take:

$$\frac{146,000}{59} = \text{approx 2,475 hours}$$

Time saving 2,600 – 2,475   =   125 hours

Cost saving 125 × £10   =   £1,250

This increase in productivity therefore could bring about a labour cost saving of £1,250.

Method 2 – Productivity per employee

Productivity per employee   = $\dfrac{\text{Output in the period}}{\text{No of employees working on output}}$

	Factory A	Factory B
=	$\dfrac{285,000}{30}$	$\dfrac{146,000}{16}$
=	9,500 units per employee	9,125 units per employee

Again comparison can be made between the two factories, to productivity in previous periods or to budgeted productivity levels.

Which method to use?

In a manufacturing situation, the most useful method of measuring productivity is normally method 1, productivity per labour hour, as on the factory floor each employee will be likely to be doing different tasks. It is probably not the case, in the previous example, that each of the 30 production workers in Factory A actually produced 9,500 units.

However method 2, the productivity per employee, is most appropriate in a situation where each employee is doing an identical job and the job in question can take a varied amount of time.

HOW IT WORKS

Harris Engineering has a sales department which processes all orders for goods. In June the six members of the telephone sales team processed 1,240 orders.

Productivity per employee   = $\dfrac{\text{Output} = \text{number of orders}}{\text{Number of employees}}$

                                 = $\dfrac{1,240 \text{ orders}}{6 \text{ employees}}$

                                 =   207 orders per employee

Task 1

An advertising company has produced 216 advertisements in Quarter 2 using 26 advertising executives. In Quarter 1 only 188 advertisements were produced when there were 22 executives.

What is the productivity of the company for this quarter and the previous quarter?

Current quarter

Previous quarter

Value added

A further method of measuring productivity is to calculate the VALUE ADDED per employee.

When a business buys raw materials and services from suppliers, it is buying them at their value to the supplier. The business will then process or work on these raw materials, incorporating any bought-in services, and will aim to sell the final goods for more than the materials and services cost, in order to make a profit.

Value added is the difference between the value of the inputs in a business and the value of the outputs. The inputs are the cost of materials and bought in services and the value of the outputs is the sales revenue of the business.

Value added = Sales revenue – (cost of materials and bought in services)

The value added therefore is the extra value that the employees of the business have added to the materials and services in order to bring them to the value of their selling price. Value added can therefore be used as a measure of overall company performance and often the value added per employee is a performance indicator used by management in order to measure productivity.

HOW IT WORKS

You are given the following information about a small manufacturing business for the year ending 30 June 20X8.

Sales revenue	£835,400
Cost of materials used	£466,700
Cost of bought in services	£265,000
Number of employees	12

What is the total value added and the value added per employee?

Value added	=	Sales revenue – (cost of materials and bought in services)
	=	£835,400 – (466,700 + 265,000)
	=	£103,700
Value added per employee	=	£103,700/12
	=	£8,642

Note: No deduction is made for the wages paid to the employees

CONTROL RATIOS: EFFICIENCY, CAPACITY AND ACTIVITY

A further method of measuring the productivity of the workforce is to calculate what are generally known as the CONTROL RATIOS of efficiency, capacity and activity.

Remember from an earlier chapter that the labour efficiency variance was calculated to determine whether the workforce had been more or less efficient than the standard efficiency. This was calculated by comparing:

- the standard hours for the actual production, and
- the actual hours worked

These three ratios of efficiency, capacity and activity are calculated using these same two figures, together with the budgeted total hours.

Efficiency ratio

As the name implies the EFFICIENCY RATIO is a measure of how efficiently the workforce has operated during a period and is expressed as a percentage. It is calculated as:

$$\text{Efficiency ratio} = \frac{\text{Standard hours for actual production}}{\text{Actual hours worked}} \times 100$$

If the ratio is 100% this means that the workforce has worked as efficiently as the standard that was set. If the ratio is more than 100% then they have worked more efficiently and if it is less than 100%, less efficiently.

Capacity ratio

The CAPACITY RATIO measures whether the workforce has worked to full planned capacity or not. This is done by comparing the actual hours worked to the hours that were budgeted for and is expressed as a percentage.

$$\text{Capacity ratio} = \frac{\text{Actual hours worked}}{\text{Budgeted hours}} \times 100$$

If the ratio is less than 100% then the workforce have not worked for as long as was budgeted for and if it is more than 100%, they have worked for longer.

Activity ratio

The ACTIVITY RATIO is an indicator of how the actual output compares to the budgeted output. It is calculated as:

$$\text{Activity ratio} = \frac{\text{Standard hours for actual production}}{\text{Budgeted hours}} \times 100$$

This ratio can also be calculated from actual and budgeted output levels, in which case it is known as the PRODUCTION VOLUME RATIO.

$$\text{Production volume ratio} = \frac{\text{Actual output}}{\text{Budgeted output}} \times 100$$

HOW IT WORKS

Harris Engineering has a third factory, Factory C, which produces a product made from the components produced by Factories A and B. The production figures for June for this factory are as follows:

	Factory C
Budgeted production in units	4,800
Actual production in units	4,500
Labour hours worked	10,000
Standard hours for each unit	2

Efficiency ratio

$$\text{Efficiency ratio} = \frac{\text{Standard hours for actual production}}{\text{Actual hours worked}} \times 100$$

$$= \frac{4,500 \text{ units} \times 2 \text{ hours per unit}}{10,000} \times 100$$

$$= \frac{9,000}{10,000} \times 100$$

$$= 90\%$$

The workforce has worked well below standard levels, taking 10,000 hours to produce output that should have taken only 9,000 hours.

Capacity ratio

$$\text{Capacity ratio} \quad = \quad \frac{\text{Actual hours worked}}{\text{Budgeted hours}} \times 100$$

$$= \quad \frac{10,000}{4,800 \text{ units} \times 2 \text{ hours}} \times 100$$

$$= \quad \frac{10,000}{9,600} \times 100$$

$$= \quad 104.17\%$$

The capacity ratio shows that more hours have been worked than were budgeted. The

workforce has exceeded the budgeted capacity level.

Activity ratio

$$\text{Activity ratio} \quad = \quad \frac{\text{Standard hours for actual production}}{\text{Budgeted hours}} \times 100$$

$$= \quad \frac{4,500 \text{ units} \times 2 \text{ hours}}{4,800 \text{ units} \times 2 \text{ hours}} \times 100$$

$$= \quad \frac{9,000}{9,600} \times 100$$

$$= \quad 93.75\%$$

This shows that actual output was only 93.75% of the budgeted output.

This could also be calculated as the production volume ratio:

$$\text{Production volume ratio} \quad = \quad \frac{\text{Actual output}}{\text{Budgeted output}} \times 100$$

$$= \quad \frac{4,500 \text{ units}}{4,800 \text{ units}} \times 100$$

$$= \quad 93.75\%$$

Relationship between the control ratios

The three control ratios are related to each other as follows:

$$\boxed{\text{Efficiency ratio}} \times \boxed{\text{Capacity ratio}} = \boxed{\text{Activity ratio}}$$

This means that we can explain the activity ratio by referring to the other two ratios.

HOW IT WORKS

Using the figures for Factory C, remember that the three control ratios were calculated as:

Efficiency ratio	90%
Capacity ratio	104.17%
Activity ratio	93.75%

These are related as follows:

$$\boxed{\text{Efficiency ratio}} \times \boxed{\text{Capacity ratio}} = \boxed{\text{Activity ratio}}$$

$$90\% \times 104.17\% = 93.75\%$$

The activity ratio shows production was only 93.75% of the budgeted level. We can now explain that this was due to the significantly lower level of efficiency than budgeted for, despite the workforce working for more hours than budgeted for.

Task 2

A manufacturing organisation had a budgeted output planned for the month of October of 288,000 units. 268,000 units were in fact produced. The standard production time for each unit is 3 hours.

What is the activity ratio for the month?

$$\frac{804000}{864000}$$

93.06	%

EFFECTIVENESS

In addition to considering productivity and efficiency, an organisation may want to measure effectiveness. This considers the extent to which the objectives of the organisation are being met.

The measure used will depend on the nature of the organisation:

Organisation	Measure of effectiveness
Parts manufacturer	% of production free from defects
Furniture retailer	% of goods delivered to customer within 10 days of ordering
Training college	% of students passing exams first time
Parcel delivery company	% of parcels delivered on time
Train service provider	% of trains run to timetable

Task 3

A hospital wants to monitor the performance of its out-patients department.

Suggest appropriate effectiveness measures that could be used to assess:

(i) the booking of appointments

(ii) the service received by the patient

PROFITABILITY MEASURES

The aim of most businesses is to make a profit, therefore management will be interested in profitability performance measures. The profitability measures could also be described as efficiency indicators, as they are measuring the efficiency with which the business has used its assets to earn profits.

Gross profit margin

The GROSS PROFIT of a business is the sales for the period less the cost of those sales. In a manufacturing business, the cost of sales figure will be the manufacturing cost of goods sold, and in a retail business, the cost of sales will be the cost of the products that were actually sold during the period. The cost of sales is calculated as follows:

Cost of sales	£
Opening inventory (stock)	X
Add: Purchases/Production cost	X
	X
Less: closing inventory (stock)	(X)
	X

For a service organisation the sales for the period will be the amount of revenue that is billed to customers for the service provided. However, the cost of sales figure will not be based upon physical goods, as rather than selling goods, a service organisation trades in providing the service, for example an accountancy firm,. The cost of sales figure in such an organisation is likely to be made up of the direct salaries of those employees providing the service, together with any other direct costs of providing the service.

The GROSS PROFIT MARGIN is calculated by showing the gross profit as a percentage of the sales figure for the period:

$$\text{Gross profit margin} = \frac{\text{Gross profit}}{\text{Sales}} \times 100$$

Operating profit margin

The OPERATING PROFIT of a business is the gross profit less the selling, distribution and administration costs. This is also the same as the profit before any interest payable or any tax.

The OPERATING PROFIT MARGIN is calculated by showing the operating profit as a percentage of the sales figure for the period:

$$\text{Operating profit margin} = \frac{\text{Operating profit}}{\text{Sales}} \times 100$$

Net profit margin

The NET PROFIT of a business is the profit shown in the income statement (profit and loss account) after all of the expenses, usually including interest and tax for the period, have been deducted. The NET PROFIT MARGIN is calculated by showing the net profit as a percentage of the sales figure for the period:

$$\text{Net profit margin} = \frac{\text{Net profit}}{\text{Sales}} \times 100$$

Expenses

It is also sometimes useful to express individual items of expenses as a percentage of the sales figure, in order to determine how these expenses have changed. This is done by the following calculation:

$$\text{Expense percentage} = \frac{\text{Expense}}{\text{Sales}} \times 100$$

If this percentage is being compared over time, when sales and production levels are changing, it is important to be aware of the difference between variable expenses and fixed expenses. If sales and production are increasing then we would also expect to see:

- similar increases in variable expenses therefore the expense percentage should remain fairly constant

- fixed expenses should be remaining reasonably constant thereby giving a decrease in the expense percentage

HOW IT WORKS

The income statement (profit and loss account) for Hampton Manufacturing for the year ending 30 September 20X8 is given below:

Hampton Manufacturing – income statement for the year ended 30 September 20X8

	£	£
Revenue		1,350,400
Cost of sales		
Opening inventory (stock)	144,300	
Purchases	849,200	
	993,500	
Less: closing inventory (stock)	156,300	
		837,200
Gross profit		513,200
Less: expenses		
Selling and distribution costs	168,400	
Administration expenses	105,600	
		274,000
Operating profit		239,200

What is the gross profit margin, the operating profit margin and the expense percentage for each category of expense?

Note that the term "revenue" in the income statement is just the technical accounting name for sales.

$$\text{Gross profit margin} \quad = \quad \frac{£513,200}{£1,350,400} \times 100$$

$$= \quad 38.0\%$$

$$\text{Operating profit margin} \quad = \quad \frac{\text{Operating profit}}{\text{Sales}} \times 100$$

$$= \quad \frac{£239,200}{£1,350,400} \times 100$$

$$= \quad 17.7\%$$

$$\text{Selling costs percentage} \quad = \quad \frac{\text{Selling cost}}{\text{Sales}} \times 100$$

$$= \quad \frac{£168,400}{£1,350,400} \times 100$$

$$= \quad 12.5\%$$

$$\text{Administration costs percentage} = \frac{\text{Administration cost}}{\text{Sales}} \times 100$$

$$= \frac{£105,600}{£1,350,400} \times 100$$

$$= 7.8\%$$

If the expenses were being compared over a number of periods in which sales were rising, we would probably expect to see the selling costs percentage remain fairly stable, as this is a variable cost, and the administration costs percentage fall, as most administration costs are likely to be fixed.

Comparison of gross profit margin and operating profit margin

It has already been noted that when performance indicators are calculated it will normally be for the purposes of comparison either with previous periods, budgeted figures or those of another organisation or an industry average.

If the gross profit margin is compared over time, any changes or differences are likely to be due to:

- changes in the selling price of the goods
- changes in the sales mix of the goods
- changes in the production costs or price of the goods
- a combination of these factors

Any movement in the operating profit margin will be explained in part by changes in the gross profit margin. If the operating profit does not move in line with the gross profit margin, then this will be due to changes in the expense percentages which may be due to the expenses being either variable or fixed.

Task 4

A business has a gross profit of £58,700 and net profit of £22,500 for the month of November, after deducting interest of £2,500 and tax of £4,750. The sales for the month were £133,400.

What is the gross profit margin, the operating profit margin and the net profit margin?

Gross profit margin   [   ] %

Operating profit margin [   ] %

Net profit margin   [   ] %

Improvement of gross profit margin

If the gross profit margin for a business can be increased by raising selling prices or reducing cost of sales, then the overall profitability of the business can be increased.

HOW IT WORKS

Hampton Manufacturing has a gross profit margin of 38% (calculated above) on sales of £1,350,000. However other firms in the same line of business have a gross profit margin of 40%. If Hampton were to improve its gross profit margin to 40%, it would make additional profit for the year.

	£
Current gross profit	513,200
Gross profit @ 40% margin (1,350,400 × 40%)	540,160
Additional profit	26,960

Based on the current year's sales level, if the gross profit margin can be increased by 2% points, the profits can be increased by almost £27,000.

Note that one way in which the gross profit margin can be increased is by an increase in selling price. This will have no effect on any costs, either variable or fixed, so will feed through to an increase in profit provided that sales volume is maintained. However from a commercial point of view, an increase in selling price may render the company's products uncompetitive. Another method of increasing total profit is to increase sales volume. This will have no effect on the gross profit margin as any increase in volume will be matched by increased variable costs (cost of sales). However this could lead to an increase in operating and net profit margin, as many expenses are fixed and will not lead to an increase if volume increases.

Return on capital employed

The RETURN ON CAPITAL EMPLOYED is sometimes known as the primary ratio as it is of great importance to the business. It is calculated as:

$$\text{Return on capital employed (ROCE)} \quad = \quad \frac{\text{Profit}}{\text{Capital employed}} \times 100$$

As such it is relating the profit that has been earned for the period to the capital from the statement of financial position (balance sheet) to determine what return has been made on the owners' investment in the business. As the capital figure is made up of the assets minus the liabilities then the ROCE can also be seen to be showing the profit that has been generated from the net assets of the business and is therefore sometimes known as Return on Net assets.

ROCE can be calculated in different ways. Both the return element (the profit), and the capital can be calculated in different ways and it is important to ensure that the return being used matches with the capital figure used.

HOW IT WORKS

Given below is the full income statement (profit and loss account) for Hampton Manufacturing for the year ending 30 September 20X8 and the statement of financial position (balance sheet) at that date.

Hampton Manufacturing – income statement for the year ended 30 September 20X8

	£	£
Revenue		1,350,400
Cost of sales		
Opening inventory (stock)	144,300	
Purchases	849,200	
	993,500	
Less: closing inventory (stock)	156,300	
		837,200
Gross profit		513,200
Less: expenses		
Selling and distribution costs	168,400	
Administration expenses	105,600	
		274,000
Operating profit		239,200
Interest payable		50,000
Profit after interest payable		189,200
Tax		56,000
Profit after tax		133,200

Hampton Manufacturing – statement of financial position as at 30 September 20X8

	£	£
Non-current (fixed) assets		2,428,300
Current assets:		
Inventory (stock)	156,300	
Receivables (debtors)	225,000	
Bank	10,200	
	391,500	
Payables (creditors)	(169,800)	
Net current assets		221,700
		2,650,000
Less: Long term loan		400,000
		2,250,000
Capital		1,500,000
Reserves		200,000
Retained earnings		550,000
		2,250,000

What is the return on capital employed?

Method 1

The most common method of calculating ROCE is to compare the operating profit (before interest and tax), to the capital provided by all the providers of funds. This is not only the shareholders, whose funds are the capital plus all reserves including the retained earnings, but also any long term capital within the business such as long term loans. The reason for this is that we are looking at the profits that are available for all of the providers of funds for the business.

This capital employed figure can be calculated in one of two ways:

From the capital side of the statement of financial position (balance sheet):

	£
Capital	1,500,000
Reserves	200,000
Retained earnings	550,000
Long term loan	400,000
Capital employed	2,650,000

From the asset side of the statement of financial position (balance sheet):

	£
Non-current (fixed) assets	2,428,300
Current assets	391,500
Less: current liabilities	(169,800)
Capital employed	2,650,000

As you can see the same figure is reached under each method.

Now the Return on Capital Employed is the operating profit as a percentage of this capital employed:

$$\text{ROCE} \quad = \quad \frac{\text{Operating profit}}{\text{Share and loan capital + reserves = capital employed}}$$

$$= \quad \frac{239,200}{2,650,000} \times 100$$

$$= \quad 9.0\%$$

It is **recommended** that you use this method of calculating ROCE in assessments.

Method 2

A less common method of calculating a return is to use as the capital figure just the capital relating to the shareholders – capital, reserves and the retained earnings. This is then matched with the profit available for the shareholders, which is the profit after interest payable (and tax). Technically the ratio is known as the RETURN ON SHAREHOLDERS' FUNDS .

$$\text{Return on shareholders' funds} \quad = \quad \frac{\text{Profit after tax}}{\text{Shareholders' funds}} \times 100\%$$

$$= \quad \frac{£133,200}{£2,250,000}$$

$$= \quad 5.9\%$$

Task 5

A business has made an operating profit of £365,800 for the year. The statement of financial position (balance sheet) shows that shareholders' funds total £1,700,000 and that there is a long term loan outstanding of £600,000, upon which annual interest of 12% is paid.

What is the return on capital employed using each of the methods above?

Method 1 [   ] %

Method 2 [   ] %

RESOURCE UTILISATION

Performance measures relating to RESOURCE UTILISATION show how efficiently and effectively an organisation is using the various resources at its disposal.

These measures concentrate on the statement of financial position (balance sheet) but also relate the statement of financial position (balance sheet) figures to sales and cost of sales in the income statement (profit and loss account). We will start with measures that consider the overall assets and liabilities of the business and then consider the more detailed elements of the working capital of the business.

Asset turnover

ASSET TURNOVER is a performance indicator which compares the sales or revenue of the business to the capital employed. The measure is calculated as follows:

$$\text{Asset turnover} = \frac{\text{Revenue}}{\text{Capital employed}}$$

Remember that total capital from the statement of financial position (balance sheet) is equal to the assets of the organisation less the current liabilities or alternatively shareholders' funds + long term loans.

You will note that asset turnover is an absolute figure and not a percentage. What this figure is showing is the amount of sales revenue that is being earned by every £1 of capital or every £1 of investment in assets and liabilities.

Asset turnover and return on capital employed

Asset turnover is an important indicator in its own right, as it shows how effectively the assets and liabilities of the business have been used to create revenue during the period. It is also an important figure as it is one of the elements that makes up ROCE as can be seen below:

$$\boxed{\text{ROCE}} = \boxed{\text{Asset turnover}} \times \boxed{\text{Operating profit margin}}$$

If we look at how each of these figures is calculated you will see how this works:

$$\frac{\text{Operating profit}}{\text{Capital employed}} = \frac{\text{Turnover}}{\text{Capital employed}} \times \frac{\text{Operating profit}}{\text{Turnover}}$$

The importance of this relationship is that we can then explain any change in ROCE by changes in asset turnover and changes in operating profit margin.

HOW IT WORKS

Given below is a summary of these three performance indicators for Jason Enterprises for the last two years:

	20X6	20X5
Operating profit margin	13%	15%
Asset turnover	1.40	1.44
Return on capital employed	18.2%	21.6%

The return on capital employed has been significantly reduced over the period, and by looking at its component elements we can see that the reduction is due not only to a decrease in the operating profit margin of 2% but also a fall in asset turnover from the assets earning £1.44 for every £1 invested in 20X5, to only earning £1.40 per £1 invested in 20X6.

This combination of factors has caused the fall in return on capital employed.

Non-current (fixed) asset turnover

Another useful indicator to management of how effectively the organisation is using its resources is a measure of how much the non-current (fixed) assets, the major long term assets of the business, are earning.

NON-CURRENT (FIXED) ASSET TURNOVER is measured as an absolute figure rather than a percentage, and shows the amount of revenue earned for each £1 invested in non-current (fixed) assets:

$$\text{Non-current (fixed) asset turnover} = \frac{\text{Revenue}}{\text{Net book value of non-current (fixed) assets}}$$

HOW IT WORKS

We will now return to the statement of financial position (balance sheet) of Hampton Manufacturing:

Hampton Manufacturing – statement of financial position as at 30 September 20X8

	£	£
Non-current (fixed) assets		2,428,300
Current assets:		
Inventory (stock)	156,300	
Receivables (debtors)	225,000	
Bank	10,200	
	391,500	
Payables (creditors)	(169,800)	
Net current assets		221,700
		2,650,000
Less: Long term loan		400,000
		2,250,000
Capital		1,500,000
Reserves		200,000
Retained earnings		550,000
		2,250,000

Remember that revenue for the year was £1,350,400, the operating profit margin was 17.7% and ROCE was 9.0%. We can now calculate the asset turnover and non-current (fixed) asset turnover and show how the ROCE is made up.

$$\text{Asset turnover} = \frac{\text{Turnover}}{\text{Capital employed}}$$

$$= \frac{£1,350,400}{£2,650,000}$$

$$= 0.51 \text{ times}$$

This tells us that for every £1 invested in the assets and liabilities, or the capital of the business, 51 pence of sales revenue has been earned.

We can now relate the ROCE to the net profit margin and asset turnover:

ROCE	$=$	Asset turnover	$\times$	Operating profit margin
9.0%	$=$	0.51	$\times$	17.7%

Finally we can calculate the non-current (fixed)asset turnover:

$$\text{Non-current (fixed) asset turnover} = \frac{\text{Revenue}}{\text{Net book value of non-current (fixed) assets}}$$

$$= \frac{£1,350,400}{£2,428,300}$$

$$= 0.56$$

For every £1 invested in the non-current (fixed) assets, 56 pence of sales revenue is being earned. This figure can be used in comparison with previous periods' non-current (fixed) asset turnover or with that of a similar organisation.

Working backwards through a ratio

In the computer based tests you may be given a certain amount of information about a ratio and from this information be expected to work backwards to calculate a figure from the income statement (profit and loss account) or the statement of financial position (balance sheet).

HOW IT WORKS

A business has an asset turnover of 2 times and capital employed of £450,000. What is the revenue of the business?

$$\text{Asset turnover} = \frac{\text{Revenue}}{\text{Capital employed}}$$

$$2 = \frac{\text{Revenue}}{£450,000}$$

$$\text{Revenue} = 2 \times £450,000 = £900,000$$

Task 6

An accountancy firm has revenue of £420,000 in the month of June and the capital of the firm totals £350,000.

What is the asset turnover for the month?

☐ times

WORKING CAPITAL RATIOS

Continuing with the calculation of ratios indicating the resource utilisation of a business, we will now consider the WORKING CAPITAL of the business in more detail.

Working capital is the total of the current assets of the business less the current liabilities. It is the amount of money invested in inventory (stock) and receivables (debtors) less the credit allowed from payables (creditors) and it is a necessary part of most business's investment.

The component elements of working capital are constantly changing as the diagram below illustrates:

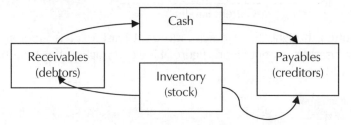

- inventory (stock) is turned into receivables (debtors) when it is sold
- inventory (stock) is purchased on credit which means we have payables (creditors)
- receivables (debtors) will eventually be turned into cash
- cash will be used to pay payables (creditors)

We will consider the overall working capital situation first and then look at the individual elements of inventory (stock), receivables (debtors) and payables (creditors).

The overall working capital performance indicators are a measure of the LIQUIDITY of the business. Liquidity is a measure of how safe the business is in terms of its cash availability. Even if a business is profitable, it must still have enough cash to be able to pay its payables (creditors) when they fall due.

The current ratio

The CURRENT RATIO relates the total current assets to the total current liabilities:

$$\text{Current ratio} = \frac{\text{Current assets}}{\text{Current liabilities}}$$

This is normally expressed as a ratio, for example 2.4 : 1. It shows how many times the current liabilities are covered by the current assets.

It is often said that a current ratio of 2 : 1 is 'safe'. However although this can be used as a benchmark figure, care should be taken with the type of business that you are dealing with. For example, supermarkets will tend to have much lower current ratios than this, as they have few, if any, receivables (debtors), rapid inventory (stock) movements and large amounts of payables (creditors).

Quick ratio

One problem with using the current ratio as a measure of liquidity is that the inventory (stock) of a business, although a current asset, is not a particularly liquid asset. For inventory (stock) to be turned into cash, it must first be processed or manufactured, then it must be sold and turned into receivables (debtors) and only finally will it become cash when the customers pay.

Due to the lack of liquidity of inventory (stock), a further ratio, the QUICK RATIO (sometimes known as the acid test ratio), is calculated which excludes inventory (stock) from the current assets figure.

$$\text{Quick ratio} = \frac{\text{Current assets - inventory (stock)}}{\text{Current liabilities}}$$

Again it is often thought that a quick ratio of at least 1 : 1 is 'safe' and this can certainly be used as a benchmark figure. However, again, the type of business must be considered.

Inventory (stock)

Moving now to the individual elements of working capital.

We will start with inventory (stock). It is useful for management to have an indication of how long inventories (stocks) are being held. In some businesses inventory (stock) must be sold, or turned over, quickly, for example if the inventory (stock) is made up of perishable foods. However in other businesses inventory (stock) may be held for some considerable period before it is sold (eg in the construction industry).

A business needs to control how long inventory (stock) is being held, as capital is being tied up in the inventory (stock), while it is waiting to be sold. Therefore an INVENTORY (STOCK) DAYS ratio can be calculated to show the length of time that inventory (stock) is held in the business.

$$\text{Inventory (stock) days} = \frac{\text{Average inventory (stock)}}{\text{Cost of sales}} \times 365$$

This will indicate the number of days on average that the inventory (stock) is being held before sale. You will note that 'average inventory (stock)' has been used here. This is calculated as:

Average inventory (stock) =

$$\frac{\text{Opening inventory (stock) + closing inventory (stock)}}{2}$$

In some tests you may not have information about the opening inventory (stock) and therefore the closing inventory (stock) figure can be used in the calculation rather than average inventory (stock). However if the opening inventory (stock) figure is available, then use average inventory (stock) in your calculation.

Rather than being expressed in terms of the number of days for which inventory (stock) is held, inventory (stock) turnover can also be expressed as the number of times a year that the inventory (stock) is turned over:

$$\text{Inventory (stock) turnover} = \frac{\text{Cost of sales}}{\text{Average/closing inventory (stock)}}$$

A high inventory (stock) turnover figure calculated on this basis indicates that inventory (stock) is moving in and out of the business quickly whereas a low figure indicates that inventory (stock) is in the business for some time before it is sold.

Receivables' (debtors') collection period

The RECEIVABLES' (DEBTORS') COLLECTION PERIOD, also known as receivables' (debtors') days, is a measure that shows how long it is taking for the credit customers of the business to pay.

$$\text{Receivables' (debtors') collection period} = \frac{\text{Trade receivables (debtors)}}{\text{Credit sales}} \times 365 \text{ days}$$

There are a number of potential problems with this calculation. Firstly a separate figure for credit sales may not be available, in which case total sales must be used. However if the total sales include a large proportion of cash sales this will distort the picture shown. A further problem may be with the use of year end receivables (debtors). These may not be representative of the average amounts owing throughout the year. Therefore if possible, use the average of opening and closing receivables (debtors) but in tests it is rare for this information to be available.

The receivables (debtors) collection period can be compared over time in order to assess how well receivables (debtors) are being managed. It can also be compared to the stated credit terms, for example if invoices are due to be paid within 60 days we would not wish to see receivables (debtors) days being much more than this figure. Finally a business would try, if possible to match its receivables (debtors) and payables (creditors) days, so that it is not giving away more credit than it is receiving from suppliers.

Payables' (creditors') payment period

Management may also wish to know how long we take to pay our credit suppliers. This is calculated by the PAYABLES' (CREDITORS') PAYMENT PERIOD ratio, or payables (creditors) days.

$$\text{Payables' (creditors') payment period} = \frac{\text{Trade payables}}{\text{Credit purchases (creditors)}} \times 365 \text{ days}$$

As with sales, we may not have a separate figure for credit purchases, therefore total purchases will need to be used. In some cases there will not even be a separate figure for purchases, in which case cost of sales must be used even though this is not so appropriate. In many tests only cost of sales will be available, so use this figure. If the average of opening and closing payables (creditors) is available this is again a better figure than just the closing figure but normally only the closing statement of financial position (balance sheet) figure will be available.

The payables' (creditors') payment period can be compared over time to determine the trend in payment times. It can also be compared to the receivables' (debtors') collection period. If customers are taking 75 days on average to pay, then we would not wish to have a payables' (creditors') payment period of just 15 days, as this means that money is being paid out of the business much more rapidly than it is being received.

HOW IT WORKS

Given below are the income statement (profit and loss account) and statement of financial position (balance sheet) for Hampton Manufacturing again:

Hampton Manufacturing – income statement for the year ended

30 September 20X8

	£	£
Revenue		1,350,400
Cost of sales		
Opening inventory (stock)	144,300	
Purchases	849,200	
	993,500	
Less: closing inventory (stock)	156,300	
		837,200
Gross profit		513,200
Less: expenses		
Selling and distribution costs	168,400	
Administration expenses	105,600	
		274,000
Operating profit		239,200
Interest payable		50,000
Profit after interest payable		189,200
Tax		56,000
Profit after tax		133,200

Hampton Manufacturing – statement of financial position as at 30 September 20X8

	£	£
Non-current (fixed) assets		2,428,300
Current assets:		
Inventory (stock)	156,300	
Receivables (debtors)	225,000	
Bank	10,200	
	391,500	
Payables (creditors)	(169,800)	
Net current assets		221,700
		2,650,000
Less: Long term loan		400,000
		2,250,000
Capital		1,500,000
Reserves		200,000
Retained earnings		550,000
		2,250,000

We will now calculate all of the working capital ratios.

$$\text{Current ratio} = \frac{\text{Current assets}}{\text{Current liabilities}}$$

$$= \frac{\pounds391,500}{\pounds169,800}$$

$$= 2.3 : 1$$

$$\text{Quick ratio} = \frac{\text{Current assets - inventory (stock)}}{\text{Current liabilities}}$$

$$= \frac{\pounds391,500 - \pounds156,300}{\pounds169,800}$$

$$= 1.4 : 1$$

$$\text{Average inventory (stock)} = \frac{\pounds144,300 + \pounds156,300}{2}$$

$$= \pounds150,300$$

$$\text{Inventory (stock) days} = \frac{\text{Average inventory (stock)}}{\text{Cost of sales}} \times 365$$

$$= \frac{£150,300}{£837,200} \times 365$$

$$= 66 \text{ days}$$

$$\text{Inventory (stock) turnover (times)} = \frac{\text{Cost of sales}}{\text{Average inventory (stock)}}$$

$$\frac{£837,200}{£150,300}$$

$$= 5.6 \text{ times}$$

$$\text{Receivables' (debtors') collection period} = \frac{\text{Trade receivables (debtors)}}{\text{Credit sales}} \times 365$$

$$= \frac{£225,000}{£1,350,400} \times 365$$

$$= 61 \text{ days}$$

$$\text{Payables' (creditors') payment period} = \frac{\text{Trade payables (creditors)}}{\text{Credit purchases}} \times 365$$

$$= \frac{£169,800}{£849,200} \times 365$$

$$= 73 \text{ days}$$

Task 7

A business has opening inventory (stock) of £13,500 and closing inventory (stock) of £17,000. Purchases during the year were £99,000.

What is the inventory (stock) turnover in days?

[   ] days

Improvement in working capital management

As we saw at the start of this section, the components of working capital are constantly changing but will eventually become cash receipts and cash payments. We have seen how performance indicators for individual elements of working capital – inventory (stock), receivables (debtors) and payables (creditors) – can be calculated.

If the management of working capital can be improved, for example by shortening inventory (stock) turnover days or receivables (debtors) collection period or by extending the payables'(creditors) payment period, then this will mean that the business will have additional cash available.

HOW IT WORKS

The performance indicators for Hampton Manufacturing show the following:

Inventory (stock) turnover 66 days

Receivables' (debtors') collection period 61 days

Payables' (creditors') payment period 73 days

The industry average figures for working capital are:

Inventory (stock) turnover 50 days

Receivables' (debtors') collection period 48 days

Payables' (creditors') payment period 80 days

If Hampton were to improve its working capital practices in order to be in line with the industry average figures, what effect would this have on the cash balance?

Reduction in inventory (stock) turnover period (66 days – 50 days) = 16 days

The value of 16 days of inventory (stock) is:

$$\frac{\text{Cost of sales}}{365} \times 16 \qquad = \qquad \frac{837,200}{365} \times 16$$

$$= \qquad £36,699$$

Reduction in receivables' (debtors') collection period (61 days – 48 days) = 13 days

The value of 13 days of receivables (debtors) is:

$$\frac{\text{Credit sales}}{365} \times 13 \qquad = \qquad \frac{1,350,400}{365} \times 13$$

$$= \qquad £48,096$$

Increase in payables' (creditors') payment period (80 days – 73 days) = 7 days

The value of 7 days of payables (creditors) is:

$$\frac{\text{Credit purchases}}{365} \times 7 \qquad = \qquad \frac{849,200}{365} \times 7$$

$$= \qquad £16,286$$

If all three improvements were made there would be an improvement in the cash balance of £101,081 (£36,699 + 48,096 + 16,286).

Months not days

In the test you may be asked to calculate inventory (stock) turnover, receivables' (debtors') collection period or payables' (creditors') payment period in months rather than in days. In these situations simply substitute 12 months for 365 days in the formula and the answer will automatically be expressed in months.

HOW IT WORKS

A business has payables (creditors) of £24,000 and purchases during the year were £101,000. What is the payables' (creditors') payment period in months?

$$\text{Payables' (creditors') payment period} = \frac{\text{Payables (creditors)}}{\text{Purchases}} \times 12$$

$$= \frac{£24,000}{£101,000} \times 12$$

$$= 2.9 \text{ months}$$

GEARING

Some companies are not only financed by share capital from the shareholders but also by long term loans, for example from banks or in the form of debentures. These long term loans are shown separately as such in a company's statement of financial position (balance sheet).

When long term loans are taken out this produces additional commitments for a company:

- the company needs to be able to pay the annual interest on the loan
- the company needs to be able to pay off the loan when it falls due.

These additional commitments mean that companies with long term loan capital are often viewed as more risky than those companies without any long term loans or with smaller amounts of loan capital. For this reason there are two main performance indicators that measure the effect of long term loan capital on a company.

Interest cover

INTEREST COVER is a measure of how easily the company can make its interest payments out of annual profits. It is measured as:

$$\text{Interest cover} = \frac{\text{Profit before interest charges}}{\text{Interest charges}}$$

This will give an indication of how safe the annual interest payments are in terms of the profit that the company is making.

Gearing ratio

The GEARING RATIO is a measure of the amount of long term loan capital that a company has compared to the other sources of long term finance, being the share capital and reserves of the company.

The gearing ratio can be measured in one of two ways:

Method 1   Gearing ratio $= \dfrac{\text{Long term loan finance}}{\text{Shareholders' funds}} \times 100$

This is sometimes known as the debt: equity ratio

Method 2   Gearing ratio $= \dfrac{\text{Long term loan finance}}{\text{Shareholders' funds} + \text{long term finance}} \times 100$

HOW IT WORKS

Returning to Hampton Manufacturing:

Hampton Manufacturing – income statement (profit and loss account) for the year ended 30 September 20X8

	£	£
Revenue		1,350,400
Cost of sales		
Opening inventory (stock)	144,300	
Purchases	849,200	
	993,500	
Less: closing inventory (stock)	156,300	
		837,200
Gross profit		513,200
Less: expenses		
Selling and distribution expenses	168,400	
Administration expenses	105,600	
		274,000
Operating profit		239,200
Interest payable		50,000
Profit after interest payable		189,200
Tax		56,000
Profit after tax		133,200

Hampton Manufacturing – statement of financial position (balance sheet) as at 30 September 20X8

	£	£
Non-current (fixed) assets		2,428,300
Current assets:		
Inventory (stock)	156,300	
Receivables (debtors)	225,000	
Bank	10,200	
	391,500	
Payables (creditors)	(169,800)	
Net current assets		221,700
		2,650,000
Less: Long term loan		400,000
		2,250,000
Capital		1,500,000
Reserves		200,000
Retained earnings		550,000
		2,250,000

$$\text{Interest cover} = \frac{\text{Profit before interest charges}}{\text{Interest charges}}$$

$$\text{Interest cover} = \frac{£239,200}{£50,000}$$

$$= 4.78$$

This indicates that the interest payments due for the year are just over one fifth of the profits made during the year. This would tend to indicate that the interest payments are quite safe unless there is a large fall in profits.

The gearing ratio can be measured in one of two ways:

Method 1 $\qquad$ $\dfrac{\text{Gearing}}{\text{ratio}} = \dfrac{\text{Long term loan finance}}{\text{Shareholders' funds}} \times 100$

$\dfrac{\text{Gearing}}{\text{ratio}} = \dfrac{£400,000}{£2,250,000} \times 100$

$= 17.8\%$

Method 2 $\qquad$ $\dfrac{\text{Gearing}}{\text{ratio}} = \dfrac{\text{Long term loan finance}}{\text{Shareholders' funds} + \text{long term finace}} \times 100$

$\dfrac{\text{Gearing}}{\text{ratio}} = \dfrac{£400,000}{£2,250,000 + £400,000} \times 100$

$= 15.1\%$

Whichever method is used, this indicates that the gearing ratio of the company is quite low. Compared to either the shareholders' funds or the total capital the amount of loan capital is relatively low.

RATIO ANALYSIS

As well as being able to calculate the performance indicators considered in this chapter, you will also need to be able to interpret the indicators and to comment intelligently on them. The performance indicators that you will have calculated will be compared either over time within the organisation, with target or budgeted figures, with another similar organisation or with industry average figures.

Interpreting the performance indicators

In the next example we will bring together many of the performance indicators covered in this chapter and not only calculate them but also comment on their significance to explain what picture they paint of the organisation.

HOW IT WORKS

Jamboree Ltd is a manufacturing organisation which produces a range of small plastic tricycles for children. You are given below summarised income statements (profit and loss accounts) for the years ended 31 October 20X7 and 31 October 20X8 and summarised statements of financial position (balance sheets) at those dates.

Summarised income statements

	Y/e 31 Oct 20X8	Y/e 31 Oct 20X7
	£000	£000
Revenue	420	320
Cost of sales	256	180
Gross profit	164	140
Expenses	100	89
Operating profit	64	51
Interest payable	10	10
Profit before tax	54	41
Tax	16	12
Profit after tax	38	29

Summarised statements of financial position

	31 Oct 20X8		31 Oct 20X7	
	£000	£000	£000	£000
Non-current (fixed) assets		394		369
Current assets:				
Inventory (stock)	50		30	
Receivables (debtors)	69		44	
Cash	2		12	
	121		86	
Payables (creditors)	52		30	
Net current assets		69		56
		463		425
Long term loan		100		100
		363		325
Capital		250		250
Retained earnings		113		75
		363		325

You are required to calculate the following ratios and then to comment on the performance of the company over the last two years in the light of these ratios:

- (a) gross profit margin
- (b) operating profit margin
- (c) expenses to sales
- (d) return on capital employed
- (e) asset turnover
- (f) non-current (fixed) asset turnover
- (g) current ratio
- (h) quick ratio
- (i) inventory (stock) turnover in days
- (j) receivables' (debtors') collection period
- (k) payables' (creditors') payment period
- (l) interest cover
- (m) gearing ratio

Calculate the ratios first and tabulate them so that they are easy to compare.

		20X8	20X7
(a)	Gross profit margin		
	164/420 × 100	39.0%	
	140/320 × 100		43.8%
(b)	Operating profit margin		
	64/420 × 100	15.2%	
	51/320 × 100		15.9%
(c)	Expenses to turnover		
	100/420 × 100	23.8%	
	89/320 × 100		27.8%
(d)	Return on capital employed		
	64/463 × 100	13.8%	
	51/425 × 100		12.0%
(e)	Asset turnover		
	420/463	0.91	
	320/425		0.75
(f)	Non-current (fixed) asset turnover		
	420/394	1.07	
	320/369		0.87

(g)   Current ratio

     121/52   2.3 : 1

     86/30   2.9 : 1

(h)   Quick ratio

     71/52   1.4 : 1

     56/30   1.9 : 1

(i)   Inventory (stock) days

     $50/256 \times 365$ 71 days

     $30/180 \times 365$ 61 days

(j)   Receivables' (debtors') collection period

     $69/420 \times 365$ 60 days

     $44/320 \times 365$ 50 days

(k)   Payables' (creditors') payment period

     $52/256 \times 365$ 74 days

     $30/180 \times 365$ 61 days

(l)   Interest cover

     64/10   6.4

     51/10   5.1

(m)   Gearing ratio (loans/SHF)

     100/363   27.5%

     100/325   30.8%

Now consider the whole picture – look at the movement in each ratio and decide why it might have changed and how all the movements in the ratios piece together. The main points to make are given below – you may find it useful to consider profitability, resource utilisation and working capital in separate sections. Remember that as well as summarising the movement you need to try and explain why this might have arisen.

Profitability

- Turnover has increased by 31% ($\frac{(420 - 320)}{320} \times 100\%$)

- Gross profit margin has decreased – this may be due to a lowering of prices in order to increase the turnover and market share

- Operating profit margin has decreased slightly but not as much as the gross profit margin, as the percentage of expenses to sales has decreased – this may be due to the fact that some of the expenses were fixed costs and have therefore not increased with turnover

- Return on capital employed has increased despite the fall in profit margins, due to a significant improvement in asset turnover and non-current (fixed) asset turnover

Resource utilisation

- Asset turnover has increased significantly as has non-current (fixed) asset turnover

- There has obviously been investment in non-current (fixed) assets during 20X8 as the non-current (fixed) asset total has increased despite this year's depreciation having been charged

- Therefore the increase in asset and non-current (fixed) asset turnover may be due to efficiencies as a result of the new non-current (fixed) assets

Working capital

- In overall terms both the current ratio and the quick ratio have fallen, although they are still at healthy levels – the main reasons for this are the reduction in cash and the significant increase in payables (creditors)

- Investment in inventory (stock) has increased with inventory (stock) now being held for 71 days rather than 61 – there is no obvious reason for this although it could be due to the company stocking a wider range of tricycles.

- Receivables' (debtors') collection period has also increased by 10 days to 60 days, which may be due to offering longer credit periods to attract new customers

- Payables' (creditors') payment period has increased by 13 days to 74 days which may be due to the lack of cash, evidenced by the significantly reduced level of cash at the year-end

Gearing

Gearing is relatively low and interest cover quite high. Therefore the company looks quite safe in this area.

Task 8

A business had a gross profit margin of 38.7% for the year ending 30 June 20X7 and a gross profit margin of 35.2% for the year ending 30 June 20X8.

Suggest reasons for the change in gross profit margin.

LIMITATIONS OF RATIO ANALYSIS

It has been noted throughout this chapter that care must be taken when using ratios in order to draw conclusions about an organisation for a variety of reasons. These limitations of ratio analysis are now summarised below:

Comparing like with like – if ratios are to be compared then they must have been calculated in the same way and using comparable figures. When comparing ratios over time in an organisation, if there has been any change in accounting policies over the period then this may impact upon the ratios. If comparing the accounts of two different companies it is likely that they will have different accounting policies and strict adjustments should be made to bring the accounting policies in line before calculating the ratios.

Inflation – if ratios are being compared over time on the basis of historical cost accounting figures then adjustments must be made using an appropriate index in order to restate all the figures in terms of one particular price.

Representative figures – in many cases we are using year end statement of financial position (balance sheet) amounts to calculate ratios and these may not necessarily be representative of the value throughout the year.

Accounting adjustments – as year end figures are used for the ratios, just one significant accounting adjustment or transaction before the year end can alter the position shown by the statement of financial position (balance sheet) and the resulting ratios. For example if a large cash payment were made to suppliers just before the year end, this would significantly improve the payables' (creditors') payment period.

Age of non-current (fixed) assets – if we are comparing one company to another using ratio analysis, the figures may not be entirely comparable unless the non-current (fixed) assets are of similar age.

Key performance indicators and the behaviour of managers – the way in which managers are assessed on their performance can have a major influence on the decisions that they make. If key performance indicators such as ROCE are used to assess a manager then there is the possibility of a lack of goal congruence in decision making. For example a new piece of machinery may benefit the business as a whole as it will reduce costs and improve quality but the manager in charge of that department may be reluctant to invest if it will reduce his department's ROCE on which he is assessed.

THE BALANCED SCORECARD

So far in this chapter we have considered a variety of performance indicators, both financial and non-financial, which can be used to provide information to management to help them to control costs and enhance value.

The BALANCED SCORECARD is a framework that can be used to determine which performance indicators are important to a business. The balanced scorecard approach is to recognise that there is not just one perspective – the financial one – but four different perspectives of a business, all of which must be monitored.

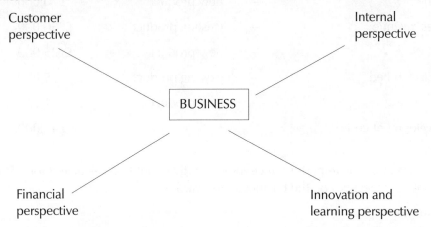

We will now consider the types of performance indicator that might be calculated to measure these four perspectives.

Perspective	Concerned with:	Possible performance indicators
Customer	Customer satisfaction and loyalty therefore quality, delivery, after-sales service	▪ number of repeat orders ▪ average delivery period ▪ number of complaints
Internal	Internal processes and technical excellence	▪ value added ▪ number of units rejected in quality inspections
Financial	Profits and satisfying the needs of shareholders or owners	▪ ROCE ▪ gross, operating and net profit margins
Innovation and learning	Improvement of existing products and development of new products	▪ training costs per employee ▪ percentage of sales from new products

HOW IT WORKS

Lampoon Productions has in the past produced just one fairly successful product. Recently, however, a new version of this product has been launched. Development work continues to add a related product to the product range. Given below are some details of the activities during the month of November.

Units produced	—	existing product	25,000
	—	new product	5,000
Cost of units produced	—	existing product	£375,000
	—	new product	£70,000
Sales revenue	—	existing product	£550,000
	—	new product	£125,000
Hours worked	—	existing product	5,000
	—	new product	1,250
Development costs			£47,000

Suggest and calculate performance indicators that could be calculated for each of the four perspectives on the balanced scorecard.

Customer

- Percentage of sales represented by new products

$$= \frac{£125,000}{£550,000+£125,000} \times 100$$

$$= 18.5\%$$

Internal

- Productivity   –   existing product $= \dfrac{25,000 \text{ units}}{5,000 \text{ hours}}$

  $= 5$ units per hour

  –   new product $= \dfrac{5,000 \text{ units}}{1,250 \text{ hours}}$

  $= 4$ units per hour

- Unit cost   –   existing product $= \dfrac{£375,000}{25,000 \text{ units}}$

  $= £15$ per unit

  –   new product $= \dfrac{£70,000}{5,000 \text{ units}}$

  $= £14$ per unit

Financial

- Gross profit – existing product $= \dfrac{£550,000 - 375,000}{£550,000}$

$= 32\%$

          – new product $= \dfrac{£125,000 - 70,000}{£125,000}$

$= 44\%$

Innovation and learning

- Development costs as % of sales $= \dfrac{£47,000}{£675,000}$

$= 7\%$

SERVICE ORGANISATIONS

So far in this chapter we have concentrated on performance indicators for manufacturing organisations. Performance indicators obviously also have to be calculated for organisations that provide a service rather than a tangible product, such as accountancy firms, a transport provider, a hotel or a college of education.

Many of the performance indicators considered in this chapter will be relevant to service industries, although they will need to be expressed slightly differently. For example, the cost per unit in a manufacturing industry might become the cost per chargeable hour in an accountancy firm or the cost per passenger mile in a transport provider.

Productivity will also be assessed in service organisations, adapted to suit their circumstances – in an accountancy firm it might be measured as the percentage of chargeable hours to total hours; in a college of education the number of students enrolled per lecturer; in a transport company the number of passengers transported per month.

Service organisations will normally expect to make a profit and therefore most of the financial performance indicators will be relevant to service organisations.

It should be noted, however, that often the main revenue-generating assets of a service business are its employees. As the 'worth' of employees is not generally reflected on the statement of financial position (balance sheet), measures such as ROCE, asset turnover and non-current (fixed) asset turnover are perhaps not as relevant or significant in the service sector.

The main difference between manufacturing and service organisations however is that the service organisations will probably be more interested in non-financial performance indicators. For example, an accountancy firm will monitor the number of clients that leave the firm for another firm, a transport provider will be concerned about delays on routes, a college of education will take particular note of the students' assessments of the lecturers.

Service organisations are sometimes the scenario in an assessment for a number of tasks. Use the information in the scenario and the techniques that you have learnt in this chapter to adapt performance indicators to the requirements of the organisation being considered. However the AAT have made it clear that if the formula for performance indicator is not obvious then it will be given.

WHAT IF ANALYSIS

Throughout the chapter we have covered a variety of performance indicators. In an assessment, in addition to calculating and comparing performance indicators you may be required to

- Forecast performance indicators based on the assumptions you are given

- Recalculate performance indicators to take account of changes to a business eg the purchase of new machinery

- Use performance indicators to evaluate and recommend the best course of action in a given situation

- Show what the results of the business would have looked like if certain performance targets (benchmarks) had been achieved

CHAPTER OVERVIEW

- Performance indicators can be calculated to summarise productivity, profitability and resource utilisation – some of the performance indicators will be financial measures and some will be non-financial measures

- Productivity can be measured as units produced per hour or units produced per employee – productivity can also be measured by considering the value added per employee

- A further method of measuring productivity is to use the three control ratios – efficiency, capacity and activity

- The gross profit margin measures the profitability of the trading element of the organisation and the operating and net profit margins give a measure of profitability after deduction of expenses

- The return on capital employed relates the operating profit to the amount of capital invested in the business to give an overall return to the providers of that capital – the return on capital employed is made up of the asset turnover multiplied by the operating profit margin

- Measures of resource utilisation include asset turnover and non-current (fixed) asset turnover which show the amount of revenue earned for each £1 investment

- Working capital overall can be monitored by calculation of the current ratio and the quick ratio – individual elements of the working capital can be controlled by monitoring of inventory (stock) turnover, receivables (debtors) collection period and payables (creditors) payment period

- The gearing level (amount of debt finance) can be measured using either interest cover or the gearing ratio

- Not only must the performance indicators be calculated but they must also be interpreted using ratio analysis. In order to do this comparative figures (or benchmarks) are required.

- The balanced scorecard is an approach to monitoring performance indicators which recognises that there are four distinct perspectives to the business – the customer perspective, internal perspective, the financial perspective and the innovation and learning perspective

- Service organisations will also require performance indicators but they may be slightly different from those for manufacturing or retail organisations due to the nature of the organisation.

- "What if?" analysis involves forecasting performance indicators or results given certain assumptions about a business or recalculating these to take account of given changes to the business in order to assess the impact of different courses of action.

Key words

Performance indicators – ways of summarising elements of performance using a formula

Benchmarking – comparison of actual figures to a pre-determined target or industry best practice

Productivity – a measure of how hard the employees are working

Value added – sales value less the cost of materials and bought in services

Control ratios – the productivity measures of efficiency, capacity and activity

Efficiency ratio – a measure of how efficiently the employees have worked compared to standard efficiency

Capacity ratio – a measure indicating whether the employees have worked to full capacity

Activity ratio – an indicator of how the actual output compares to budgeted output

Effectiveness – a measure of the extent to which the objectives of the organisation are being met.

Gross profit – sales value minus cost of sales

Gross profit margin – gross profit as a percentage of sales

Operating profit – profit after deduction of cost of sales, selling, administration and distribution expenses (or profit before interest and tax)

Operating profit margin – operating profit as a percentage of sales

Net profit – profit after deduction of expenses, interest and tax

Net profit margin – net profit as a percentage of sales

Return on capital employed – operating profit as a percentage of total capital

Return on shareholders' funds – net profit as a percentage of shareholders' funds

Resource utilisation – how productively and effectively an organisation uses its resources

Asset turnover – the amount of sales revenue earned for each £1 invested in the capital of the business

Non-current (fixed) asset turnover – the amount of sales revenue earned for each £1 invested in non-current (fixed) assets

Working capital – current assets less current liabilities

Liquidity – how much cash the business can access

Current ratio – ratio of current assets to current liabilities

Quick ratio – ratio of current assets less inventory to current liabilities

Inventory (stock) turnover – number of days inventory (stock) is held or the number of times a year inventory (stock) is turned over

Receivables' (debtors') collection period – the number of days it takes customers to pay

Payables' (creditors') payment period – the number of days before suppliers are paid

Interest cover – is the number of times that the annual interest charge is covered by the annual profit.

Gearing ratio – is a measure of the percentage of long term loan capital in the capital structure

Balanced scorecard – a framework for performance indicators which recognises that there are four perspectives of a business (customer, internal, financial and innovation & learning)

What if analysis – a technique that is used to assess the impact of potential changes before they are actually made.

TEST YOUR LEARNING

1   Given below are the production figures for a factory for the last four months.

	August	September	October	November
Output in units	257,300	251,400	262,300	258,600
Budgeted output	250,000	255,000	260,000	260,000
Hours worked	24,400	24,600	26,700	25,600

The standard time for each unit of production is 6 minutes.

Complete the table below showing the performance indicators for each of the four months:

	Aug	Sept	Oct	Nov
Productivity per labour hour	10.5	10.2	9.8	10.1
Efficiency ratio				
Capacity ratio				
Activity ratio				

2   Given below are the production figures for a factory for the last three months.

	April	May	June
Production costs	£418,300	£424,500	£430,500
Production wages	£83,700	£86,000	£86,300
Output in units	121,700	123,500	128,000
Hours worked	11,200	11,500	11,500
Budgeted output	120,000	125,000	125,000
Sales revenue	£625,000	£634,000	£656,000
Number of employees	81	83	83

Production costs are made up of the materials for production and the bought in services required in the month. It is estimated that 11 units should be produced each hour.

Complete the table to calculate the following performance indicators for each of the last three months and for the three months in total:

(a) (i) productivity per labour hour
(ii) efficiency ratio
(iii) capacity ratio
(iv) activity ratio
(v) value added per employee

	April	May	June	Total
Productivity per labour hour	10·9	10·7	11·3	11·2
Efficiency ratio	98·8%	97·6%	102%	99·5
Capacity ratio	102·7%	101·2%	101·2%	101·7
Activity ratio				
Value added per employee				

(b) The labour rate is £7.50 per hour. Production for July will be the same as in June. If productivity can be increased to 11.5 units per hour, what is the cost saving in production wages?

£ [   ]

3   A travel firm employs five sales representatives. Sales of holidays are seasonal and you are provided with the following figures for the last year:

	July – Sept	Oct – Dec	Jan – March	April – June
Holidays sold	6,200	4,100	7,700	5,900
Total costs	£113,200	£115,400	£125,500	£120,400

(a) For each quarter of the year complete the following table to calculate:

(i) the productivity per sales representative
(ii) the cost per holiday sold

	July - Sept	Oct - Dec	Jan - Mar	Apr – June	
Productivity	1240	820	1540	1180	
Cost per holiday	18·25	28·15	16·30	20·41	

(b) Comment upon why you think the cost per holiday sold fluctuates so much.

4   Given below is a summary of a business's performance for the last six months:

	Jan	Feb	Mar	April	May	June
	£000	£000	£000	£000	£000	£000
Revenue	400	480	450	510	560	540
Cost of sales	210	270	260	320	340	330
Expenses	140	144	141	136	157	152
Interest	–	–	–	3	3	3
Shareholders' funds	240	290	319	353	406	434
Loan	–	–	–	40	40	40

For each month of the year you are to complete the table calculate the following performance indicators:

(a) gross profit margin
(b) operating profit margin
(c) percentage of expenses to turnover
(d) return on capital employed
(e) asset turnover

Comment on what the performance measures indicate about the business activities for the last six months.

	Jan	Feb	Mar	April	May	June
Gross profit margin	47.5%					
Net profit margin	12.5%					
% expenses to turnover	35%					
Return on capital employed	20.8					
Asset turnover	1.7					

5   Given below is a summary of the performance of a business for the last three years:

	20X6	20X7	20X8
	£000	£000	£000
Revenue	820	850	900
Cost of sales	440	445	500
Expenses	290	305	315
Interest	—	3	3
Capital and reserves	500	560	620
Long term loan	—	50	50
Non-current assets	385	453	498
Receivables	85	112	128
Inventory	50	55	67
Payables	30	34	41
Bank balance	10	24	18

For each of the three years complete the table to calculate the following performance measures and comment on what the measures indicate about the performance of the business over the period:

(a)   gross profit margin
(b)   operating profit margin
(c)   return on capital employed
(d)   asset turnover
(e)   non-current (fixed) asset turnover
(f)   current ratio
(g)   quick ratio
(h)   receivables' (debtors') collection period
(i)   inventory (stock) turnover in days
(j)   payables' (creditors') payment period
(k)   interest cover
(l)   gearing ratio

	20X6	20X7	20X8
Gross profit margin			
Operating profit margin			
Return on capital employed			
Asset turnover			
Non-current (fixed) asset turnover			
Current ratio			
Quick ratio			
Receivables' (debtors') collection period			
Inventory (stock) days			
Payables' (creditors') payment period			
Interest cover			
Gearing ratio			

6   A retail business has three small department stores in Flimwell, Hartfield and Groombridge. The figures for the first six months of 20X8 are given below:

	Flimwell	Hartfield	Groombridge
Financial details	£	£	£
Revenue	540,000	370,000	480,000
Opening inventory (stock)	51,000	45,000	30,000
Closing inventory (stock)	56,000	50,000	32,000
Purchases	210,000	165,000	192,000
Expenses	270,000	175,000	225,000
Capital	550,000	410,000	510,000
Payables (creditors)	25,800	27,500	30,500

Non-financial details

Floor area	2,400 sq m	1,700 sq m	2,000 sq m
Employees	28	13	26
Hours worked	30,500	14,100	28,300

(a) Complete the table to calculate the following performance indicators for each store:

   (i)   gross profit margin
   (ii)   operating profit margin
   (iii) return on capital employed
   (iv) asset turnover
   (v)   inventory (stock) turnover in days
   (vi) payables' (creditors') payment period
   (vii) sales per square metre of floor area
   (viii) sales per employee
   (ix) sales per hour worked.

	Flimwell	Hartfield	Groombridge
Gross profit margin	38%		
Operating profit margin	12%		
Return on capital employed	11.8%		
Asset turnover	1		
Inventory (stock) turnover	93 days		
Payables' (creditors') payment period	17 days		
Sales per sq m			
Sales per employee			
Sales per hour worked			

(b) Use the performance indicators calculated in (a) to write a report to the sales director of the chain comparing the performances of the three stores for the six month period. In the report explain the effect on the cash balance if the payables payment period in Flimwell were increased to that of Hartfield.

7 (a) A business operates on a gross profit margin of 44% and sales for the period were £106,500. What is the gross profit?

£ [46860]

(b) A business operates on a gross profit margin of 37.5% and the gross profit made in the period was £105,000. What was the figure for revenue for the period?

£ [   ]

(c) A business had revenue of £256,000 in a month, with a gross profit margin of 41% and an operating profit margin of 13.5%. What were the expenses for the month?

£ [   ]

(d) A business has a return on capital employed of 12.8% and made an operating profit for the period of £50,000. What is the capital employed?

£ [   ]

(e) A business has an operating profit percentage of 10% and a return on capital employed of 15%. What is the asset turnover of the business?

[   ] times

(f) A business has opening inventory (stock) and closing inventory (stock) of £118,000 and £104,000 respectively and made purchases during the year totalling £465,000. How many times did inventory (stock) turnover during the year?

[   ] times

(g) A business has a receivables' (debtors') collection period of 64 days and the closing receivables (debtors) figure is £64,000. What is the figure for revenue for the year?

£ [   ]

8   Given below is the summarised income statement (profit and loss account) and statement of financial position (balance sheet) of a manufacturing company for the year ended 30 September 20X8:

Income statement

	£000	£000
Revenue		372
Opening inventory (stock) of finished goods	19	
Materials	28	
Labour	40	
Production overheads	14	
	101	
Closing inventory (stock) of finished goods	21	
Cost of sales		80
Gross profit		292
Administration costs	184	
Interest payable	6	
Training costs	9	
Research costs	25	
		224
		68

Statement of financial position

	£000	£000
Non-current (fixed) assets		232
Current assets:		
Inventory (stock) of finished goods	21	
Receivables (debtors)	62	
Cash	9	
	92	
Payables (creditors)	24	
Net current assets		68
		300
Long term loan		(100)
		200
Capital and reserves		200

You are to complete the table to calculate the following performance indicators and for each one to identify which balanced scorecard perspective is being measured.

(a) operating profit margin
(b) return on capital employed
(c) inventory (stock) turnover in days
(d) asset turnover
(e) research costs as a percentage of production costs
(f) training costs as a percentage of the labour cost

		Balanced scorecard perspective
Net profit margin		
Return on capital employed		
Inventory (stock) turnover		
Asset turnover		
Research costs as % of production costs		
Training costs as a % of labour cost		

chapter 8:
COST MANAGEMENT

---

chapter coverage 📖

In this chapter we will look at a variety of final aspects of financial performance – largely the topics of quality and target costing.

The topics we shall cover are:

✍ What is quality?

✍ Costs of quality

✍ Performance indicators for quality

✍ Total Quality Management

✍ Target costing

✍ Product life cycle

WHAT IS QUALITY?

So far in this Course Companion we have been considering the production of products and the provision of services, from the point of view of the maker of the product or the provider of the service. Here we move onto considerations of quality, which means that we must now consider the product or service from the customer's perspective.

Quality and value

QUALITY could be described as the 'degree of excellence of the product or service' or 'how well the product or service serves its purpose'.

Quality is therefore judged by the customer. The product or service will only be perceived as having quality if it satisfies the customer. To do this the product or service must have two main elements:

- it must be fit for the purpose for which it has been acquired
- it must represent value for money to the customer.

This does not mean that products or services need to be made more expensive by using better materials or more highly skilled staff. Provided that the product or service does what it is meant to do and is viewed as value for money by the customer, then this product or service will have quality.

HOW IT WORKS

Let us consider travelling by aeroplane from London to Zurich. The basic requirements of this service to a customer are:

- the customer reaches his destination safely
- the flight departs and arrives on time.

Provided that these requirements are met, then the service will be fit for its purpose.

The price that the customer will pay for the flight however will depend upon the customer's perspective of value. One customer may choose a low cost 'no frills' flight which includes no food or refreshment and probably less leg-room in the seats. This will represent value to that customer.

Alternatively another customer may choose a first class seat on a scheduled flight as their perception of value is the luxury of the first class lounge, additional space, more comfortable seats and the provision of refreshments.

Both services will have quality if they serve their purpose and are perceived as value for money by the customer.

Enhancement of value

As value is important in judging whether a product or service has quality, then it is important to consider what the customer expects from the product or service.

Many industries are now highly competitive, with many businesses providing the same type of goods or service and competing for customers. In these situations, value can be enhanced by considering what the customer requires and improving the perceived value of the product or service.

HOW IT WORKS

If we consider the banking system, there are many High Street banks and building societies that provide the same basic services of current and deposit accounts, cheque books and cheque guarantee cards. In order to compete for customers, many of these banks have attempted to enhance the value of the service that they provide, by offering additional services that are thought to enhance the value of the basic service to the customer, with no additional cost to the customer. Therefore many banks now try to compete by offering services such as telephone banking, internet banking and text messaging banking.

Managing for quality

Returning now to the perspective of the producer of goods or the provider of a service, it is obviously essential that the goods or services are fit for their purpose. In order to ensure this quality of the goods or services management needs to embrace the principle of GETTING IT RIGHT FIRST TIME.

This means accepting that the cost of prevention of defective goods should be recognised as less than the cost of correction when faulty goods are sold to customers. We will return to this principle of getting it right first time later in the chapter.

COSTS OF QUALITY

The COSTS OF QUALITY are the costs of ensuring and assuring quality and also any losses incurred when quality is not achieved.

There are generally thought to be four main areas of quality related costs and for computer based assessments these are the terms that you need to be able to define. The four types of quality costs are:

- prevention costs
- appraisal costs
- internal failure costs
- external failure costs

Prevention costs

PREVENTION COSTS are the costs incurred prior to, or during, production in order to investigate, prevent or reduce defects in products or mistakes in services.

These costs might include any of the following:

- improvements in product design or specification to reduce defective products
- improvements in systems designed to reduce mistakes in the provision of services
- design, development and maintenance of quality control or inspection equipment
- administration of quality control
- provision of training for quality control

Appraisal costs

APPRAISAL COSTS are the costs incurred in initially ascertaining how the product or service conforms to quality requirements. They are all of the costs associated with assessing the level of quality achieved.

These costs will include:

- inspection of goods and raw materials received
- inspection of production processes and work in progress
- inspection or performance testing of finished goods
- appraisal of the quality of services provided
- sample testing finished production, perhaps to the point of destruction

Internal failure costs

INTERNAL FAILURE COSTS are the costs arising from inadequate quality before the goods or services are sold to the customer. Therefore they are costs arising within the organisation due to the failure to achieve the required level of quality.

Internal failure costs will include:

- investigation and analysis of failed units
- re-work costs
- re-inspection costs
- lost contribution on defective units scrapped or sold at a lower price than normal
- losses due to faults in raw materials purchased
- costs of reviewing product design or specification after finding defective units
- costs of production delays

External failure costs

EXTERNAL FAILURE COSTS are costs arising from inadequate quality discovered after the goods or services have been sold to the customer.

These costs might include:

- costs of running a customer service department
- costs of administering customer complaints
- product liability costs
- costs of replacing or repairing goods returned from customers
- loss of future custom from dissatisfied customers

Task 1

Categorise the following examples in terms of the four different types of quality costs

(a) improvements in product design or specification to reduce defective products *prevention*

(b) loss of future custom from dissatisfied customers *external failure*

(c) lost contribution on defective units scrapped or sold at a lower price than normal *internal failure*

(d) sample testing finished production *appraisal*

HOW IT WORKS

Smithson Ltd is a manufacturer of small electrical items of kitchen equipment such as toasters, food processors, microwave ovens etc.

A number of events that occurred recently are given below.

(a) One line of microwave ovens has had to be recalled due to a few isolated incidents where the oven has caught fire. It is highly likely that the company may have to pay damages to the customers involved in the fires. It is unlikely that any of the owners of the recalled products will buy Smithson goods again.

(b) The company engineers have designed a new motor for one of the food processors which should ensure far fewer breakdowns and a longer life of the machine.

(c) It has been discovered that the external surface of one of the toasters, which has been made with a new material from a new supplier, gets scratched in the production process and all of these toasters can only be sold at a lower price as seconds.

(d) The company has introduced more detailed inspection procedures for microwave ovens following the recall incident.

(e) The company produces a range of different food mixers and it has been discovered that one particular line fails more often than others and the cause is to be investigated and put right.

We will now analyse each of these events and determine what effects they are likely to have on the various categories of quality costs – prevention, appraisal, internal failure and external failure.

(a) **Recall of microwaves**

Prevention costs – these will increase as the fault must be eliminated which may require redesign of the product

Appraisal costs – these will probably increase as this microwave will require closer monitoring in future to ensure that the problem has been eliminated

Internal failure costs – these will increase due to investigation of the failure, repairs to any ovens in stock which may cause disruption to the production process and re-inspection costs

External failure costs – the costs of repairing the microwaves, any damages claims received from customers and the loss of these customers for future sales

(b) **Design of new motor**

Prevention costs – these would be the cost of the design and its implementation

Internal failure costs – these should be reduced as the product is more reliable

External failure costs – these should be reduced as the product is more reliable and has a longer lifespan

(c) **Scratched toasters**

Prevention costs – new design or finding a new supplier

Internal failure costs – the lost contribution from having to sell the toasters at a lower price

(d) **Inspection procedures for microwaves**

Appraisal costs – these will increase with the costs of inspection procedures

Internal failure costs – these should reduce as the benefits of the inspection are felt

External failure costs – these should reduce as fewer defective products will be sold to customers

(e) **Food mixers**

Prevention costs – these will be incurred in the re-design of the product once the cause has been identified

Internal failure costs – these will increase due to investigation of the problem

External failure costs – these should reduce as fewer defective products are sold to customers

---

Task 2

A car manufacturer recalls a particular make of car due to the fact that the handbrake fails if the car door is slammed shut.

Complete the table to show what effect will this have on the different categories of quality cost.

Cost of quality	Effect
Prevention costs	increase
Appraisal costs	increase
Internal costs	increase
External costs	increase

Measuring the costs of quality

Now we have been able to analyse the costs of quality into their constituent elements we will need to consider how we can measure these costs.

Normally the cost accounting system of an organisation will have to be adapted in order to be able to find the costs of quality.

For example, in a traditional cost accounting system, normal losses will be allowed for in the production costs. Therefore, the costs of wasted materials, scrapping of defective products and reworking of products with faults are all included in the production cost and are not separately identifiable or highlighted for management attention. Similarly costs of inspections will be included in production overheads without being separately identified.

Therefore if the costs of quality are to be measured, the cost accounting system must be amended in order that the various relevant costs can be separately identified.

Explicit and implicit costs of quality

The costs of quality that can be quantified from the cost accounting records are known as EXPLICIT COSTS. However, there are other types of cost which are not recorded in the accounting records and which can only be estimated – these are known as IMPLICIT COSTS.

Implicit costs might include:

- the opportunity cost of lost sales to existing customers who are dissatisfied due to faulty goods and will not purchase from the organisation again

- loss of goodwill or reputation due to factors such as the widespread recall of one of an organisation's products, affecting potential customers

- costs of production disruption due to reworking of faulty products – these costs will be included in the production costs but cannot be separately identified

- costs incurred due to the practice of holding higher levels of inventory (stock) of raw materials in order to allow faulty materials to be replaced without disruption to production.

HOW IT WORKS

Given below is a summary of the costs of quality identified earlier for Smithson Ltd. Now we will decide which are explicit costs and which are implicit costs.

	Explicit	Implicit
(a) **Recall of microwaves**		
Prevention costs – redesign costs	✗	
Appraisal costs – inspection costs	✗	
Internal failure costs –		
investigation of the failure	✗	
disruption of production process from reworking		✗
re-inspection costs	✗	
External failure costs –		
cost of repairs to the microwaves	✗	
damages claims		✗
loss of customers		✗

		Explicit	*Implicit*
(b)	**Design of new motor**		
	Prevention costs –		
	cost of the design/implementation	✗	
	Internal failure costs – reduced due to design		✗
	External failure costs – reduced due to design		✗
(c)	**Scratched toasters**		
	Prevention costs –		
	new design	✗	
	finding a new supplier		✗
	Internal failure costs – lost contribution	✗	
(d)	**Inspection procedures for microwaves**		
	Appraisal costs – costs of inspection procedures	✗	
	Internal failure costs – reduced due to inspections		✗
	External failure costs – reduced as fewer defective products will be sold		✗
(e)	**Food mixers**		
	Prevention costs – re-design of the product	✗	
	Internal failure costs – investigation of the problem	✗	
	External failure costs –		
	reduced as fewer defective products are sold to customers		✗

This analysis of the costs of quality highlights a few areas:

- the explicit costs should all be available from the accounting records
- some of the implicit costs can also be estimated, such as the amount of likely claims for damages from customers of the microwaves
- other implicit costs may not be possible to estimate such as the lost microwave customers or the disruption to the production process from repairs and reworking
- some of the implicit elements are not costs but reductions of quality costs such as the reduction of external quality costs as less defective products are sold – it will not often be possible to put a value to these.

> ## Task 3
>
> Give two examples of explicit quality costs and two examples of implicit quality costs.
>
> **Explicit costs**
>
> (1)
>
> (2)
>
> **Implicit costs**
>
> (1)
>
> (2)

Calculating the costs of quality

As we have just seen, in practice determining the costs of quality is a complicated business. However in tests the situation will be simplified and you may be required to identify and total the costs of quality.

HOW IT WORKS

Scooby Products estimates that 2 out of every 1,000 of its products that are sold are defective in some way. When the goods are returned they are replaced free of charge. It is estimated that every customer who buys a faulty product will return it and will not buy Scooby Products' goods again. Each unit costs £30 to manufacture and is sold at a price of £40.

Due to quality inspections it is also estimated that 10,000 defective units a year are discovered before they are sold and these can then be sold as 'seconds' at a price of £25. The quality inspections cost £450,000 each year.

The unit sales of the product are 20 million each year.

We will analyse and calculate the explicit costs of quality:

If units sales are 20 million and 2 out of every 1,000 units sold are defective then the number of defective units is $20,000,000/1,000 \times 2 = 40,000$ units.

	£
Appraisal costs – inspection costs	450,000
Internal failure costs – lost contribution on seconds (10,000 units × (£40 – £25))	150,000
External failure costs – cost of replacement products (40,000 × £30)	1,200,000
	1,800,000

There is also the implicit cost of the loss of 40,000 customers each year who will not buy Scooby Products' items again.

Task 4

A manufacturing business estimates that it has to sell 3,000 defective units of its product at a "seconds" price of £12 per unit. The normal selling price is £25 per unit and the inspection procedure that identifies these defective units costs £20,000.

What is the total cost of quality and what type of quality costs has the business incurred ?

£ [   ]

Type of quality costs [   ]

PERFORMANCE INDICATORS FOR QUALITY

In just the same way as performance indicators are produced to summarise the production operations for a business so performance indicators can be produced to value the quality of the organisation's products or services. Most of these performance indicators will be measures of customer satisfaction.

If we start by thinking about performance indicators for the quality of physical goods these can be a mixture of financial and non-financial performance indicators.

Financial indicators

Financial indicators to assess customer satisfaction with the products and therefore their quality might include the following:

- cost per customer of the customer service department
- cost per customer of after-sales service
- the percentage of the sales value of returned goods to total sales value
- unit cost of returned goods
- unit cost of repair of returned goods
- cost of reworking defective goods as a percentage of total production cost

Non-financial indicators

- number of goods returned
- percentage of number of goods returned to number of goods sold
- number of warranty claims as a percentage of total units sold
- number of customer complaints as a percentage of total number of sales

Quality control and inspections

At this stage a distinction should be drawn between quality control (prevention - before the event) and quality inspections (detection – after the event). Quality control is about prevention of defective products or mistakes in provision of a service. Quality inspections are to do with detection and identification of defective products or mistakes in provision of a service. Whilst ideally an organisation would plan to have zero defects, the costs of the quality assurance needed to guarantee this may be so high as to be prohibitive and so some defects may be tolerated.

Quality inspections

If a manufacturing business carries out quality inspections this will often be done by taking a sample of the production and testing this for defective products. Quality inspections normally take place at three points in the production process:

- receiving inspections when raw materials and components are received from suppliers

- production floor or process inspections for work in progress

- final inspection of finished goods

From these inspections, and using the sample results, further performance indicators can be established such as:

- percentage of defective materials compared to total materials
- number of anticipated defective units
- percentage of defective units to total of units produced

Measuring quality of services

Finding performance indicators for quality for manufactured goods is much more straightforward than finding performance indicators for the quality of services.

Measuring the quality of a service again involves measuring customer satisfaction, therefore the first stage is to ensure that the organisation knows what it is that the customer expects from the service.

Some of the performance indicators for quality of a service may be qualitative, such as surveys of customer opinion. A further method of assessing the quality of a service may be by inspection, either by an internal or an external body, such as OFSTED inspections of schools.

There can also be quantitative, although normally non-financial, performance indicators for a service, such as average waiting times for hospital operations or the percentage of train journeys that did not run on time.

Task 5

What type of quality performance indicators might a taxi firm consider?

TOTAL QUALITY MANAGEMENT

TOTAL QUALITY MANAGEMENT (TQM) is a quality management system in an organisation that involves all areas of the organisation not just the production element. The philosophy behind quality management must be applied in all the activities of the business – design, production, marketing, administration, purchasing, sales and even the finance function.

TQM can be defined as a continuous improvement in quality, productivity and effectiveness obtained by establishing management responsibility for processes as well as output. In this system every process has an identified process owner and every person in an entity operates within a process and contributes to its improvement (CIMA *Official Terminology*).

Principles of TQM

As we have seen, defective products or mistakes in production or provision of a service are costly. These costs include:

- materials wastage
- idle time
- reworking costs
- production disruption costs
- re-inspection costs
- costs of dealing with complaints
- costs of replacing faulty goods
- costs of loss of customer goodwill

The basic principle behind TQM is that of continuous improvement. This can be described as the concept of 'getting it right first time' and 'getting it even more right next time'. By getting it right first time the costs outlined above will be reduced to the point where they should not occur at all. Costs of prevention are less than the costs of correction.

TQM seeks to ensure that the goods produced or the services supplied are of the highest quality.

Training

In order for TQM to work in all areas of an organisation, training and motivation of staff is vital in order for each individual to have the attitude of constantly seeking improvement in what they do. All staff within the organisation must be taught that they have customers. These may be external customers of the business or internal customers in the form of colleagues in the business that use an individual's work. Each individual should endeavour to ensure that they get it right first time and therefore that their excellent work is passed on in the chain.

Quality circles

Another important concept behind TQM is that every employee is involved and anyone with an idea should be allowed to put this forward. This is often done by groups of employees being formed within the organisation known as QUALITY CIRCLES.

These quality circles normally consist of about ten employees with a range of skills, roles and seniority who meet regularly to discuss problems of quality and quality control and to perhaps suggest ways of improving processes and output. This means that there is input from all levels within the organisation and from different disciplines such as marketing, design, engineering, information technology and office administration as well as production.

TARGET COSTING

If the selling price of a product is fixed by market forces, then the product must be made at a cost that is lower than the market selling price, in order for the business to make a profit. The TARGET COST is determined by taking the fixed selling price and deducting the required profit margin. This target cost is then presented to the product designers for them to achieve. This may be done by the use of value analysis.

Task 6

A car manufacturer wants to calculate a target cost for a new car, the price of which will be set at £27,950. The company requires an 8% profit margin.

The target cost is £ [   ]

Value analysis

The aim behind VALUE ANALYSIS is to reduce the cost of a product or service without any reduction in the value to the customer. Value analysis is where every aspect of a product or service is analysed to determine whether it does provide value to the customer and whether its function can be achieved in any other way at a lower cost.

Value engineering

Technically, value analysis is applied to products or services already being produced or provided. If this process takes place during the design stage of a product or in the planning stage of a service then it is known as VALUE ENGINEERING.

Specialists in design, engineering, work methods and technology, amongst others, will be involved in this process. When designing a product or planning a service each element of the product or service must be considered to determine whether it does add value to the product or service for the consumer and then to ensure that this is included in the product or service at the lowest possible cost.

Cost reduction

The aim of value analysis is cost reduction; however, care must be taken to ensure that short term cost reduction does not affect long term profitability. For example, costs could be reduced by cutting back on staff training. However, this could lead to inefficiencies, wastage, low morale or high labour turnover.

The aim should be long term cost reduction by improving productivity and the efficiency with which all of the resources of the organisation are used.

Assessment of cost reductions

A variety of methods can be used to assess whether cost reductions are possible including:

- work study
- organisation and method study
- variety reduction

Work study

Work study can be used in manufacturing processes to determine factors such as:

- the most efficient layout of the factory and the stores function
- the most efficient usage of materials, labour and machinery to reduce wastage and idle time
- the most efficient work methods and procedures

Organisation and method study

This is similar to work study but it is used in the administrative functions of the business in order to improve office procedures and determine factors such as:

- maximising the benefits from computerisation
- determining the most efficient office layout, work flows and communications
- elimination of unnecessary or duplicated office procedures
- minimising the amount of paperwork

Variety reduction

The aim of variety reduction is to reduce either the number of products produced, or the number of types of components used, in order to reduce costs.

By reducing the range of products that are produced and concentrating on just a small number of products, this can increase economies of scale of production, but this must be balanced with value to the customer. If consumers require a wide range of choices of a product then such cost cutting will not be of benefit due to lost sales and goodwill.

Often a more effective way of cutting costs is to standardise the components used in the products. If the same basic components are used in many of the products, then cost savings can be made by bulk buying from suppliers and a smaller variety of inventories (stock) being held.

Benefits of value analysis

If value analysis and cost reduction procedures are successfully carried out in an organisation this can have a number of benefits for both the organisation and the customer:

- reduced costs for the organisation and potentially reduced prices for the customer with no loss of value
- continuous improvement in the design and manufacture of products
- improvement of customer service due to the use of standard components
- design of products and services with customer value always considered

Value analysis and value engineering can help an organisation to reduce costs while still maintaining the quality of the product or service that it provides.

PRODUCT LIFE CYCLE

Most products have a limited PRODUCT LIFE CYCLE which will show different sales and profitability patterns at different stages of the life cycle.

The product life cycle is generally thought to split naturally into five separate stages:

- development
- launch (or introduction)
- growth
- maturity
- decline

Development and launch stages

During this period of the product's life there are large outgoings in terms of development expenditure, purchase of non-current (fixed) assets necessary for production, the building up of inventory (stock) levels and advertising and promotion expenses. Costs are incurred but no revenue is generated.

Launch/introduction stage

The product is introduced to the market. It is likely that even after the launch sales will be quite low and the product will be making a loss at this stage. Further amounts will need to be spent on advertising to make potential customers aware of the product.

Growth stage

If the launch of the product is successful then during the growth stage there will be fairly rapid increases in sales and a move to profitability as the costs of the earlier stages are covered. These sales increases however are not likely to continue indefinitely.

Maturity stage

In the maturity stage of the product life cycle, the growth in demand for the product will probably start to slow down and sales volumes will become more constant. It will continue to be profitable. In many cases this is the stage where the product is modified or improved, in order to sustain demand, and this may then result in a small surge in sales.

Decline stage

At some point in a product's life, unless it is a consumable item such as chocolate bars, the product will reach the end of its sale life. The market will have bought enough of the product and it will reach saturation point where sales will decline. This is the point where the business should consider no longer producing the product.

The level of sales and profits earned over a life cycle can be illustrated diagrammatically as follows.

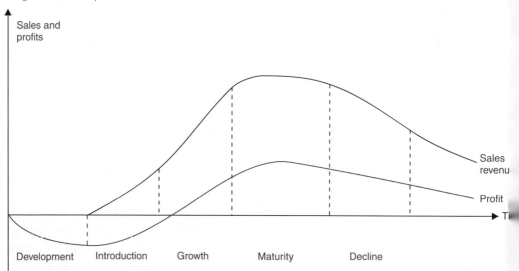

The horizontal axis measures the duration of the life cycle, which can last from, say, 18 months to several hundred years. Children's crazes or fad products have very short lives while some products, such as binoculars (invented in the eighteenth century) can last a very long time.

Market considerations

It is also important to consider the overall market for a particular product. Is the market a new, emerging market for a new product, an established market for a long-standing product or a declining market for a product which is no longer of great interest to consumers?

For example no matter how technologically advanced a VHS video recorder is, DVD players mean that demand for video recorders is in terminal decline.

Lifecycle costing

Under traditional costing methods the costs of a product are only recorded and analysed once production of the product has begun. However a product's life cycle costs are incurred from its design stage through development to market launch, production and sales, and finally to its eventual withdrawal from the market. It is recognised that in reality a large proportion of the costs of a product are incurred before production has started in the early stages of the product life cycle.

Life cycle costing recognises all of these pre-production costs of the product such as:

- design costs
- prototyping
- programming
- process design
- equipment acquisition

Traditional cost accumulation systems are based on the financial accounting year and tend to dissect a product's life cycle into a series of 12-month periods. This means that traditional management accounting systems do not accumulate costs over a product's entire life cycle and do not therefore assess a product's profitability over its entire life. Instead they do it on a periodic basis.

The aim of life cycle costing is to ensure that all the costs of the product are accumulated over the whole of its life cycle in order to ensure that all costs are covered by revenue from the product.

CHAPTER OVERVIEW

- Quality of a product or service is what is perceived from the customer's perspective – is the product/service fit for its purpose and value for money?

- An aspect of a product has value if the customer perceives it as being worth paying money for

- Costs of quality are of four types – prevention costs, appraisal costs, internal failure costs and external failure costs

- In order to measure the costs of quality the cost accounting system may have to be modified in order to highlight the relevant figures – figures that can be taken from the accounting records are explicit costs of quality but there may also be other implicit costs of quality which cannot be found from the accounting records

- An organisation can monitor its quality levels and costs of quality by a variety of financial and non-financial performance indicators – for an organisation which provides a service some of the performance indicators will tend to be qualitative rather than quantitative

- Total quality management is an ethos whereby every person in an organisation strives for continuous improvement by trying to get it right first time

- Target costing involves setting a target for the cost of a product or service by deducting the desired profit margin from the market selling price. The target cost represents the maximum amount of cost that the organisation can incur and still make the desired level of profit.

- Value analysis is a method of analysing the constituent elements of a product or service in order to try to reduce the cost with no loss in value to the customer Most products have a limited lifecycle which involves the stages of development and launch, growth, maturity and decline. The position of the product within its life cycle will affect sales and profitability patterns and be an important factor in cost management

- The aim of life cycle costing is to ensure that all the costs of a product (including development costs) are accumulated over the whole of its life cycle in order to ensure that all costs are covered by revenue from the product.

Keywords

Quality – the degree of excellence of a product/service and how well it serves its purpose

Getting it right first time – the basic concept behind total quality management – the costs of prevention are less than the costs of correction

Costs of quality – costs of ensuring quality and any losses incurred when quality is not achieved

Prevention costs – costs incurred to investigate, prevent and reduce defects or mistakes

Appraisal costs – costs associated with assessing the level of quality achieved

Internal failure costs – costs arising within the organisation due to the failure to achieve quality, eg reworking

External failure costs – costs arising from inadequate quality discovered after the goods/services have been sold, eg repairs

Explicit costs – costs that can be found within the accounting records

Implicit costs – costs not recorded in the accounting records

Total quality management – a system of continuous improvement in quality, productivity and effectiveness

Quality circles – groups of employees who meet regularly to discuss quality issues

Target cost – the desired cost of a product which the designers must achieve, based on deducting the desirable profit margin from the market selling price

Value analysis – analysis of every aspect of existing products/services in order to reduce the cost with no reduction in value to the customer

Value engineering – value analysis in the design stage of a product or planning stage of a service

Life cycle costing – accumulation of all costs including pre-production costs

TEST YOUR LEARNING

1   For each of the following state which type of cost of quality it is (prevention, appraisal, internal failure or external failure):

Type of cost

(a)	products scrapped due to faulty raw materials	*internal*
(b)	training for quality control staff	*prevention*
(c)	costs of customer after sales service department	*external*
(d)	lost contribution on defective products sold as seconds	*internal.*
(e)	costs of inspection of raw materials	*appraisal.*
(f)	maintenance of quality control equipment	*prevention*
(g)	cost of replacing faulty products returned by customers	*external.*
(h)	costs of production delays due to re-working defective products discovered in quality inspection	*internal*
(i)	claims from customers relating to defective products	*external.*
(j)	performance testing of finished goods	*apprasal.*

int
ext
app

2. A business estimates that one in 3,000 of its products are found to be faulty after sale. Of these it is estimated that 60% are returned by customers and can be repaired at a cost of £20 per product. It is felt that the customers who do not return the products will not buy the company's products again and the cost of advertising for replacement customers is £40,000 per annum.

Total sales of the product are 5 million units each year.

Complete the table to list all of the costs of quality and the amount of that cost where possible. State into which category of cost of quality each cost falls.

Cost of quality	Amount £	Category of cost

3   A manufacturing organisation carries out quality inspections on product A. In the last year 2,000 defective units were discovered and had to be sold as seconds at a price of £45, compared with the normal selling price of £80. The costs of the quality inspections totalled £60,000 for the year.

Sales of product A are 1 million units each year and it is estimated that a further 1 in every 1,000 sales will be defective. Of these it is expected that 75% will be returned by customers and will be replaced at no cost to the customer. The cost of producing a unit of product A is £50. The customers who do not return their products are unlikely to buy the company's products again.

Complete the table to list all of the costs of quality incurred by the business and the amount of each cost if possible. State which type of cost of quality each cost is and whether it is an explicit cost or an implicit cost.

Cost of quality	Amount £	Category of cost	Explicit or implicit

4 A manufacturing business has the following details for the period just ended:

Total sales	£1,500,000
Cost of customer after sales service department	£280,000
Total sales returns (sales value)	£120,000
Costs of repairs of returned products	£40,000
Number of after sales service customers	60,000
Total units sold	50,000 units
Number of units returned	4,000
Number of customer complaints	3,000

Complete the table to calculate performance indicators for quality from the information provided.

Cost per after sales service customer	
Sales returns as a % of sales	
Repair cost per returned units	
Complaints as a % of unit sales	

5 Explain what is meant by Total Quality Management.

6 Explain the stages of a product life cycle including the likely effect of each stage on sales quantity and profitability.

CHAPTER 1   Costs

1   **Fixed cost per unit:**

Production level	Cost £
20,000 units	5.00
40,000 units	2.50
80,000 units	1.25

Working

Production level		Cost £		
20,000 units	£100,000/20,000	=	£5.00 per unit	
40,000 units	£100,000/40,000	=	£2.50 per unit	
80,000 units	£100,000/80,000	=	£1.25 per unit	

2   The **relevant range** of a cost is the activity levels over which the cost is fixed.

3

Cost	Behaviour
Stores department costs which include £5,000 of insurance premium and an average of £100 cost per materials receipt or issue	Semi-variable
Machinery depreciation based upon machine hours used	Variable
Salary costs of lecturers in a training college where one lecturer is required for every 200 students enrolled	Stepped
Buildings insurance for a building housing the stores, the factory and the canteen	Fixed
Wages of production workers who are paid per unit produced, with a guaranteed weekly minimum wage of £250	Fixed then semi-variable

4

Sales	Monthly salary £
4 sales	880
8 sales	960
15 sales	1,100

Working

Sales		Monthly salary £
4 sales	£800 + (4 × £20) =	£880
8 sales	£800 + (8 × £20) =	£960
15 sales	£800 + (15 × £20) =	£1,100

5

The variable rate of production costs is

£6 per unit

The fixed amount of production costs is

£23,000

Workings

	Activity level – units		Cost – £
Highest	28,000		191,000
Lowest	20,000		143,000
Increase	8,000		48,000
Variable rate	=	£48,000/8,000 =	£6 per unit

Fixed amount using highest level:

Variable cost 28,000 units × £6	£168,000
Total cost	£191,000
Fixed cost	£23,000

CHAPTER 2 Methods of costing

1

Costing method	Cost per unit £
Absorption costing	15.00
Marginal costing	10.00

Workings
Cost per unit – absorption costing

	£
Direct materials	12,000
Direct labour	15,000
Variable overheads	23,000
Fixed overheads	25,000
Total cost	75,000
Cost per unit =	£75,000/5,000
= £15 per unit	

Cost per unit – marginal costing

	£
Direct materials	12,000
Direct labour	15,000
Variable overheads	23,000
Total cost	50,000
Cost per unit =	£50,000/5,000
= £10 per unit	

2

	£
Absorption cost profit	504,000
Change in inventory (stock) :	
Decrease in inventory (stock) 2,500 – 1,500 = 1,000 units × fixed cost per unit £2	(2,000)
Marginal cost profit	506,000

3

(a) The overhead absorption rate based on direct labour hours is £0.90 per direct labour hour.

(b) Use the picklists to complete the sentences:

The **over** absorption of £**2,500** should be **added to** profit

Workings

(a) Overhead absorption rate = $\dfrac{£54,000}{60,000h}$ (budgeted direct labour hours)

$\qquad\qquad\qquad\qquad\quad = £0.90$ per direct labour hour

(b)   £

	£
Actual overheads	47,000
Absorbed overheads (55,000h × £0.90 per h)	49,500
Over absorption	2,500

The amount over absorbed will be an addition to profit.

4

(a)

Overhead included in Product A	£5,000
Overhead included in Product B	£26,000

Workings

Cost per inspection	=	£74,000/370
	=	£200 per inspection
Overhead included in A's cost	=	£200 × 25
	=	£5,000
Overhead included in B's cost	=	£200 × 130
	=	£26,000

(b)

Product A overhead cost per unit	£0.50
Product B overhead cost per unit	£2.00

Product A £5,000/10,000 units = £0.50

Product B £26,000/13,000 units = £2.00

CHAPTER 3 Decision making

1 Break-even point $= \dfrac{£360,000}{£28 - £19}$

$= 40,000$ units

2 Target profit output $= \dfrac{£250,000 + £150,000}{£80 - £60}$

$= 20,000$ units

3 Break-even point $= \dfrac{£480,000}{£32 - £24}$

$= 60,000$ units

Margin of safety $= \dfrac{£75,000 - 60,000}{75,000} \times 100$

$= 20\%$

4 Profit volume ratio $= \dfrac{£36 - £27}{£36} \times 100$

$= 25\%$

Break-even point $= \dfrac{£360,000}{0.25}$

$= £1,440,000$

5

(a)

Product	Units produced
R	1,000
S	4,000
P	2,000
Q	3,750

Workings

	P	Q	R	S
Contribution per kg	£4.00	£3.75	£9.00	£7.00
Ranking	3	4	1	2

Production plan

	Units produced	Kgs used
R	1,000	1,000
S	4,000	8,000
P	2,000	6,000
Q (balance = 15000/4)	3,750	15,000
		30,000

(b)   The profit earned from this production plan will be £115,250

Working

Profit

	£
P (2,000 × £12)	24,000
Q (3,750 × £15)	56,250
R (1,000 × £9)	9,000
S (4,000 × £14)	56,000
Contribution	145,250
Less: fixed costs	30,000
Profit	115,250

6   A

	A	B	C
	£	£	£
Direct materials	1.60	2.00	0.80
Direct labour	3.20	3.60	1.60
Direct overheads	0.80	1.20	0.40
Variable cost of production	5.60	6.80	2.80
External price	5.50	8.40	4.00

On the basis of costs alone only product A should be purchased externally as it is cheaper to buy than to make.

7

Year	0	1	2	3	4
Cash flow	-400,000	-45,000	-45,000	-45,000	105,000
Discount factor	1.000	0.952	0.907	0.864	0.823
Present value	-400,000	-42,840	-40,815	-38,880	86,415
Net present cost	-436,120				

CHAPTER 4 Statistical methods

1. A cyclical variation in a time series is due to the long term fluctuations of the economy as a whole. A seasonal variation is a regular variation in the results due to the nature of the business, and will repeat itself within a short-term period, eg a week, quarter, year.

2.

Month	Actual	Three month moving average
	£	£
March	226,500	
April	251,600	238,767
May	238,200	245,800
June	247,600	242,100
July	240,500	250,300
August	262,800	

3.

	Actual	Four year moving average	Centred moving average – trend
	£	£	£
20X1	226,700		
20X2	236,500		
		236,500	
20X3	240,300		238,175
		239,850	
20X4	242,500		240,988
		242,125	
20X5	240,100		243,038
		243,950	
20X6	245,600		244,663
		245,375	
20X7	247,600		
20X8	248,200		

4

Month	Cost £
January	228,800
February	217,830
March	205,700

Workings

January	£205,600 + 23,200	=	£228,800
February	£208,600 + 9,230	=	£217,830
March	£209,200 − 3,500	=	£205,700

5

		Profit £	Index
20X7	Quarter 1	86,700	100.0
	Quarter 2	88,200	101.7
	Quarter 3	93,400	107.7
	Quarter 4	90,500	104.4
20X8	Quarter 1	83,200	96.0
	Quarter 2	81,400	93.9
	Quarter 3	83,200	96.0
	Quarter 4	85,000	98.0

Workings

20X7	Quarter 1	86,700	100.0
	Quarter 2	88,200/86,700 × 100	101.7
	Quarter 3	93,400/86,700 × 100	107.7
	Quarter 4	90,500/86,700 × 100	104.4
20X8	Quarter 1	83,200/86,700 × 100	96.0
	Quarter 2	81,400/86,700 × 100	93.9
	Quarter 3	83,200/86,700 × 100	96.0
	Quarter 4	85,000/86,700 × 100	98.0

6

		Costs	RPI	Restated costs
		£		£
20X7	June	133,100	171.1	133,100
	July	133,800	170.5	134,271
	Aug	133,600	170.8	133,835
	Sept	134,600	171.7	134,130
	Oct	135,800	171.6	135,404
	Nov	135,100	172.1	134,315
	Dec	135,600	172.1	134,812
20X8	Jan	134,700	171.1	134,700
	Feb	135,900	172.0	135,189
	Mar	136,200	172.2	135,330
	April	136,500	173.1	134,923
	May	136,700	174.2	134,267

Workings

		£	£
20X7	June	$133,100 \times 171.1/171.1$	133,100
	July	$133,800 \times 171.1/170.5$	134,271
	Aug	$133,600 \times 171.1/170.8$	133,835
	Sept	$134,600 \times 171.1/171.7$	134,130
	Oct	$135,800 \times 171.1/171.6$	135,404
	Nov	$135,100 \times 171.1/172.1$	134,315
	Dec	$135,600 \times 171.1/172.1$	134,812
20X8	Jan	$134,700 \times 171.1/171.1$	134,700
	Feb	$135,900 \times 171.1/172.0$	135,189
	Mar	$136,200 \times 171.1/172.2$	135,330
	Apr	$136,500 \times 171.1/173.1$	134,923
	May	$136,700 \times 171.1/174.2$	134,267

7

		Costs	RPI	Restated costs
		£		£
20X7	June	133,100	171.1	135,512
	July	133,800	170.5	136,704
	Aug	133,600	170.8	136,259
	Sept	134,600	171.7	136,560
	Oct	135,800	171.6	137,858
	Nov	135,100	172.1	136,749
	Dec	135,600	172.1	137,255
20X8	Jan	134,700	171.1	137,141
	Feb	135,900	172.0	137,638
	Mar	136,200	172.2	137,782
	April	136,500	173.1	137,367
	May	136,700	174.2	136,700

Workings

Adjusted figures

		£	£
20X7	June	$133,100 \times 174.2/171.1$	135,512
	July	$133,800 \times 174.2/170.5$	136,704
	Aug	$133,600 \times 174.2/170.8$	136,259
	Sept	$134,600 \times 174.2/171.7$	136,560
	Oct	$135,800 \times 174.2/171.6$	137,858
	Nov	$135,100 \times 174.2/172.1$	136,749
	Dec	$135,600 \times 174.2/172.1$	137,255
20X8	Jan	$134,700 \times 174.2/171.1$	137,141
	Feb	$135,900 \times 174.2/172.0$	137,638
	Mar	$136,200 \times 174.2/172.2$	137,782
	Apr	$136,500 \times 174.2/173.1$	137,367
	May	$136,700 \times 174.2/174.2$	136,700

8   It is generally assumed that the level of sales will depend on the advertising undertaken, so:

- ■ Dependent variable – sales volume
- ■ Independent variable – advertising costs

9   Production costs   = $63,000 + (3.2 \times 44,000)$

=   £203,800

10 The first 2 years account for x = 1 to x = 24

Thus the x values in which we are interested are x = 25, 26, 27

Month 1	x = 25 :	y = 4.8 + 1.2(25)	= 34.8 ie £34,800
Month 2	x = 26 :	y = 4.8 + 1.2(26)	= 36.0 ie £36,000
Month 3	x = 27 :	y = 4.8 + 1.2(27)	= 37.2 ie £37,200

CHAPTER 5 Standard costing

1   If ideal standards are used to calculate variances, then the result will be adverse variances. This will tend to mean that these adverse variances become the norm and are accepted without questioning. Ideal standards will also tend to be demotivating to managers and employees, as they cannot hope to meet the standards.

2   (a) Total materials cost variance   £

Standard cost for actual production

24,000 × 12 × £20.50   5,904,000

Actual cost   6,240,000

336,000 Adv

(b) Materials price variance

Actual quantity at standard price

312,000 × £20.50   6,396,000

Actual cost   6,240,000

156,000 Fav

(c) Materials usage variance

Standard quantity for actual production at standard price

24,000 × 12 × £20.50   5,904,000

Actual quantity at standard price

312,000 × £20.50   6,396,000

492,000 Adv

3

    (a)   Materials price variance £5,000 favourable

    (b)   Materials usage variance £2,000 adverse

Workings

    (a)

Actual quantity purchased at standard price	80,000
8,000kg × £10.00	
Actual quantity purchased at actual price	75,000
Materials price variance	5,000 Fav

    (b)

	£
Standard quantity for actual production at standard price	75,000
1,500 ×5 kg × £10.00	
Actual quantity used for actual production at standard price 7,700 kg × £10.00	77,000
Materials usage variance	2,000 Adv

4   (a)   Total direct labour cost variance

	£	
Standard cost for actual production		
12,000 × 4 × £6.50	312,000	
Actual cost	306,000	
	6,000 Fav	

    (b)   Labour rate variance

Actual hours at standard rate		
45,000 × £6.50	292,500	
Actual cost	306,000	
	13,500 Adv	

    (c)   Labour efficiency variance

Standard hours for actual production at standard rate		
12,000 × 4 × £6.50	312,000	
Actual hours at standard rate		
45,000 × £6.50	292,500	
	19,500 Fav	

5   (a)   Budgeted fixed overhead   =   2,400 units × 2 hours × £5.00

                                             =   £24,000

(b)   Total fixed overhead variance   £

Fixed overhead incurred   26,000

Fixed overhead absorbed

2,500 × 2 × £5.00   25,000

1,000 Adv

(c)   Fixed overhead expenditure variance

Budgeted fixed overhead   24,000

Actual fixed overhead   26,000

2,000 Adv

(d)   Fixed overhead volume variance

Actual production at standard absorption rate

2,500 × 2 hours × £5.00   25,000

Budgeted production at standard absorption rate

2,400 × 2 × £5.00   24,000

1,000 Fav

6   (a)   Budgeted direct labour hours   =   2,400 × 2

=   4,800 hours

(b)   Fixed overhead efficiency variance   £

Standard hours for actual production at standard absorption rate

2,500 × 2 × £5.00   25,000

Actual hours for actual production at standard absorption rate

5,500 × £5.00   27,500

2,500 Adv

(c)   Fixed overhead capacity variance

Actual hours at standard absorption rate

5,500 × £5.00   27,500

Budgeted hours at standard absorption rate

4,800 × £5.00   24,000

3,500 Fav

7   If the starting point for the reconciliation is the standard cost of the actual production and there is a favourable variance this means that the actual cost was less than the standard cost and therefore the favourable variance is deducted.

8   D

CHAPTER 6 Standard costing – further aspects

1   D

2   The favourable labour rate variance could be due to the manager responsible for hiring labour taking on a lower grade of worker, hence the lower rate of pay per hour.

The less skilled workers may have taken longer to do the job and been more inefficient in their usage of material, causing the adverse labour efficiency and materials usage variances.

An independent investigation would need to be carried out into the grade of labour hired and the normal hourly rate for such labour. Other independent factors that may have caused material wastage (e.g. poor quality material) or labour inefficiency (machine breakdowns) should also be investigated.

Note: since this is the first period for the new contract it is possible that the manager responsible for hiring workers has provided valid information and that the other variances are caused by the fact that the standards set were inaccurate or that there was some learning process involved

3   (a)   The total materials price variance was £3,080 adverse

(b)   The planning variance due to the price increase was £3,680 adverse

The control variance due to other factors was £600 favourable

Workings

Total materials price variance	£
Standard price of actual quantity	
4,600 kg × £8.20	37,720
Actual cost	40,800
	3,080 Adv
Planning variance due to the price increase	
Standard price of actual quantity	
4,600 kg × £8.20	37,720
Adjusted price for actual quantity	
4,600 kg × £9.00	41,400
	3,680 Adv

Control variance due to other causes   £

Adjusted price for actual quantity

4,600 kg × £9.00	41,400
Actual cost	40,800
	600 Fav

4   (a)   The total materials price variance was £7,700 adverse

      (b)   The planning variance due to the seasonal price change was £9,270 adverse

          The control variance due to other factors was £1,570 favourable

Workings

Total materials price variance   £

Standard price of actual quantity

10,300 kg × £6.00	61,800
Actual cost	69,500
	7,700 Adv

Planning variance due to seasonal price

Standard price of actual quantity

10,300 kg × £6.00	61,800

Adjusted price for actual quantity

10,300 kg × (£6.00 + £0.90)	71,070
	9,270 Adv

Control variance due to other factors

Adjusted price for actual quantity

10,300 kg × (£6.00 + £0.90)	71,070
Actual cost	69,500
	1,570 Fav

5   (a)   The total labour efficiency variance was £37,200 adverse

      (b)   The planning variance due to early production problems was £65,100 adverse

          The control variance due to other causes was £27,900 favourable

Workings

Total labour efficiency variance £

Standard hours for actual quantity at standard rate

    12,000 × 3.5 × £6.20   260,400

Actual hours at standard rate

    48,000 × £6.20   297,600

                                          37,200 Adv

Planning variance due to early production problems

Standard hours for actual quantity at standard rate

    12,000 × 3.5 × £6.20   260,400

Adjusted hours for actual quantity at standard rate

    12,000 × (3.5 × 1.25) × £6.20   325,500

                                          65,100 Adv

Control variance due to other causes £

Adjusted hours for actual quantity at standard rate

    12,000 × (3.5 × 1.25) × £6.20   325,500

Actual hours at standard rate

    48,000 × £6.20   297,600

                                          27,900 Fav

6   (a)   The total labour rate variance was £2,500 adverse

     (b)   The planning variance due to the labour rate increase was £13,125 adverse

         The control variance due to other causes was £10,625 favourable

Total labour rate variance £

Standard rate for actual hours

    21,000 × £7.50   157,500

Actual cost   160,000

                                          2,500 Adv

Planning variance due to rate increase

Standard rate for actual hours

21,000 × £7.50   157,500

Adjusted price for actual hours

21,000 × (£7.50 × 130/120)   <u>170,625</u>

       <u>13,125</u> Adv

Control variance due to other causes

Adjusted price for actual hours

21,000 × (£7.50 × 130/120)   170,625

Actual cost   <u>160,000</u>

       <u>10,625</u> Fav

CHAPTER 7 Performance indicators

1   Quarter 2   Quarter 1

Productivity

216/26   8.3 per executive

188/22   8.5 per executive

2   Activity ratio $= \dfrac{\text{Standard hours for actual production}}{\text{Budgeted hours}} \times 100$

$= \dfrac{268,000 \times 3}{288,000 \times 3} \times 100$

$=$ 93.1%

3   Possible effectiveness measures might include:

(i)   Booking system:

% of patients offered an appointment within a week

% of appointments cancelled

(ii)   Service:

% of patients seen on time

Average waiting times

% of patients requiring a second visit (measures effectiveness of treatment)

4   Gross profit margin $= \dfrac{£58,700}{£133,400} \times 100$

$= 44.0\%$

Operating profit $=$ Profit before interest and tax $= 22500 + 2500 + 4750$
$= 29750$

Operating profit margin $= \dfrac{£29,750}{£133,400} \times 100$

$= 22.3\%$

Net profit margin $= \dfrac{£22,500}{£133,400} \times 100$

$= 16.9\%$

5   ROCE $= \dfrac{£365,800}{£1,700,000 + £600,000} \times 100$ $= 15.9\%$ (Method 1)

or

ROCE $= \dfrac{£365,800 - 12\% \times (£600,000)}{£1,700,000} \times 100 = 17.3\%$ (Method 2)

6   Asset turnover $= \dfrac{£420,000}{£350,000}$

$= 1.20$

7   Average inventory (stock) $= \dfrac{£13,500 + £17,000}{2}$

$= £15,250$

Cost of sales $= £13,500 + 99,000 - 17,000$

$= £95,500$

Inventory turnover $= \dfrac{£15,250}{£95,500} \times 365$

$= 58$ days

8   Possible reasons for a decrease in gross profit margin include:

- decrease in selling price
- increase in purchases or production costs
- large write off of inventories

CHAPTER 8 Cost management

1

   (a) improvements in product design or specification to reduce defective products = prevention cost

   (b) loss of future custom from dissatisfied customers = external failure cost

   (c) lost contribution on defective units scrapped or sold at a lower price than normal = internal failure cost

   (d) sample testing finished production = appraisal cost

2

Cost of quality	Effect
Prevention costs	Increase as product design must be modified to eliminate the problem in future
Appraisal costs	There may be none, although could increase if this product line has to be more closely monitored in future
Internal costs	Increase due to investigation of problem, review of product design, repairs and re-inspection
External costs	Increase due to cost of repairs, any claims relating to the failure and loss of customer goodwill

3   Explicit quality costs

- costs of quality inspections
- costs of repairs to faulty products returned
- costs of replacing faulty products
- costs of design review to ensure quality

Implicit quality costs –

- loss of customer goodwill
- disruption of production process due to repairs/reworking
- potential claims from customers

(Note: Only two examples of each were required)

	£
4	
Inspection costs – Appraisal cost	20,000
Lost contribution on seconds – Internal failure cost	
3,000 units × (£25 – £12)	39,000
Total quality cost	59,000

5   Quality performance indicators for a taxi firm:

- percentage of taxis arriving on time compared to total taxi journeys
- percentage of repeat customers compared to total customers
- survey results of customer satisfaction
- number of customer complaints

6   The target cost is £25,714

Working

Profit required = 8% × £27,950 = £2,236

Target cost = £ 27,950 - £2,236 = £25,714

TEST YOUR LEARNING
– ANSWERS

CHAPTER 1   Costs

1

True ✓

False ☐

10,000 units	Cost per unit £43,600/10,000	=	£4.36
12,000 units	Cost per unit £52,320/12,000	=	£4.36

As the cost per unit is the same at each level of production this would appear to be a purely variable cost.

2

Activity level	Total fixed cost £	Fixed cost per unit £
3,000 units	64,000	21.33
10,000 units	64,000	6.40
16,000 units	64,000	4.00

Working

3,000 units   £64,000/3,000 = £21.33

10,000 units   £64,000/10,000 = £6.40

16,000 units   £64,000/16,000 = £4.00

3   (a)   The variable element of the production cost is

> £3 per unit

The fixed element of the production cost is

> £169,000

(b)

Level of production	Production cost £
120,000 units	529,000
150,000 units	619,000

Workings

(a)

		£
Highest level	126,000	547,000
Lowest level	101,000	472,000
Increase	25,000	75,000

$$\text{Variable rate} - \frac{£75,000}{25,000} = £3 \text{ per unit}$$

Using highest level:

	£
Variable cost 126,000 × £3	378,000
Fixed costs (balancing figure)	169,000
Total cost	547,000

(b)   (i)   120,000 units

	£
Variable cost 120,000 × £3	360,000
Fixed cost	169,000
Total forecast cost	529,000

(ii)   150,000 units

	£
Variable cost 150,000 × £3	450,000
Fixed cost	169,000
Total forecast cost	619,000

(c) The estimate of costs for 120,000 units is likely to be more accurate than that for 150,000 units. This is due to the fact that 120,000 is within the range of activity levels used to calculate the variable costs and fixed costs (interpolation) whereas 150,000 units is outside that range (extrapolation). We cannot be sure that the costs will still behave in the same manner at an activity level of 150,000 units.

CHAPTER 2   Methods of costing

1   (a) B

    (b) C

Workings

$$\text{Department P1} = \frac{£50,000}{2,500 \text{ h}}$$

$$= £20 \text{ per direct labour hour}$$

$$\text{Department P2} = \frac{£60,000}{4,000 \text{ h}}$$

$$= £15 \text{ per machine hour}$$

2

	Amount of under/over absorption £	Under or over absorption	Add or subtract in income statement (P&L a/c)
An overhead absorption rate of £3 per unit, based on expected production levels of 500 units. Actual overheads turn out to be £1,600, and actual production is 650 units.	350.00	Over	Add
The budget is set at 1,000 units, with £9,000 overheads recovered on the basis of 600 direct labour hours. At the end of the period, overheads amounted to £8,600, production achieved was only 950 units and 590 direct labour hours had been worked.	250.00	Over	Add

Workings

(a)

	£
Actual overheads	1,600
Absorbed overheads (650 units @ £3 per unit)	1,950
Over absorption	350

The over absorption of £350 would be added to profit (a credit) in the income statement (profit and loss account).

(b)

	£
Actual overheads	8,600
Absorbed overheads (590h × £15* per h)	8,850
Over absorption	250

$$* \text{ Overhead absorption rate} = \frac{£9,000}{600 \text{ direct labour hours}} = £15 \text{ per direct labour hour}$$

The over absorption of £250 would be added to profit (a credit) in the income statement (profit and loss account).

3   In an absorption costing system all fixed production overheads are absorbed into the cost of the products and are included in unit cost. In a marginal costing system the fixed production overheads are written off in the income statement (profit and loss account) as a period cost.

4

Method of costing	Budgeted cost £
Absorption costing	59.70
Marginal costing	57.11

Workings

Absorption costing – unit cost

	£
Direct materials	12.50
Direct labour assembly (4 × £8.40)	33.60
finishing	6.60
Assembly overheads (£336,000/60,000)	5.60
Finishing overheads (£84,000/60,000)	1.40
	59.70

Marginal costing – unit cost

		£
Direct materials		12.50
Direct labour assembly (4 × £8.40)		33.60
finishing		6.60
Assembly overheads	$\dfrac{£336,000 \times 60\%}{60,000}$	3.36
Finishing overheads	$\dfrac{£84,000 \times 75\%}{60,000}$	1.05
		57.11

5   Unit cost

	£
Direct materials	12.00
Direct labour	8.00
Variable overhead (£237,000/15,000)	15.80
Marginal costing unit cost	35.80
Fixed overhead (£390,000/15,000)	26.00
Absorption costing unit cost	61.80

(a) (i) Absorption costing – income statement (profit and loss account)

	November		December	
	£	£	£	£
Sales (12,500/18,000 × £75)		937,500		1,350,000
Less: cost of sales				
Opening inventory (stock)				
(2,000 × £61.80)	123,600			
(4,500 × £61.80)			278,100	
Production costs				
(15,000 × £61.80)	927,000		927,000	
	1,050,600		1,205,100	
Less: closing inventory (stock)				
(4,500 × £61.80)	278,100			
(1,500 × £61.80)			92,700	
		772,500		1,112,400
Profit		165,000		237,600

(ii)   Marginal costing – income statement (profit and loss account)

	November		December	
	£	£	£	£
Sales		937,500		1,350,000
(12,500/18,000 × £75)				
Less: cost of sales				
Opening inventory (stock)				
(2,000 × £35.80)	71,600			
(4,500 × £35.80)			161,100	
Production costs				
(15,000 × £35.80)	537,000		537,000	
	608,600		698,100	
Less: closing inventory (stock)				
(4,500 × £35.80)	161,100			
(1,500 × £35.80)			53,700	
		447,500		644,400
Contribution		490,000		705,600
Less: fixed overheads		390,000		390,000
Profit		100,000		315,600

(b)

	November	**December**
	£	£
Absorption costing profit	165,000	237,600
Inventory (stock) changes	(65,000)	78,000
Marginal costing profit	100,000	315,600

Working

	November	December
	£	£
Increase in inventory (stock) × fixed cost per unit		
((4,500 – 2,000) × £26)	(65,000)	
Decrease in inventory (stock) × fixed cost per unit		
((4,500 – 1,500) × £26)		78,000

6

Product	Budgeted cost per unit £	Budgeted overhead per unit £
LM	9.78	3.68
NP	27.41	20.81

Workings

Stores cost = $\dfrac{£140,000}{320}$

= £437.50 per material requisition

Production set-up costs = $\dfrac{£280,000}{280}$

= £1,000 per set up

Quality control costs = $\dfrac{£180,000}{90}$

= £2,000 per inspection

Product costs		*LM*	*NP*
		£	£
Direct materials	50,000 × £2.60	130,000	
	20,000 × £3.90		78,000
Direct labour	50,000 × £3.50	175,000	
	20,000 × £2.70		54,000
Stores costs	100 × £437.50	43,750	
	220 × £437.50		96,250
Production set-up costs	80 × £1,000	80,000	
	200 × £1,000		200,000
Quality control costs	30 × £2,000	60,000	
	60 × £2,000		120,000
Total cost		488,750	548,250
Cost per unit		488,750	548,250
		50,000	20,000
		= £9.78	= £27.41

Analysis of total unit cost

Direct costs	(2.60 + 3.50)	6.10	
	(3.90 + 2.70)		6.60
Overheads	$\dfrac{(43,750 + 80,000 + 60,000)}{50,000}$	3.68	
	$\dfrac{(96,250 + 200,000 + 120,000)}{20,000}$		20.81
		9.78	27.41

CHAPTER 3   Decision making

1   As activity levels increase, the total fixed costs will be split amongst more units, and the amount of fixed costs absorbed into the cost of a unit will get smaller. With no change in selling cost or variable cost, the total unit cost will decrease.

2   The break-even point is 30,000 units

The margin of safety is 21%

Workings

Break-even point	$=$	$\dfrac{£360,000}{£57-£45}$
	$=$	30,000 units

Margin of safety	$=$	$\dfrac{38,000-30,000}{38,000}$
	$=$	21%

3   D

Target profit sales	$=$	$\dfrac{£910,000+£500,000}{£24-£17}$
	$=$	201,429 units

4   The sales revenue required in order to make a profit of £200,000 is £1,500,000

Profit volume ratio	$=$	$\dfrac{£(40-32)}{£40}\times100$
	$=$	20%

Target profit sales revenue	$=$	$\dfrac{£100,000+£200,000}{0.20}$
	$=$	£1,500,000

Alternatively: Units required to make £200,000 profit = £300,000/8 = 37,500 units

Total revenue required = 37,500 x £40 = £1,500,000

5 (a) The limiting factor of production resources is materials/labour hours/**machine hours**?

Working

Resource requirements for maximum demand

	R	S	T	Total
Materials	80,000 kg	120,000 kg	25,000 kg	225,000 kg
Labour hours	20,000 hours	80,000 hours	5,000 hours	105,000 hours
Machine hours	60,000 hours	80,000 hours	15,000 hours	155,000 hours

Therefore the machine hours available are the limiting factor.

(b)

Product	Units produced
S	20,000
T	5,000
R	4,166

Workings

Contribution per machine hour

	R	S	T
Contribution	£6	£12	£6
Machine hours	6	4	3
Contribution/machine hour	£1.00	£3.00	£2.00
Ranking	3	1	2

Production plan

Product	Units produced	Machine hours used
S	20,000	80,000
T	5,000	15,000
R (balance 25,000 / 6 = 4166.67 = 4166 complete units))	4,166	24,996
		119,996

(c)   The profit that will be earned under this production plan is £244,996

Workings

Product contribution:	£
R (4,166 × £6)	24,996
S (20,000 × £12)	240,000
T (5,000 × £6)	30,000
Total Contribution	294,996
Less: fixed costs	50,000
Profit	244,996

6

Year	Cash flows £	Discount factor at 7%	Present value £
0	(340,000)	1.000	(340,000)
1	80,000	0.9346	74,768
2	70,000	0.8734	61,138
3	90,000	0.8163	73,467
4	120,000	0.7629	91,548
5	60,000	0.7130	42,780
Net present value			**3,701**

Remember that depreciation is not a cash flow and is therefore excluded from the net present value calculations.

7

(a)

Year	Cash flows £	Discount factor at 11%	Present value £
0	(90,000)	1.000	(90,000)
1	23,000	0.9009	20,721
2	31,000	0.8116	25,160
3	40,000	0.7312	29,248
4	18,000	0.6587	11,857
Net present value			(3,014)

(b) As the investment in the new plant and machinery has a negative net present value at the cost of capital of 11%, then the investment should not take place.

CHAPTER 4 Statistical methods

1

	Actual £	Three month moving average £
July	397,500	
August	403,800	400,300
September	399,600	402,900
October	405,300	403,667
November	406,100	406,633
December	408,500	407,500
January	407,900	408,933
February	410,400	411,433
March	416,000	413,167
April	413,100	415,533
May	417,500	417,467
June	421,800	

2

		Actual	Four quarter moving average	Centred moving average – TREND	Seasonal variations
		£	£	£	£
20X5	Quarter 1	383,600			
	Quarter 2	387,600			
			365,400		
	Quarter 3	361,800		365,688	-3,888
			365,975		
	Quarter 4	328,600		366,575	-37,975
			367,175		
20X6	Quarter 1	385,900		366,013	+19,887
			364,850		
	Quarter 2	392,400		366,125	+26,275
			367,400		
	Quarter 3	352,500		368,225	-15,725
			369,050		
	Quarter 4	338,800		371,288	-32,488
			373,525		
20X7	Quarter 1	392,500		375,575	+16,925
			377,625		
	Quarter 2	410,300		378,325	I 31,975
			379,025		
	Quarter 3	368,900		379,750	-10,850
			380,475		
	Quarter 4	344,400		382,388	-37,988
			384,300		
20X8	Quarter 1	398,300			
	Quarter 2	425,600			

Working

Seasonal variations:

	Quarter 1	Quarter 2	Quarter 3	Quarter 4
	£	£	£	£
20X5	–	–	–3,888	–37,975
20X6	+19,887	+26,275	–15,725	–32,488
20X7	+16,925	+31,975	–10,850	–37,988
	+36,812	+58,250	–30,463	–108,451
Average	+ 18,406	+ 29,125	–10,154	–36,150

Total of seasonal variations 18,406 + 29,125 – 10,154 – 36,152 = 1,227

Adjustment required   = 1,227/4

                                            =   307

	Quarter 1	Quarter 2	Quarter 3	Quarter 4
	£	£	£	£
Unadjusted	+18,406	+29,125	–10,154	–36,150
Adjustment	–307	–307	–306	–307
Seasonal variation	+18,099	+28,818	–10,460	–36,457

3

	Cost	Index
	£	
January	59,700	100.0
February	62,300	104.4
March	56,900	95.3
April	60,400	101.2
May	62,400	104.5
June	66,700	111.7

4   (a)

	Wages cost	RPI	Adjusted cost
	£		£
January	126,700	171.1	126,848
February	129,700	172.0	129,172
March	130,400	172.2	129,718
April	131,600	173.0	130,307
May	130,500	172.1	129,893
June	131,600	171.3	131,600

Workings

(a)

	Wages cost	Adjusted cost
	£	£
January	126,700 × 171.3/171.1	126,848
February	129,700 × 171.3/172.0	129,172
March	130,400 × 171.3/172.2	129,718
April	131,600 × 171.3/173.0	130,307
May	130,500 × 171.3/172.1	129,893
June	131,600 × 171.3/171.3	131,600

(b)

	Adjusted cost	Index
	£	
January	126,848	100.0
February	129,172	101.8
March	129,718	102.3
April	130,307	102.7
May	129,893	102.4
June	131,600	103.7

5

	Production	Costs
	Units	£
January	5,400	17,320
February	5,600	17,480
March	5,700	17,560
April	6,000	17,800
May	5,500	17,400
June	6,100	17,880

Workings

Stores costs:

January	13,000 + (0.8 × 5,400)	17,320
February	13,000 + (0.8 × 5,600)	17,480
March	13,000 + (0.8 × 5,700)	17,560
April	13,000 + (0.8 × 6,000)	17,800
May	13,000 + (0.8 × 5,500)	17,400
June	13,000 + (0.8 × 6,100)	17,880

6

	Value of x	Trend	Seasonal variation	Forecast sales
Quarter 1 20X9	13	2,785	− 200	2,585
Quarter 2 20X9	14	2,830	+ 500	3,330
Quarter 3 20X9	15	2,875	+ 350	3,225
Quarter 4 20X9	16	2,920	− 650	2,270

Workings

Value of x for quarter 1, 20X9

Quarter 1 20X6	=	1
Add: 3 years of 4 quarters	=	$\frac{12}{13}$

Trend for quarter 1, 20X9

$2,200 + (45 \times 13) = 2,785$

CHAPTER 5   Standard costing

1   The information for the amount of labour time for each cost unit would come from payroll records such as time sheets or from physical observations such as time and motion studies. Factors that should be taken into account include:

- the level of skill or training of the labour grade to be used on the product
- any anticipated changes on the grade of labour used on the product
- any anticipated changes in work methods or productivity levels
- the effect of any bonus scheme on productivity

The hourly rate for the direct labour can be found from payroll records but the following factors should be considered:

- anticipated pay rises
- anticipated changes in grade of labour
- effect of any bonus scheme on the labour rate
- whether any anticipated overtime is built into the hourly rate.

2   Ideal standards are set on the basis of perfect working conditions. No allowance is made for normal wastage or inefficiencies. Attainable standards are standards that are set on the basis of normal working conditions by building in some element to reflect normal wastage or inefficiencies. Attainable standards are capable of being met by efficiency operations. Basic standards are the original historical standards based upon the original expectations of cost for the product.

3   (a)   Total materials cost variance

	£
Standard cost of actual production	
1,800 × 7 kg × £6.00	75,600
Actual cost	70,800
	4,800 Fav

(b)   Materials price variance

	£
Actual usage at standard price	
12,000 × £6.00	72,000
Actual cost	70,800
	1,200 Fav

(c)   Materials usage variance

Standard usage for actual production at standard cost

1,800 × 7 kg × £6.00	75,600
Actual usage at standard cost	
12,000 × £6.00	72,000
	3,600 Fav

4   (a)   Total labour cost variance   £

Standard cost of actual production

15,400 × 2.5 hours × £6.80	261,800
Actual cost	265,200
	3,400 Adv

(b)   Labour rate variance

Actual hours at standard rate

41,000 × £6.80	278,800
Actual hours at actual rate	265,200
	13,600 Fav

(c)   Labour efficiency variance

Standard hours for actual production at standard rate

15,400 × 2.5 × £6.80	261,800
Actual hours at standard rate	
41,000 × £6.80	278,800
	17,000 Adv

5   (a)   Budgeted fixed overhead   =   7,000 units × 3 hours × £2.50

                                          =   £52,500

(b)   Fixed overhead expenditure variance   £

Budgeted fixed overhead	52,500
Actual fixed overhead	56,000
	3,500 Adv

(c)   Fixed overhead volume variance

Actual product at standard absorption rate

6,400 units × 3 hours × £2.50	48,000

Budgeted production at standard absorption rate

7,000 units × 3 hours × £2.50	52,500
	4,500 Adv

(d)   Fixed overhead efficiency variance

Standard hours for actual production at standard absorption rate

6,400 units × 3 × £2.50	48,000

Actual hours at standard absorption rate

20,000 × £2.50	50,000
	2,000 Adv

(e)   Fixed overhead capacity variance

Actual hours at standard absorption rate

20,000 × £2.50	50,000

Budgeted hours at standard absorption rate

7,000 × 3 × £2.50	52,500
	2,500 Adv

6   (a)   Materials price variance   £

Actual quantity at standard price

7,500 × £3.60	27,000
Actual cost	25,900
	1,100 Fav

Materials usage variance

	£
Standard usage for actual production at standard price	
1,750 × 4.2 × £3.60	26,460
Actual usage at standard price	
7,500 × £3.60	27,000
	540 Adv

(b) Labour rate variance

Actual hours at standard rate	
2,580 × £7.80	20,124
Actual cost	20,600
	476 Adv

Labour efficiency variance

Standard hours for actual production at standard rate	
1,750 × 1.5 × £7.80	20,475
Actual hours at standard rate	
2,580 × £7.80	20,124
	351 Fav

(c) Fixed overhead expenditure variance

Actual fixed overhead	8,100
Budgeted fixed overhead	
1,800 × 1.5 × £2.80	7,560
	540 Adv

Fixed overhead efficiency variance

Standard hours for actual production at standard absorption rate	
1,750 × 1.5 × £2.80	7,350
Actual hours at standard absorption rate	
2,580 × £2.80	7,224
	126 Fav

Fixed overhead capacity variance

	£
Actual hours at standard absorption rate	
2,580 × £2.80	7,224
Budgeted hours at standard absorption rate	
1,800 × 1.5 × £2.80	7,560
	336 Adv

(d) Standard cost of actual production

Direct materials 1,750 × 4.2 × £3.60	26,460
Direct labour 1,750 × 1.5 × £7.80	20,475
Fixed overhead 1,750 × 1.5 × £2.80	7,350
Total cost 1,750 × £31.02	54,285

Reconciliation statement

	Adverse variances	Favourable variances	
	£	£	
Standard cost of production			54,285
Variances :			
Materials price		1,100	
Materials usage	540		
Labour rate	476		
Labour efficiency		351	
Fixed overhead expenditure	540		
Fixed overhead efficiency		126	
Fixed overhead capacity	336		
	1,892	1,577	
Add: adverse variances			1,892
Less: favourable variances			(1,577)
Actual cost of production			54,600

7 (a) Total direct materials cost variance £

Standard cost of actual production

2,400 × 12 × £4.80   138,240

Actual cost   145,000

      6,760 Adv

Materials price variance

Actual quantity at standard price

29,600 × £4.80   142,080

Actual cost   145,000

      2,920 Adv

Materials usage variance

Standard quantity for actual production at standard price

2,400 × 12 × £4.80   138,240

Actual quantity at standard price

29,600 × £4.80   142,080

      3,840 Adv

(b) Total direct labour variance

Standard cost of actual production

2,400 × 3 × £8.00   57,600

Actual cost   56,200

      1,400 Fav

Labour rate variance

Actual hours at standard rate

6,900 × £8.00   55,200

Actual cost   56,200

      1,000 Adv

Labour efficiency variance

Standard hours for actual production at standard rate

2,400 × 3 × £8.00	57,600

Actual hours at standard rate

6,900 × £8.00	55,200
	2,400 Fav

(c) Fixed overhead expenditure variance

Actual fixed overhead	92,000
Budgeted fixed overhead	95,000
	3,000 Fav

(d) Standard cost of production

	£
Direct materials 2,400 × 12 × £4.80	138,240
Direct labour 2,400 × 3 × £8.00	57,600
Variable cost (2400 x 81.60)	195,840
Fixed overheads	95,000
Total standard cost	290,840

	Adverse variances	Favourable variances	
	£	£	£
Standard cost of actual production			290,840
Variances			
Materials price	2,920		
Materials usage	3,840		
Labour rate	1,000		
Labour efficiency		2,400	
Fixed overhead expenditure	____	3,000	
	7,760	5,400	
Add adverse variances			7,760
Less: favourable variances			(5,400)
Total actual cost			**293,200**

8   Material usage variance, variable overhead efficiency variance and idle time variance. The material price variance is recorded in the stores control account. The labour rate variance is recorded in the wages control account. The sales variances do not appear in the books of account.

CHAPTER 6   Standard costing – further aspects

1   **REPORT**

To: Managing Director

From: Accountant

Date: xx.xx.xx

Subject: November production cost variances

The November production cost is 5% more than the standard cost for the actual production, due to a number of fairly significant adverse variances.

The main cause appears to have been the labour that was used in production for the month which was a more junior grade than normal due to staff shortages. Although this has given a favourable labour rate variance, it has also caused adverse labour efficiency and materials usage variances due to inefficiencies and wastage from the staff. This inefficiency in labour hours has also led to the fixed overhead efficiency adverse variance.

For future months we should either ensure that we have enough of the normal grade of labour for production of this product or train the junior staff in the production process.

There is also an adverse materials price variance which has been due to an increase in the price of our materials. As it is believed that this is a permanent price increase by all suppliers, we should consider altering the direct materials standard cost to reflect this, otherwise each month we will have adverse materials price variances.

The factory now has an additional rent cost which has presumably caused the adverse fixed overhead expenditure variance. If the additional inventory requirement and hence the additional rent is a permanent change then this should be built into the budgeted fixed overhead figure.

Due to the labour inefficiency, more hours have been worked than were budgeted for, leading to the favourable capacity variance. This indicates that the factory has more capacity than we have been making use of which, if the inefficiencies are sorted out, could be used to increase monthly production if required.

2   (a)   The total materials price variance was £4,900 adverse

(b)   The planning variance due to the price increase was £5,600 adverse

The control variance due to other factors was £700 favourable

Workings

Total materials price variance

	£
Standard price for actual quantity used	
14,000 × £2.40	33,600
Actual cost	38,500
	4,900 Adv

Planning variance due to price increase

Standard price of actual quantity used	
14,000 × £2.40	33,600
Adjusted price for actual quantity	
14,000 × £2.80	39,200
	5,600 Adv

Control variance due to other causes

Adjusted price for actual quantity

14,000 × £2.80	39,200
Actual cost	38,500
	700 Fav

3   (a) The total materials price variance is £3,200 favourable

(b) The planning variance due to the seasonal variation is £4,920 favourable

The control variance due to other factors is £1,720 adverse

Workings

Total materials price variance

	£
Standard price for actual quantity used	
12,300 × £8.00	98,400
Actual cost	95,200
	3,200 Fav

Planning variance due to seasonal variation

Standard price for actual quantity used	
12,300 × £8.00	98,400
Adjusted price for actual quantity	
12,300 × (£8.00 - £0.40)	93,480
	4,920 Fav

Control variance due to other factors

	£
Adjusted price for actual quantity	
12,300 × (£8.00 - £0.40)	93,480
Actual cost	95,200
	1,720 Adv

4   (a)   The total labour efficiency variance was £36,720 adverse

(b)   The planning variance due to the learning process was £32,640 adverse

The control variance due to other factors was £4,080 adverse

Workings

Total labour efficiency variance

	£
Standard hours for actual production at standard rate	
2,400 × 9 × £6.80	146,880
Actual hours at standard rate	
27,000 × £6.80	183,600
	36,720 Adv

Planning variance due to learning process

	£
Standard hours for actual production at standard rate	
2,400 × 9 × £6.80	146,880
Adjusted hours for actual production at standard rate	
2,400 × 11 × £6.80	179,520
	32,640 Adv

Control variance due to other causes

Adjusted hours for actual production at standard cost	
2,400 × 11 × £6.80	179,520
Actual hours at standard cost	183,600
	4,080 Adv

5 (a) The total materials price variance was £20,000 adverse

(b) The planning variance due to price changes was £40,000 adverse

The control variance due to other factors was £20,000 favourable

Workings

Total materials price variance

	£
Standard price for actual quantity used	
100,000 × £6.50	650,000
Actual cost	670,000
	20,000 Adv

Planning variance due to price change

Standard price for actual quantity used

    100,000 × £6.50   650,000

Adjusted price for actual quantity

    100,000 × (£6.50 × 138/130)   690,000

                                           40,000 Adv

Control variance due to other causes

Adjusted price for actual quantity

    100,000 × (£6.50 × 138/130)   690,000

Actual cost   670,000

                                           20,000 Fav

CHAPTER 7 Performance indicators

1

	Aug	Sept	Oct	Nov
Productivity per labour hour	10.5 units	10.2 units	9.8 units	10.1 units
Efficiency ratio	105.4%	102.2%	98.2%	101.0%
Capacity ratio	97.6%	96.5%	102.7%	98.5%
Activity ratio	102.9%	98.6%	100.9%	99.5%

Workings

		August	September	October	November
(a)	Productivity per labour hour	$\dfrac{257,300}{24,400}$	$\dfrac{251,400}{24,600}$	$\dfrac{262,300}{26,700}$	$\dfrac{258,600}{25,600}$
		= 10.5 units	= 10.2 units	= 9.8 units	= 10.1 units
(b)	Standard hours for actual	$\dfrac{257,300}{10}$	$\dfrac{251,400}{10}$	$\dfrac{262,300}{10}$	$\dfrac{258,600}{10}$
		= 25,730	= 25,140	= 26,230	= 25,860
	Efficiency ratio	$\dfrac{25,730}{24,440} \times 100$	$\dfrac{25,140}{24,600} \times 100$	$\dfrac{26,230}{26,700} \times 100$	$\dfrac{25,860}{25,600} \times 100$
		= 105.4%	= 102.2%	= 98.2%	= 101.0%

(c) Budgeted hours

$$\frac{250,000}{10} \qquad \frac{255,000}{10} \qquad \frac{260,000}{10} \qquad \frac{260,000}{10}$$

$$= 25,000 \qquad = 25,500 \qquad = 26,000 \qquad = 26,000$$

Capacity ratio

$$\frac{24,400}{25,000} \times 100 \qquad \frac{24,600}{25,500} \times 100 \qquad \frac{26,700}{26,000} \times 100 \qquad \frac{25,600}{26,000} \times 100$$

$$= 97.6\% \qquad = 96.5\% \qquad = 102.7\% \qquad = 98.5\%$$

(d) Activity ratio

$$\frac{25,730}{25,000} \times 100 \qquad \frac{25,140}{25,500} \times 100 \qquad \frac{26,230}{26,000} \times 100 \qquad \frac{25,860}{26,000} \times 100$$

$$= 102.9\% \qquad = 98.6\% \qquad = 100.9\% \qquad = 99.5\%$$

2

	April	May	June	Total
Productivity per labour hour	10.9 units	10.7 units	11.1 units	10.9 units
Efficiency ratio	98.8%	97.6%	101.2%	99.2%
Capacity ratio	102.7%	101.2%	101.2%	101.7%
Activity ratio	101.4%	98.8%	102.4%	100.9%
Value added per employee	£2,552	£2,524	£2,717	£2,598

Workings

(a)

		April	May	June	Total

(i) Productivity per labour hour

$$\frac{121,700}{11,200} \qquad \frac{123,500}{11,500} \qquad \frac{128,000}{11,500} \qquad \frac{373,200}{34,200}$$

$$= 10.9 \text{ units} \quad = 10.7 \text{ units} \quad = 11.1 \text{ units} \quad = 10.9 \text{ units}$$

(ii) Standard hours for actual production

$$\frac{121,700}{11} \qquad \frac{123,500}{11} \qquad \frac{128,000}{11} \qquad \frac{373,200}{11}$$

$$= 11,064 \qquad = 11,227 \qquad = 11,636 \qquad = 33,927$$

Efficiency ratio

$$\frac{11,064}{11,200} \times 100 \qquad \frac{11,227}{11,500} \times 100 \qquad \frac{11,636}{11,500} \times 100 \qquad \frac{33,927}{34,200} \times 100$$

$$= 98.8\% \qquad = 97.6\% \qquad = 101.2\% \qquad = 99.2\%$$

(iii) Budgeted hours

$\dfrac{120{,}000}{11}$	$\dfrac{125{,}000}{11}$	$\dfrac{125{,}000}{11}$	$\dfrac{370{,}000}{11}$
$= 10{,}909$	$= 11{,}364$	$= 11{,}363$	$= 33{,}636$

Capacity ratio

$\dfrac{11{,}200}{10{,}909} \times 100$	$\dfrac{11{,}500}{11{,}364} \times 100$	$\dfrac{11{,}500}{11{,}363} \times 100$	$\dfrac{34{,}200}{33{,}636} \times 100$
$= 102.7\%$	$= 101.2\%$	$= 101.2\%$	$= 101.7\%$

(iv) Activity ratio

$\dfrac{11{,}064}{10{,}909} \times 100$	$\dfrac{11{,}227}{11{,}364} \times 100$	$\dfrac{11{,}636}{11{,}363} \times 100$	$\dfrac{33{,}927}{33{,}636} \times 100$
$= 101.4\%$	$= 98.8\%$	$= 102.4\%$	$= 100.9\%$

(v) Value added

£625,000 – £418,300	£206,700		
£634,000 – £424,500		£209,500	
£656,000 – £430,500			£225,500	£641,700

Value added per employee

$\dfrac{206{,}700}{81}$	$\dfrac{209{,}500}{83}$	$\dfrac{225{,}500}{83}$	$\dfrac{641{,}700}{247}$
$= £2{,}552$	$= £2{,}524$	$= £2{,}717$	$= £2{,}598$

The value added per employee for the total three months could also have been calculated as the value added over the three month period divided by the 82 employees, the average for the three months, giving £641,700/82 = £7,826.

(b) £2,767.50

Hours at increased productivity level	=	$\dfrac{128{,}000 \text{ units}}{11.5}$
	=	11,131 hours
June hours		11,500
Saving in hours		369

Cost saving 369 @ £7.50 = £2,767.50

3

	July – Sept	Oct – Dec	Jan – Mar	Apr – June	
Productivity	1,240	820	1,540	1,180	
Cost per holiday	£18.26	£28.15	£16.30	£20.41	

Workings

(a)

		July – Sept	Oct – Dec	Jan – Mar	Apr – June
(i)	Productivity	$\dfrac{6,200}{5}$	$\dfrac{4,100}{5}$	$\dfrac{7,700}{5}$	$\dfrac{5,900}{5}$
		= 1,240	= 820	= 1,540	= 1,180
(ii)	Cost per holiday	$\dfrac{113,200}{6,200}$	$\dfrac{115,400}{4,100}$	$\dfrac{125,500}{7,700}$	$\dfrac{120,400}{5,900}$
		= £18.26	= £28.15	= £16.30	= £20.41

(b) The cost per holiday booking fluctuates from £16.30 to £28.15 depending upon the quarter in question. This is due to the fact that the large majority of the costs appear to be fixed costs with similar total costs each quarter. However, as the output (the holiday bookings) change, these fixed costs will remain the same and will simply be spread over more or fewer holiday bookings depending upon the quarter. For example in October to December the costs are similar to those of the other quarters but they are only being spread over 4,100 holiday bookings.

4

	Jan	Feb	Mar	April	May	June
Gross profit margin	47.5%	43.8%	42.2%	37.3%	39.3%	38.9%
Net profit margin	12.5%	13.8%	10.9%	10.6%	11.3%	10.7%
% expenses to turnover	35.0%	30.0%	31.3%	26.7%	28.0%	28.1%
Return on capital employed	20.8%	22.8%	15.4%	15.3%	15.5%	13.4%
Asset turnover	1.67	1.66	1.41	1.30	1.26	1.14

Workings

		Jan	Feb	Mar	Apr	May	June
(a)	Gross profit margin	$\dfrac{190}{400}$	$\dfrac{210}{480}$	$\dfrac{190}{450}$	$\dfrac{190}{510}$	$\dfrac{220}{560}$	$\dfrac{210}{540}$
		47.5%	43.8%	42.2%	37.3%	39.3%	38.9%
(b)	Operating profit margin	$\dfrac{50}{400}$	$\dfrac{66}{480}$	$\dfrac{49}{450}$	$\dfrac{54}{510}$	$\dfrac{63}{560}$	$\dfrac{58}{540}$
		12.5%	13.8%	10.9%	10.6%	11.3%	10.7%
(c)	Expenses to turnover	$\dfrac{140}{400}$	$\dfrac{144}{480}$	$\dfrac{141}{450}$	$\dfrac{136}{510}$	$\dfrac{157}{560}$	$\dfrac{152}{540}$
		35.0%	30.0%	31.3%	26.7%	28.0%	28.1%
(d)	Return on capital employed	$\dfrac{50}{240}$	$\dfrac{66}{290}$	$\dfrac{49}{319}$	$\dfrac{54}{393}$	$\dfrac{63}{446}$	$\dfrac{54}{474}$
		20.8%	22.8%	15.4%	13.7%	14.1%	12.2%
(e)	Asset turnover	$\dfrac{400}{240}$	$\dfrac{480}{290}$	$\dfrac{450}{319}$	$\dfrac{510}{393}$	$\dfrac{560}{446}$	$\dfrac{540}{474}$
		1.67	1.66	1.41	1.30	1.26	1.14

There has been a rapid rise in revenue of 35% over the six-month period which has been partly funded by additional loan capital in April. This increase in revenue however has not yet been matched by increases in profits.

The gross profit margin has reduced over the period and at its lowest was almost 10% below the margin for January. The operating profit margin has been steadily decreasing but not as dramatically as the gross profit margin due to the fact that expenses appear to be being well controlled. The decrease in the expenses to sales percentage indicates that many of the expenses are fixed and are therefore not rising in line with the increase in turnover.

Return on capital employed has also declined over the period partly due to the decrease in operating profit margin but also due to a significantly worsening asset turnover. This may be due to the fact that the new assets that have been funded by the loan have not yet become fully functional and we will see an improvement in asset turnover when the benefit of these new assets starts to be seen.

5

	20X6	20X7	20X8
Gross profit margin	46.3%	47.6%	44.4%
Operating profit margin	11.0%	11.8%	9.4%
Return on capital employed	18.0%	16.4%	12.7%
Asset turnover	1.64	1.39	1.34
Non-current (fixed) asset turnover	2.13	1.88	1.81
Current ratio	4.8:1	5.6:1	5.2:1
Quick ratio	3.2: 1	4.0:1	3.6:1
Receivables' (debtors') collection period	38 days	48 days	52 days
Inventory (stock) days	41 days	45 days	49 days
Payables' (creditors') payment period	25 days	28 days	30 days
Interest cover	N/a	33.3	28.3
Gearing ratio	N/a	8.9%	8.1%

Workings

		20X6	20X7	20X8
(a)	Gross profit margin	$\frac{380}{820} \times 100$	$\frac{405}{850} \times 100$	$\frac{400}{900} \times 100$
		46.3%	47.6%	44.4%
(b)	Operating profit margin	$\frac{90}{820} \times 100$	$\frac{100}{850} \times 100$	$\frac{85}{900} \times 100$
		11.0%	11.8%	9.4%
(c)	Return on capital employed	$\frac{90}{500} \times 100$	$\frac{100}{610} \times 100$	$\frac{85}{670} \times 100$
		18.0%	16.4%	12.7%
(d)	Asset turnover	$\frac{820}{500}$	$\frac{850}{610}$	$\frac{900}{670}$
		1.64	1.39	1.34

(e)	Non-current asset turnover	$\dfrac{820}{385}$	$\dfrac{850}{453}$	$\dfrac{900}{498}$
		2.13	1.88	1.81
(f)	Current ratio	$\dfrac{145}{30}$	$\dfrac{191}{34}$	$\dfrac{213}{41}$
		4.8 : 1	5.6 : 1	5.2 : 1
(g)	Quick ratio	$\dfrac{95}{30}$	$\dfrac{136}{34}$	$\dfrac{146}{41}$
		3.2 : 1	4.0 : 1	3.6 : 1
(h)	Receivables' (debtors') collection period	$\dfrac{85}{820} \times 365$	$\dfrac{112}{850} \times 365$	$\dfrac{128}{900} \times 365$
		38 days	48 days	52 days
(i)	Inventory (stock) days	$\dfrac{50}{440} \times 365$	$\dfrac{55}{445} \times 365$	$\dfrac{67}{500} \times 365$
		41 days	45 days	49 days
(j)	Payables' (creditors') payment period	$\dfrac{30}{440} \times 365$	$\dfrac{34}{445} \times 365$	$\dfrac{41}{500} \times 365$
		25 days	28 days	30 days
(k)	Interest cover	n/a	100/3	85/3
			= 33.3	= 28.3
(l)	Gearing ratio	n/a	$50/560 \times 100$	$50/620 \times 100$
			=8.9%	=8.1%

PROFITABILITY

Between 20X6 and 20X7 there was an increase in both gross profit margin and operating profit margin. However in 20X8, when revenue grew by 6%, both gross profit margin and operating profit margin decreased. However, the fall in the operating profit margin was relatively a great deal larger than that of the gross profit margin, indicating that expenses are increasing.

Return on capital employed did not follow the increases in profitability in 20X7 but instead fell due to a significant decrease in the asset turnover in that year. Asset turnover and non-current (fixed) asset turnover both stabilised a little in 20X8 but ROCE still decreased due to the falling profit levels.

WORKING CAPITAL

One of the main problems with the business appears to be control of its working capital. Both the current ratio and the quick ratio are excessively high showing that there are large amounts of capital being tied up in receivables (debtors), inventory (stock) and cash balances which could perhaps be used more profitably in other areas of the business.

The main problem areas appear to be receivables (debtors) and payables (creditors). The receivables' (debtors') collection period has increased from 38 to 52 days over the period whereas suppliers were being paid after just 25 days in 20X6 and still after only 30 days in 20X8. This means that cash is flowing out of the business much earlier than it is coming in.

Added to this the inventory (stock) holding period has also increased from 41 to 49 days over the three years meaning that even more cash is being tied up in these inventories (stock).

6

	Flimwell	Hartfield	Groombridge
Gross profit margin	62.0%	56.8%	60.4%
Operating profit margin	12.0%	9.5%	13.5%
Return on capital employed	11.8%	8.5%	12.7%
Asset turnover	0.98	0.90	0.94
Inventory (stock) turnover	95 days	108 days	60 days
Payables' (creditors') payment period	45 days	61 days	58 days
Sales per sq m	£225	£218	£240
Sales per employee	£19,286	£28,462	£18,462
Sales per hour worked	£17.70	£26.24	£16.96

(a) **Working**

	Flimwell	Hartfield	Groombridge
Cost of sales	51 + 210 − 56 = £205,000	45 + 165 − 50 = £160,000	30 + 192 − 32 = £190,000

(i) Gross profit margin

$$\frac{335,000}{540,000} \times 100 \qquad \frac{210,000}{370,000} \times 100 \qquad \frac{290,000}{480,000} \times 100$$

62.0% 56.8% 60.4%

(ii) Operating profit margin

$$\frac{65,000}{540,000} \times 100 \qquad \frac{35,000}{370,000} \times 100 \qquad \frac{65,000}{480,000} \times 100$$

12.0% 9.5% 13.5%

(iii)	Return on capital employed	$\dfrac{65{,}000}{550{,}000} \times 100$	$\dfrac{35{,}000}{410{,}000} \times 100$	$\dfrac{65{,}000}{510{,}000} \times 100$
		11.8%	8.5%	12.7%
(iv)	Asset turnover	$\dfrac{540{,}000}{550{,}000}$	$\dfrac{370{,}000}{410{,}000}$	$\dfrac{480{,}000}{510{,}000}$
		0.98	0.90	0.94
(v)	Average inventory (stock)	$\dfrac{51+56}{2}$	$\dfrac{45+50}{2}$	$\dfrac{30+32}{2}$
		£53,500	£47,500	£31,000
	Inventory (stock) days	$\dfrac{53{,}500}{205{,}000} \times 365$	$\dfrac{47{,}500}{160{,}000} \times 365$	$\dfrac{31{,}000}{190{,}000} \times 365$
		95 days	108 days	60 days
(vi)	Payables' (creditors') payment period	$\dfrac{25{,}800}{210{,}000} \times 365$	$\dfrac{27{,}500}{165{,}000} \times 365$	$\dfrac{30{,}500}{192{,}000} \times 365$
		45 days	61 days	58 days
(vii)	Sales per sq. m.	$\dfrac{540{,}000}{2{,}400}$	$\dfrac{370{,}000}{1{,}700}$	$\dfrac{480{,}000}{2{,}000}$
		£225	£218	£240
(viii)	Sales per employee	$\dfrac{540{,}000}{28}$	$\dfrac{370{,}000}{13}$	$\dfrac{480{,}000}{26}$
		£19,286	£28,462	£18,462
(ix)	Sales per hour worked	$\dfrac{540{,}000}{30{,}500}$	$\dfrac{370{,}000}{14{,}100}$	$\dfrac{480{,}000}{28{,}300}$
		£17.70	£26.24	£16.96

(b)   REPORT

To: Sales Director

From: Accounts assistant

Date: xx.xx.xx

Subject: Performance of stores

I have considered the performance figures for our three stores in Flimwell, Hartfield and Groombridge for the first six months of the year and have calculated a number of performance indicators (see part a). The key factors that have appeared from these figures are addressed below.

Flimwell has the highest gross profit margin but the highest operating profit margin and return on capital employed are generated by Groombridge. Clearly therefore Groombridge has better control of its expenses than the other two stores and if the Groombridge practices can be emulated in the other two stores this could improve their profitability.

The Hartfield store has problems with profitability, having significantly lower gross profit margin, operating profit margin, return on capital employed and asset turnover figures than the other two stores. Possibly one of the reasons for the lack of profitability is in the high inventory (stock) levels at Hartfield. The inventory (stock) turnover in days is almost twice as high as that for Groombridge with inventories (stock) being held for about three and half months.

Hartfield, however, does have the highest productivity levels in terms of sales per employee and sales per hour worked as these are all very much higher than the other two stores. This might imply that the Hartfield store is understaffed which may also be part of the problem with profitability. As the gross profit margin of Hartfield is much lower than the other two stores it may be that Hartfield has to charge lower prices for the goods due to the understaffing in order to attract customers.

Groombridge appears to have the best control over its working capital with inventory (stock) only held for two months and suppliers paid after a similar period. If the inventory (stock) control and payables' (creditors') control of Groombridge can be introduced into the other two stores this will help in their performance. Groombridge also has the highest sales per square metre therefore their store layout may be of interest to the other two stores.

If Filmwell's payables' (creditors') payment period of 45 days was lengthened to that of Hartfield of 61 days the cash balance of Filmwell would increase by £9,205 (£210,000/(365 × 16)).

7	(a)	Gross profit margin	=	$\dfrac{\text{Gross profit}}{\text{Revenue}}$
		44%	=	$\dfrac{\text{Gross profit}}{£106,500}$
		44% × £106,500	=	Gross profit
		Gross profit	=	£46,860

(b) Gross profit margin $= \dfrac{\text{Gross profit}}{\text{Revenue}}$

$37.5\% = \dfrac{£105,000}{\text{Revenue}}$

Revenue $= \dfrac{£105,000}{0.375}$

Revenue $= £280,000$

(c) Gross profit $= £256,000 \times 41\%$

$= £104,960$

Operating profit $= £256,000 \times 13.5\%$

$= £34,560$

Expenses $= £104,960 - 34,560$

$= £70,400$

(d) ROCE $= \dfrac{\text{Operating profit}}{\text{Capital employed}}$

$12.8\% = \dfrac{£50,000}{\text{Capital employed}}$

Capital employed $= \dfrac{£50,000}{0.128}$

$= £390,625$

(e) ROCE $=$ Operating profit margin $\times$ Asset turnover

$15\% = 10\% \times$ Asset turnover

$\dfrac{15\%}{10\%} =$ Asset turnover

Asset turnover $= 1.5$

(f) Average inventory (stock) $= \dfrac{118,000 + 104,000}{2}$

$= £111,000$

Inventory (stock) turnover $= \dfrac{\text{Cost of sales}}{\text{Average inventory (stock)}}$

$= \dfrac{£118,000 + 465,000 - 104,000}{£111,000}$

$= 4.3$ times

(g) Receivables' (debtors') collection period $= \dfrac{\text{Receivables (debtors)}}{\text{Revenue}} \times 365$

64 days $= \dfrac{64{,}000}{\text{Revenue}} \times 365$

Revenue $= \dfrac{64{,}000}{64 \text{ days}} \times 365$

$= £365{,}000$

8

		Balanced scorecard perspective
Net profit margin	19.9%	Financial or internal
Return on capital employed	24.7%	Financial
Inventory (stock) turnover	91 days	Customer
Asset turnover	1.24	Internal
Research costs as % of production costs	31.25%	Innovation and learning
Training costs as a % of labour cost	22.5%	Internal

Workings

(a) Operating profit margin $= \dfrac{\text{Operating profit}}{\text{Revenue}} \times 100$

$= \dfrac{68 + 6}{372}$

$= 19.9\%$

- financial perspective or possibly internal perspective as this is a measure of the control over the resources of the business

Note that operating profit is profit before interest therefore the interest deducted in the income statement (profit and loss account) must be added back – however if the profit after interest had been used this would be the net profit margin.

(b) Return on capital employed $= \dfrac{\text{Operating profit}}{\text{Capital employed}} \times 100$

$= \dfrac{68 + 6}{200 + 100} \times 100$

$= 24.7\%$

- financial perspective

(c)   Inventory (stock) days $= \dfrac{\text{Average inventory (stock)}}{\text{Cost of sales}} \times 365$

      Average inventory (stock) $= \dfrac{19 + 21}{2}$

                              $=$ 20

      Inventory (stock) days $= \dfrac{20}{80} \times 365$

                              $=$ 91 days

    – customer perspective – the more inventory (stock) that is held the less likely it is that   customer demand cannot be satisfied

(d)   Asset turnover $= \dfrac{\text{Revenue}}{\text{Capital employed}}$

                              $= \dfrac{372}{300}$

                              $=$ 1.24

    – internal – intensity of asset use

(e)   Research costs/production $= \dfrac{\text{Research costs}}{\text{Production costs}} \times 100$

                              $= \dfrac{25}{80} \times 100$

                              $=$ 31.25%

    – innovation and learning perspective

Note: In this calculation we have used cost of sales of £80,000 as production costs however it would also have been acceptable to use production cost of £82,000 (28 + 40 + 14)

(f)   Training costs/labour cost $= \dfrac{\text{Training costs}}{\text{Labour costs}} \times 100$

                              $= \dfrac{9}{40} \times 100$

                              $=$ 22.5%

    – internal perspective

CHAPTER 8   Cost management

1   **Type of cost**

   (a)   products scrapped due to faulty raw materials   Internal failure

   (b)   training for quality control staff   Prevention

   (c)   costs of customer after sales service department   External failure

   (d)   lost contribution on defective products sold as seconds   Internal failure

   (e)   costs of inspection of raw materials   Appraisal

   (f)   maintenance of quality control equipment   Prevention

   (g)   cost of replacing faulty products returned by customers   External failure

   (h)   costs of production delays due to re-working defective   Internal failure
        products discovered in quality inspection

   (i)   claims from customers relating to defective products   External failure

   (j)   performance testing of finished goods   Appraisal

2

Cost of quality	Amount £	Category of cost
Repair of returned goods	£20,000	External failure
Advertising costs	£40,000	External failure
Lost customers	Unknown	External failure

Working

Repair of returned goods

   5,000,000/3,000 × 60% × £20 = 20000

3

Cost of quality	Amount £	Category of cost	Explicit or implicit
Quality inspection	£60,000	Appraisal	Explicit
Lost contribution from defective units	£70,000	Internal failure	Implicit
Replacement of units	£37,500	External failure	Explicit
Lost customers	Unknown	External failure	Explicit

Workings

Lost contribution

2,000 × (£80 – £45)   £70,000

Replacement of defective units

1,000,000/1,000 × 75% × £50   £37,500

4

Cost per after sales service customer	£4.67
Sales returns as a % of sales	8%
Repair cost per returned units	£10.00
Complaints as a % of unit sales	6%

Workings

Cost per after sales service customer $= \dfrac{£280,000}{60,000} = £4.67$

Sales returns as a % of sales value $= \dfrac{£120,000}{£1,500,000} = 8\%$

Repair cost per returned unit $= \dfrac{£40,000}{4,000} = £10.00$

Complaints as a % of unit sales $= \dfrac{3,000}{50,000} = 6\%$

5   Total Quality Management (TQM) is a quality management system in an organisation that involves all areas of the organisation not just the production element. The philosophy behind quality management must be applied in all the activities of the business – design, production, marketing, administration, purchasing, sales and even the finance function.

TQM can be defined as a continuous improvement in quality, productivity and effectiveness.

Continuous improvement is the basic principle behind TQM. This can be described as the concept of "getting it right first time" and "getting it even more right next time". By getting it right first time the costs of internal failure and external failure will be reduced to the point where they should not occur at all. Costs of prevention are less than the costs of correction.

TQM seeks to ensure that the goods produced or the services supplied are of the highest quality.

In order for TQM to work in all areas of an organisation, training and motivation of staff is vital in order for each individual to have the attitude of constantly seeking improvement in what they do. All staff within the organisation must be taught that they have customers. These may be external customers of the business or internal customers in the form of colleagues in the business that use an individual's work. Each individual should endeavour to ensure that they get it right first time and therefore that their excellent work is passed on in the chain.

Another important concept behind TQM is that every employee is involved and anyone with an idea should be allowed to put this forward. This is often done by groups of employees being formed within the organisation known as quality circles.

These quality circles normally consist of about ten employees with a range of skills, roles and seniority who meet regularly to discuss problems of quality and quality control and to perhaps suggest ways of improving processes and quality. This means that there is input from all levels within the organisation and from different disciplines such as marketing, design, engineering, information technology and office administration as well as production.

6 **Development and launch stages**

During this period of the product's life there are large outgoings in terms of development expenditure, non-current (fixed) assets necessary for production, the building up of inventory (stock) levels and advertising and promotion expenses. It is likely that even after the launch sales will be quite low and the product will be making a loss at this stage.

Growth stage

If the launch of the product is successful then during the growth stage there will be a fairly rapid increase in sales and a move to profitability as the costs of the earlier stages are recovered. This sales increase, however, is not likely to continue indefinitely.

Maturity stage

In the maturity stage of the product demand for the product will probably start to slow down and become more constant. In many cases this is the stage where the product is modified or improved in order to sustain demand and this may then see a small surge in sales.

Decline stage

At some point in a product's life, unless it is a consumable items such as chocolate bars, the product will reach the end of its sale life. The market will have bought enough of the product and sales will decline. This is the point where the business should consider no longer producing the product.

INDEX

Notes

Notes

Notes

REVIEW FORM

How have you used this Text?
(Tick one box only)

☐ Home study

☐ On a course_____

☐ Other _____

Why did you decide to purchase this Text? *(Tick one box only)*

☐ Have used BPP Texts in the past

☐ Recommendation by friend/colleague

☐ Recommendation by a college lecturer

☐ Saw advertising

☐ Other _____

During the past six months do you recall seeing/receiving either of the following?
(Tick as many boxes as are relevant)

☐ Our advertisement in Accounting Technician

☐ Our Publishing Catalogue

Which (if any) aspects of our advertising do you think are useful?
(Tick as many boxes as are relevant)

☐ Prices and publication dates of new editions

☐ Information on Text content

☐ Details of our free online offering

☐ None of the above

Your ratings, comments and suggestions would be appreciated on the following areas of this Text.

	Very useful	Useful	Not useful
Introductory section	☐	☐	☐
Quality of explanations	☐	☐	☐
How it works	☐	☐	☐
Chapter tasks	☐	☐	☐
Chapter Overviews	☐	☐	☐
Test your learning	☐	☐	☐
Index	☐	☐	☐

	Excellent	Good	Adequate	Poor
Overall opinion of this Text	☐	☐	☐	☐

Do you intend to continue using BPP Products?　　Yes ☐　　No ☐

Please note any further comments and suggestions/errors on the reverse of this page. The author of this edition can be e-mailed at: suedexter@bpp.com

Please return to: Sue Dexter, Publishing Director, BPP Learning Media Ltd, FREEPOST, London, W12 8BR.

REVIEW FORM (continued)

TELL US WHAT YOU THINK

Please note any further comments and suggestions/errors below.